THE POLARITY PROCESS

Energy as a Healing Art

Franklyn Sills is the Dean of the Polarity Therapy Educational Trust and is Co-Director of Karuna, a wholistic health and therapy training centre in Devon, England.

THE POLARITY PROCESS

Energy as a Healing Art

Franklyn Sills

ELEMENT
Shaftesbury, Dorset • Rockport, Massachusetts
Brisbane, Queensland

© Franklyn Sills 1989

First Published in Great Britain in 1989 by
Element Books Limited
Longmead, Shaftesbury, Dorset

First published in the USA in 1991
by Element, Inc
42 Broadway, Rockport, MA 01966

Reprinted 1990
Reprinted 1991
Reprinted 1994

First published in Australia in 1994 by
Element Books Limited for
Jacaranda Wiley Limited
33 Park Road, Milton, Brisbane 4064

Typeset by Colset Private Limited, Singapore
Text design by Clarke Williams
Cover design by Max Fairbrother
Cover illustration by Martin Rieser
Diagrams produced by Taurus Graphics, Abingdon, Oxon
Printed and bound in Great Britain by
Redwood Books, Trowbridge, Wiltshire

British Library Cataloguing in Publication Data
Sills, Franklyn
The polarity process.
1. Life. Philosophical perspectives
I. Title
128'.5

Library of Congress Cataloging in Publication
Data available

ISBN 1-85230-052-3

Contents

List of Illustrations   vi

Acknowledgements   ix

Prologue   x

1   The Macrocosmic Connection   1
2   Wireless Anatomy: The Microcosmic Reflection   20
3   Pulsations, Fields and Transitions   34
4   The Five Elements: The Mind in Manifestation   45
5   The Movement to Health   79
6   Health and the Elements   92
7   Energy and Form   124
8   Food, Exercise and Harmony   142
9   Finishings and Final Thoughts   156

Appendix: Study Guide to Dr Stone's Writings on
    Polarity Therapy   163
Index   187

Illustrations

Fig. No.		Page
1.1	The Taoist scheme of manifestation	6
1.2	Tao and form	7
1.3	The Ayurvedic scheme of manifestation	9
1.4	The evolution and involution of energy	10
1.5	The Polarity Principle	11
1.6	The movement of energy by pulsation	12
1.7	The hologrammatic concept of the macrocosmic play of energy in its evolutionary phase	13
1.8	The mechanics of the hologram	14
1.9	Bohm's world-view	16
1.10	The explicate and implicate world	17
1.11	Heteronomy and holonomy	17
1.12	The 'torus' shape	18
1.13	Cross-section of 'Cosmic Doughnut'	19
1.14	Taoism within the 'Cosmic Doughnut'	19
2.1	The 'Cosmic Bubble'	21
2.2	The Step-Down Process	23
2.3	Impulsion and contraction	23
2.4	A cross-section through the 'Cosmic Bubble'	24
2.5	Energy is expressed at the Brow Centre and manifests as physical form	26
2.6	The Three Currents: pingala, ida and sushumna	27
2.7	The centres of the body	28
2.8	Core Energy Patterns	30
2.9	The Three Currents	33
3.1	Energy pulsates in phases of expansion and contraction	35
3.2	General polarities of the body	36
3.3	Polarity Zone Chart	37
3.4	The Oval Fields	38
3.5	Fields and transitions	42

3.6   Five posterior motor fields set up by gravity patterns and
      muscular/fascial patterns   43

4.1   The Five Element Configuration   46
4.2   Basic energy dynamics   48
4.3   The Foetal Chart   50
4.4   Chakras and Elements   52
4.5   Ether relationships   54
4.6   Centres and Triads   58
4.7   Food categories and Elements   59
4.8   The Air triad   61
4.9   Air Triad relationships   63
4.10 The Fire triad   64
4.11 Fire Triad relationships   66
4.12 Fire energy patterns   68
4.13 The Water triad   70
4.14 Water Triad relationships   73
4.15 Polarity Zone Chart   74
4.16 The Earth triad   75
4.17 Earth Triad relationships   77

5.1   Energy completion   81
5.2   The path to illness   85
5.3   Involution-Evolution in the disease process   91

6.1   General body reading   94
6.2   Constitutional types   96
6.3   Polarity Zone Chart   101
6.4   The Ether treatment relationships   103
6.5   Three types of touch   105
6.6   Anterior Air treatment relationships   106
6.7   Posterior Air treatment relationships   107
6.8   General Fire Triad relationships   110
6.9   Fire principle treatment relationships   111
6.10 Spiral current treatment relationships   112
6.11 Anterior Water treatment relationships   114
6.12 Posterior Water treatment relationships   115
6.13 Major perineal relationships   116
6.14 Five-Pointed Star patterns   117
6.15 Five-Pointed Star contraction   119
6.16 Earth pattern treatment relationships   122

7.1   The Three Life Breaths   125
7.2   The 'Interlaced Triangles'   130
7.3   Parasympathetic contact areas   132
7.4   Sympathetic contact areas   133
7.5   A cranial hold   134
7.6   Central nervous system relationships   135
7.7   The sacral keystone   137
7.8   Spinal harmonics   139
7.9   Perfect body polarity and gravity lines   141

8.1	Diet chart	146
8.2	Basic polarity squat	150
8.3	Some variations on the squat	150
8.4	Variations on the pyramid	151
8.5	Squatting Ha!	153
8.6	Woodcutter Ha!	154
8.7	Neutral sitting	155
9.1	The spectrum of consciousness	157
9.2	The 'spectrum' layers	158

Acknowledgements

To Dr Stone, the great pioneer and healer.

To Dr Jim Said whose dynamic mind has helped clarify many polarity principles.

To Cindy Rawlinson, whose gentle knowing and clear understanding of the elements has been a source of inspiration.

To Pierre Pannetier, whose emphasis on kindness and love created a heartfelt connection to polarity work.

And finally, to my wife and family, who put up with four years of my trying to put down on paper ever-changing ideas in an ever-changing format.

Prologue: Beginnings

Life is a song. It has its own rhythm of harmony. It is a symphony of all things which exist in major and minor keys of *Polarity*. It blends the discords, by opposites into a harmony which unites the whole into a grand symphony of life. To learn through experience in this life, to appreciate the symphony and lessons of life and to blend with the whole, is the object of our being here.*

I decided to write this prologue after the first draft of this book was completed. As I read the draft it seemed almost other-worldly. It took over four years of writing, rewriting, putting aside, feeling disappointed, feeling exalted and finally, feeling relieved. I didn't initially set out to write a book on polarity therapy: a publisher approached me and said that there was a need for a more in-depth introduction to the theory and practice of polarity therapy. I agreed, and he then asked me to write it. It has been a real birthing process since then. I have gone through so many changes in the four years, both personal and professional, that it seemed necessary to add new sections to the book, and to change others. What is left seems to be a reflection of various stages of my understanding, perception and clarity over a four-year period. This period sits on twelve previous years as teacher and practitioner. But it is during the last four years that major shifts in my perception, both of the world and of my work, have occurred. Because of that, the book in its various sections reflects my understanding at various stages in this period.

It was not an easy book for me to write. Who should it be aimed at? What is its purpose? The first need I perceived was for an in-depth introduction to the concepts and world-view of polarity therapy. Most

---

* This quotation and those at the beginnings of chapters are from the writings of Dr Stone.

books currently available are basically technique cook-books. Do this, do that, connect here and there. But they do not give an understanding of why you are doing these things. What relationships are you working with? What patterns are you perceiving in a client? What are the dynamics of those patterns, in their mental, emotional and physical relationships? Polarity Therapy addresses these questions in an extra-ordinarily deep and concise way. Dr Stone, the founder of Polarity Therapy had a depth of insight into the dynamics of life process. I hope to illuminate some of these dynamics in this book and to help the reader perceive the breadth and depth of polarity work.

Polarity therapy had its beginnings in the research, insight and practical application of Dr Randolph Stone D.O., D.C., N.D., but its roots are thousands of years older and the origins of its knowledge are shrouded in the veils of time. Dr Stone was born in Austria and emigrated to the USA while still a boy. It is said that he learned his English from the Bible and this is evident in the form and tempo of his later writings on polarity therapy. As a youth, he became interested in the healing arts and eventually did his degrees in osteopathy, chiropractic and the natural therapies. He felt that man was given all the healing tools needed, if only he could encourage and allow their natural functioning. Natural healing became his life-long quest and practice. To him, it was more than just a medicine: it was a healing art and, at a deeper level, a spiritual quest.

The era in which Dr Stone was studying and developing his therapeutic practice was a fascinating one. It was an era of intense investigation into the roots of the disease processes by a few avant-garde medical researchers. The common interest shared by them was not an investigation into physiology or pathology, but an intense exploration of the underlying energy matrix which underpins what we perceive as physical form. In this context, Dr Stone believed that life was much more than just chemistry and biophysics and that healing was much more than the removal of symptoms. Health, he believed, is based on our tuning in to deeper truths and a way of life which expresses these truths. It is the therapist's role to act as a facilitator, encouraging this harmonising process, which in turn implies that the therapists must also be working towards this same goal.

Early in his career, Dr Stone discovered that a solely mechanistic understanding of biological processes did not bring lasting results. He found that structural manipulation, internal cleansing programmes and dietary changes, although powerful tools, did not in themselves produce lasting changes. He realised that there was some missing ingredient, some depth of perception, of which both the allopaths and natural therapists were unaware. This realisation set Dr Stone on his quest for the key to health and well-being. He turned his gaze to the Near East and studied its medical and spiritual traditions. He then looked to the Far East and studied both the Chinese and Indian traditions. He travelled extensively and was especially impressed by the Ayurvedic medical concepts and yogic philosophy of India. In his studies and practical work he discovered, what to him, was the missing link; the vital truth which, indeed, connected both Eastern and Western thought. That link, simply put, is energy. He realised that all life is movement, and movement is a manifestation of energy or vital force. The concept of energy flow and life force is not foreign to the West, but it has not been actively pursued in its medical sciences. In the traditions of the East, not only was it actively pursued but it was the very foundation of their medical systems. With this insight, the concept of vital energy with its fields and currents became the foundation of Dr Stone's emerging healing system. As his study developed, four interrelated aspects became clear. These were: a system of therapeutic touch; cleansing and health-building diets; special 'polarity' exercises, and the creation of a positive attitude and life-style.

The system of therapeutic touch developed by Dr Stone utilises his understanding of both physical energy and 'subtle' energy anatomy. This works with energy at its various phases of manifestation. He based his work on the Ayurvedic and yogic understanding of energy centres, traditionally called 'chakras', and the pulsating fields and currents which flow from them. Dr Stone called this the 'Wireless Anatomy of Man', as subtle energy does not flow in channels, or along nerve fibres, but moves in waves of expansion and contraction in interrelated and harmonic patterns. Dr Stone once said that our hands are our greatest tools and if used with knowledge, insight and intuition, can be one of the greatest aids to healing. His system of therapeutic touch and manipulation works with three phases of energy manifestation in the body. The subtlest phase is that of the chakras and their energy fields. These relationships are traditionally described as five interrelated patterns known as the 'Five Elements'. The Five Elements are names given to the qualities and patterns of energy which arise from each chakra. Dr Stone developed diagnostic and treatment techniques which work to open blockages in their flow and bring their relationships into balance. He also worked with these energies as they step down into the nervous system. He developed techniques which affect its three phases: the parasympathetic, the sympathetic and the central nervous systems. The final phase, or level that Dr Stone worked with is physical form itself. The physical body, in his terms, is an expression of subtle energy. Imbalances in these energies are reflected in the body's fascial, muscular, bony and organ relationships. Dr Stone developed gentle techniques which bring body structure into balance. The musculo-skeletal structure is worked with as a final balancing factor. He developed a comprehensive body-work system which works on these three major phases of energy manifestation in the body.

The cleansing and health-building diets employed by Dr Stone were developed from his naturopathic background. These diets were developed as a gradual process which help to clean out body 'sludge' and toxins which accumulate in our tissues due to improper diet and way of life. The development of a healthy diet and life-style helps maintain a balanced internal chemistry.

Dr Stone also developed a unique system of stretching and releasing exercises – 'Polarity Exercises'. These help to open and balance our energies and help maintain the work done in therapy sessions. They focus on squatting and stretching postures which approximate the position of the foetus in the womb. Dr Stone believed that these were ideal postures for aiding free energy flow. Other exercises were developed to help release deeply held emotional patterns by the use of movement, sound and breath.

Overlaid on these methods was an understanding of the emotional underpinning of disease process. Dr Stone realised that processes of thought and attitude had to be taken into account. He was known for his 'Dutch Uncle' talks which were an attempt to help patients accept responsibility for their own well-being and to foster a positive mental attitude. He tried to impress upon his patients that a peaceful and aware mind, not bound by desire or need was the key to true health.

The appeal of polarity therapy is in its wholeness. It is a truly holistic health system which sees ill health as a process and not as a syndrome. It demands the active participation of the patient in his or her own health-building approach. The therapist is seen to be a teacher who helps the patient return to a balanced and vital way of life. The techniques are geared to help bring both energetic and physical imbalances to equilibrium and to give the patient tools to help maintain that balance. The movement of energy through its elemental phases can give a beautiful framework for the use of other modalities when appropriate. Herbal medicine, osteopathy, chiropractic, homoeopathy, and psychotherapy, for example, can be easily used within the polarity framework. Most of all, its appeal is found in a way of life which leads to better health, a happier state of mind and a recollection of our origins – a reconnection with our source.

The following pages are written in the hope that polarity therapy can be appreciated for its wholeness and its deep insight into the human condition.

CHAPTER ONE

The Macrocosmic Connection

Polarity is the law of opposites in their finer attraction from centre to centre. Unity is the merging of these currents into one Essence. Creation brings forth opposites by its centrifugal force, like a fountain spray of manifestation flowing out to the limits of the cosmos and of each pattern unit.

This is a book about process. The world as we experience it is a process. It is a very personal one for us all, yet follows universal laws and cycles. It is the premise of this book that this process of life, or 'becoming' as the Buddhists would say, is a flow of energy. The word 'energy' has many connotations and we will examine this key concept throughout the book.

World-Views

We, in the West, have made a very good job of exploring our material world. We have mapped its surface, explored its nooks and crannies, taken apart its constituted parts, worked out some of its physical laws, compartmentalised its processes, and magnified its smallest parts. In atomic physics we have even smashed the atom itself to explore its make-up and found still smaller parts. We have divided the world, subdivided it and compartmentalised it even further. In the last few hundred years, we have raised what we call 'science' up to a godly height and have decided that everything must measure up to its standards. The only problem with this perspective is that these standards are created by men, always changing and hence ultimately unreliable. They are useful vantage points for exploring the world but we create problems when they become elevated to the lofty heights of Universal Truth.

We have, to a large extent, based our science on a particular world-view. This view began in the seventeenth century with a mathematician named Descartes. His vision of the universe was that of a perfectly ordered and functioning mechanism. Like a clock, each part had its place and function. He saw man in the same way, a perfectly functioning mechanism. The mind, he believed, was a separate entity with no direct influence on the body. The soul was also a completely separate entity and each piece functioned in its own sphere. Thus he divided man up into pieces and saw these pieces as separate. His views deeply influenced a newly forming science. The body could be looked at as a completely closed, ordered and mechanical process. Scientists could discover the mechanisms of the disease process and 'fix' the problem as it was a problem of mechanics seen in body structure and physiology. The more they knew about the pathology the better they could cure the diseases investigated.

Later the physicist Newton explored the laws of the universe and developed an understanding of natural law which became known as 'Newtonian physics'. In his understanding, nature did indeed work in a clock-like fashion and constant laws governed its movement. Thus, if one billiard ball hit another at a constant velocity and angle, the speed and direction of the second ball would also be constant, and predictable. A whole range of physical laws were developed from this understanding: laws of gravity, thermodynamics, electromagnetism, chemical reaction, and so on. These were all found to be true at our level of knowledge in the physical world.

Modern medicine and its scientific research has been based on this Cartesian world-view and a Newtonian understanding of material dynamics. Modern physics, since Einstein and Plank, has discovered, however, a whole layer of physical reality which does not follow these laws and does not act in ways which could have been explained by the Newtonian model. At the level of atomic and subatomic physics, at this layer of subtle physical form and energy relationship, the physical laws which our senses can detect do not hold sway. These laws are true only in one 'layer' of reality. In modern physics we are discovering that there is much more to the world than we have been taught to believe.

In traditional cultures, especially in the orient, a very different world-view to that of Descartes has long held sway. In the West we compartmentalise and separate reality into its constituent parts. In the East these parts are traditionally seen to be expressions of a greater whole. Separateness is seen to be an illusion caused by our lack of understanding and a mis-perception of our experience. Our modes of thought and conceptualisation tend to create separation where none truly exists. Thus, we separate our world into mine and other, ours and theirs, good and bad, pleasure and pain. We separate things and lose touch with the 'wholeness' of their unfolding. They see the natural order, not as a mechanical process composed of multifarious parts, but as a complete, whole interrelated dynamic in which man is an integral part. The wholeness is reflected in the relationships of the world and of the cosmos. The seasons; life and death; ecosystems; the movement of the planets and stars – all partake in this wholeness and are interrelated and inter-dependent aspects of it.

We will see that this mystery of relatedness is due to the deep energetic connections that all processes share. The play of energy in mankind is a reflection of the energy in the universe as a whole. We are going to start our exploration with a look at the universal play of energy in the cosmos and in the world through a number of 'tinted' lenses. Each philosopher, each culture, has its own unique way of seeing this macro-cosmic movement of energy. Each expression is helpful as a 'way in' to understanding the movement of energy from deeper sources to more explicit form. We will explore the general concept of 'energy' first and then look at how some traditions and philosophers have described its movement.

The Concept of Energy

Dr Stone saw a deep link between Eastern and Western thought. This link is the concept and the reality of energy and its flow.

The word 'energy' has many connotations. It can mean specific types of energy such as electrical energy, X-rays, light, or atomic energy; it can also refer to the movement of subtle pulsations which inform material structures. It is these subtle pulses with which Eastern traditional approaches to healing work. No matter how subtle or coarse the mani-festation of energy is, it must follow the same basic laws of movement which behave differently in the different forms of energy we can perceive and experience.

Traditional Eastern cultures believed that underlying both mental and physical forces in the world is a whole realm of subtler relationships and energy flows. This realm is implicit within the more easily perceived physical realm. It was believed that these subtler energies must be in harmony for the physical realm to be in order. Both physical and mental imbalances start in this subtler realm. It was further believed that the subtler imbalances become manifest in the denser physical energies of both mind and matter. The process is based on one major factor. This factor is movement. For any energy to arise, for any form to come into being, there must be movement. Dr Stone based his healing system on this simple fact. He saw that in traditional thought, especially in Chinese and Ayurvedic medicine, health was seen as the fluent and harmonious *movement* of energies at subtler levels. In the East these energies have been called 'Chi' or 'prana'. We will call it 'vital energy' or 'vital forces'. All of life is based on these movements. Simply stated – 'no movement, no life'.

Dr Stone realised that this movement of energy is based on or due to a relationship which sets up two opposing fields. This relationship is called a 'polarity'. In Chinese philosophy this basic polarity relationship is called 'Yin and Yang'; in Ayurvedic philosophy it is called the 'Gunas'. A polarity is a relationship which sets up movement. These relationships are relative: one pole, or opposite, is relatively higher or more intense than the other. Another way of seeing this is that one pole directly opposes the other in the relationship and a movement is set up between them due to this opposition. This has been seen as a basic 'law' which governs all of life. Dr Stone called it the 'Polarity Principle'.

In our scientific and technologically orientated world, this principle is continuously used in very practical ways. Any kind of energy flow, no matter how coarse or how subtle, from electrical energy to atomic fission, must be guided by it. For electricity to flow, a polarity relationship of positive and negative potential must be set up. The very atom itself is nothing more nor less than positive, neutral and negative energies in dynamic relation. These polarities hold the world together – though unfortunately they can now also be used to blow it apart.

The polarity process is an expression of life itself. The nature of the cycles of our lives is an expression of this universal law. As we move through birth, growth, old age and death, we move through the basic polarities of our lives. Our conception, birth and growth is an expansive phase, a positive outpouring of life, Dr Stone, in his book *Energy*, calls it a 'fountain spray of manifestation flowing out to limits of the cosmos and of each pattern unit' (i.e. each individual being). This positive outflowing is balanced by a contractive phase, where energies reverse this pattern and we move through middle age, old age and death. It is, in a deep sense, a return to our beginnings, so that a new expansive cycle can begin. In traditions throughout the world, death is seen as this new beginning.

Dr Stone saw that for there to be an energy flow, there must be a source for this flow. Electricity must arise from a generating plant. If there is no generating plant, no movement will arise. Thus, if the heart stops beating, no blood will flow; if the brain dies, no nerve impulse will flow from it. Dr Stone looked to Eastern philosophies in order to discover how this idea of origin was expressed. He looked to the Chinese and Ayurvedic traditions for a framework to explore the realm of origins. Both these traditions postulate a movement of life force, or vital energy, which is an expression of a polarity movement. They based their understanding of this movement, and indeed of life itself, on the assumption and belief in the existence of a neutral source as its origin.

This neutral source is more than a mere source of energy; it is the very wellspring of life and of all conscious being. Life is conceived of as a movement of conscious energy from the source through stepped phases which move from subtler fields to denser physical form. Thus, this movement of vital force is seen to be imbued with consciousness or awareness which arises from the source itself.

The Taoist Tradition

In the Chinese tradition the source is called the Tao or Way. In Lao Tzu's *Tao Te Ching* we read,

> There was something formless yet complete,
> That existed before heaven and earth;
> Without sound, without substance,
> Dependent on nothing, unchanging,
> All pervading, unfailing.

The source, expressed as 'Tao' in the Chinese Taoist system, is the neutral essence of all life. It is pre-existent to being and form and is dependent on nothing. It is unchanging and thus without polarity relationships. All manifestation depends on change, yet at the source of it all is change-lessness. We also read that

> . . . the Tao is a thing impalpable, incommensurable.
> Incommensurable, impalpable.
> Yet latent in it are forms.

In it is the latent potential for all of creation. From it all of creation arises. In it is the potential for all forms of polarity relationships and thus all forms of being. There is an ancient Chinese diagram, the 'Tai Chi T'u' (see Figure 1.1) which describes the process of energy from the source. This movement steps down in intensity and quality to denser relationships until the physical world is finally formed.

In Figure 1.1 the upper circle represents the Tao and its dual aspects of Wu Chi or Non-Being and Tai Chi or Being. The Tao is the source of all things; it is the beginningless beginning. It is the mover and the movement; the source and the content. The Wu Chi is the unmanifest potential of Tao and the Tai Chi is the manifest potential, the 'uncarved block'. In a positive burst of creative energy movement, polarities arise. This upsurge is represented in the next tier down and is called yin and yang. This is akin to the 'Big Bang' theory of modern physics.

Thus, the universe begins from primordial 'stuff' (the 'uncarved block') and creation occurs with a huge, positive centrifugal bang!

Yang is the phase of energy which is outgoing, positive, expansive. Yin is the phase which is contractive, negative, receptive. They set up a process where the potential for movement arises. Dr Stone called this potential the 'poles' of the energy movement. Yang is the positive, out-going pole and yin is the negative, receptive pole. Life is based on this potential, the push and pull of gravity which holds the solar system together; the push of blood from our hearts and the receptive pull back; the movement of water from high to low; the heat of the sun and the cool of night. Yin and yang potentials underline the movement of life.

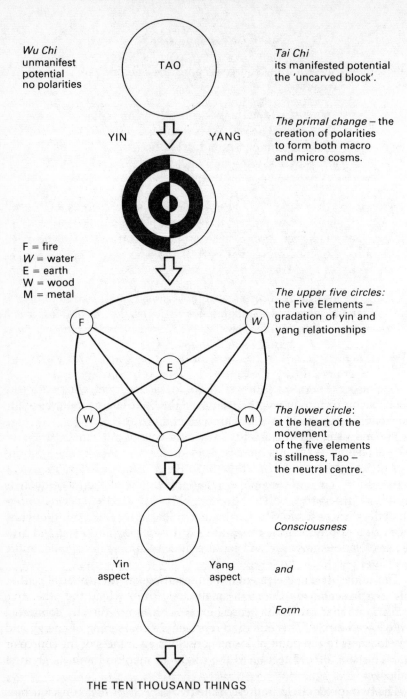

Fig. 1.1. The Taoist scheme of manifestation (from, The Way and Its Power, *Chapter XXV, translated by Arthur Waley)*

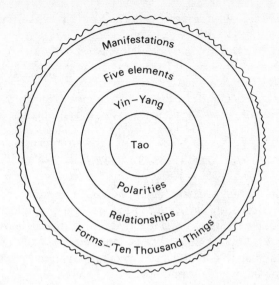

Fig. 1.2. Tao and form. Tao is the stillness at the heart of all manifesta-
tion. We tend to identify most with the outer layer of being and lose touch
with the source of the whole, Tao. We get caught up in the periphery and
lose touch with the centre.

The next phase or 'step-down' in the hierarchy is the creation of the
Five Elements or moving forces. These are the basic energy patterns of life
and from their interrelationships arise all of creation.

Yin and yang potentials set the stage for energy movement. The Five
Elements delineate this movement. They are names given to the relationships of energy movement both in the universe as a whole and in man as
its expression. Yin and yang govern the general flow of energy through its
positive and negative poles. The Five Elements are the specific differ-
entiated energy patterns which arise due to this flow. All of our thoughts,
emotions and physical processes are expressions of Yin–Yang and Five
Element relationships. We will explore these relationships in much more
detail later.

Tao underlies these elemental manifestations as their neutral centre.
This is represented by the sixth small circle from which the other five
spring. Note that earth, the densest expression, is not directly connected
to the lowest circle. This omission represents a coarsening of energy and
consciousness to the point of losing conscious awareness of the source or
Tao. This loss of connection is the plight of mankind and its greatest
challenge.

The two lower circles represent the two aspects of life, consciousness
and form. Here we see a clear cultural expression of a universal polarity
movement.

Energy arises from a source, the Tao, by a positive impulse which separates into the polarities of yin and yang. Through a series of 'step-downs' where energies become gradually denser and more physical, all of creation is formed. It is much like a transformer stepping down intense forms of energy into less intense, slower vibrations. The energy of life, or vital force, is called 'chi'. It is this chi which moves in yin/yang cycles to yield all of creation, or as the Chinese say, the Ten Thousand Things.

The Ayurvedic Tradition

In the Indian system we see much the same process occurring. The Ayurvedic version of this process comes from Sankya philosophy. In this schema the concept of the source is called Brahman. Brahman is the One, the Supreme. Brahman is the source of consciousness and life energy, and it is to the Brahman that all must return. The play of manifestation which arises from it is shown diagrammatically in Figure 1.3.

Brahman is the source of life. It has two aspects. One is Purusha. Purusha is the centre of stillness where no polarity, no movement, exists. Yet within it is the potential for all polarity relationships and therefore all manifestation. All of life is inherent within this neutral core. From it, all creation is imbued with consciousness or awareness. In a sense, Purusha contains the blueprint or plan for all polarity relationships. This blueprint or plan at a core level is seen in all living form. It is mirrored in the DNA in each cell, which has the plan for a complete organism within it. The seed for the whole is enfolded within each part.

The second aspect of Brahman is Prakriti. Prakriti performs the function of seed potential. It is the potential source of creative energy and is the vital impulse; the potential expansion from non-being into being. From this creative expansion arises Avyakta which is the 'un-carved block' or Tai Chi aspect of the hierarchy. Here the potential for polarity relationships latent in Purusha takes form through the Three Gunas. The Gunas are equivalent to the Chinese concept of yin and yang. Sattva is the neutral ground from which energy moves. It is the neutral field which allows energy movement and is the neutral or balanced aspect inherent in all polarity relationships. Rajas is the positive, expansive yang phase of the polarity movement. It is the fiery, sun aspect of the energy cycle. Tamas is the negative, contractive yin phase of polarity movement and it is the cool, moon aspect of the energy cycle. Rajas is the expansive or centrifugal phase, while Tamas is the contractive, centripetal phase.

Sattvas, Rajas and Tamas, like yin and yang, set up polarity relationships and these relationships are inherent in every aspect of our lives. Without the Gunas, no polarities could occur, no movement could take place and life as we know it could not arise.

From the Gunas there then arise planes of existence which unfold as Mahat or 'Cosmic Intellect' and then Ahamkara or ego consciousness.

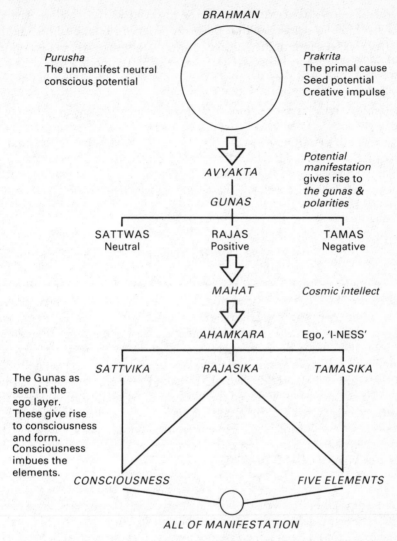

Fig. 1.3. The Ayurvedic scheme of manifestation

These two have also been called the 'Causal' and the 'Astral' planes. At Mahat, an awareness of the wholeness of existence is still in effect. Although there is a 'cosmic' knowledge of the oneness of all things, there is a subtle feeling of separation from the source. At the level of Ahamkara this separation deepens and the ego is experienced as separate from the world around it. Energy has moved so far from its source, that conscious contact is lost and the ego, or a self-sense arises. It is important to realise that this is a movement of energy which occurs within us all. It is a universal movement and a personal one also. From here, energy condenses further into physical form and the Five Elements arise. The movement of the Gunas now takes expression in the physical world via these energy relationships. We shall see that these Five Element relationships are the energetic expressions in the world of our thought processes, our emotions and our physical form. They relate to energy patterns which underlie our physical bodies and they express the quality of our consciousness at any given moment.

Imbued with consciousness, the Five Elements complete the cycle from the source to physical form. Life energy is called *prana*, which is equivalent to the Chinese term *chi*. As in the Chinese system, it is prana or chi which moves in five element cycles to bring forth all of creation. As in China, the traditional Indian medical system, called Ayurveda, or 'the teaching of life', is based on the subtle energy matrix which underlies physical form.

The Polarity Principle

So far we have talked about the outward phase of movement from the source into being. This is traditionally called the 'involutionary' phase. Here subtle energies move from the source, coarsen in various 'step-down' phases, and are finally expressed as consciousness and matter. For energy to flow, there must be a complete circuit of energy movement from the source and back to it. Thus, energy flows from the electrical generator to become heat or light and is then pulled back to the source by its negative pole. This return phase is called the 'evolutionary' phase and indicates the return of energy back to its origins. These two phases can be likened to expansion and contraction. The outward involutionary phase is the expansive phase and the inwardly returning evolutionary phase is the contractive phase (see Figure 1.4).

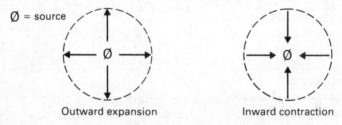

Fig. 1.4. *The evolution and involution of energy*

These two phases yield the basic pulsation of life. The change of the seasons, the pulsation of the atom, the bodily movements of respiration and circulation, even the movement of life from birth to death; all mirror this process of pulsation. Dr Stone called this basic rhythmic pulsation the Polarity Principle.

The Polarity Principle is a principle of energy flow at all levels of life.

The subtle flow of life force and vitality within man follows this principle as do coarser physical energies which are more easily measured (electricity, heat, light, etc.). No matter what form energy takes, its movement is due to some sort of polarity relationship. In other words, a relationship must be set up which has the potential for movement within it. Some examples are high and low; hot and cold; positive and negative. All these relationships have the potential for movement and change within them. They set up the potential for flow. Thus an area of high molecular excitation will flow to areas of relatively lower excitation and create a flow. This may take the form of heat, electricity, physical movement, etc. At the very core of our seemingly solid world are, as physics has discovered, pulsating fields of energy in polarity relationships. The physical world, even in a hard-nosed scientific framework, is underpinned by subtler, more intense energy pulsations. Let's define this basic movement as a principle:

Energy flows via a positive outward movement from a neutral source, through a neutral field, to some form of completion. It is then drawn back to the source by a negative, receptive pull.

In the chapters which follow we will see how this process works within us. It is set out diagrammatically in Figure 1.5.

1. Energy moves from a source via a positive expansion.
2. This impulsion pushes out energy in the form of polarities or (+) and (−) energies.
3. These energies find completion in form and express their relationship in some way (i.e. electricity, matter, atomic energy, pain, thought, etc.).
4. Once the energies have reached this point of completion, the energy pattern is exhausted in the creation of a form and is then drawn back into the source by a negative receptive pull.

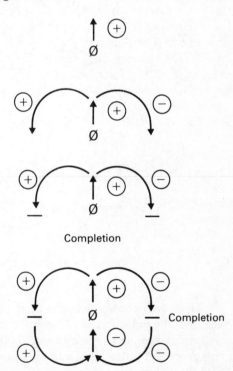

Fig. 1.5. The Polarity Principle

In this principle, Dr Stone is outlining a basic principle of energy in dynamic relationship. At the core of all movement is the vast stillness of the Source. It is from this stillness that energy movement arises. Energy moves via pulsation. All things pulsate. The world is a place of pulsation. At the heart of the physical world is a whole atomic realm of pulsation. At the heart of this realm are even subtler pulsations which underlie physical form. This pulsation moves in what Dr Stone called centrifugal and centripetal phases, that is outward and inward pulsations. In terms of yin and yang, the outward centrifugal pulsation is yang and the inward centripetal pulsation is yin. Yin and yang are phases of one movement, the grand pulsation of the universe. We too are both part of, and an expression of, that pulsation. (See Figure 1.6.)

We see this principle at work on all levels of life. Whether we are talking about energy movement as electricity or heat or about the movement of emotions from one person to another, this principle holds true. Every manifestation of life can be seen in these terms.

Our plight is that we get stuck in physical form and fail to follow the evolutionary pull back to the source. This journey has been the focus for many religious and philosophical traditions, and great works of art and poetry have arisen in an attempt to convey this truth.

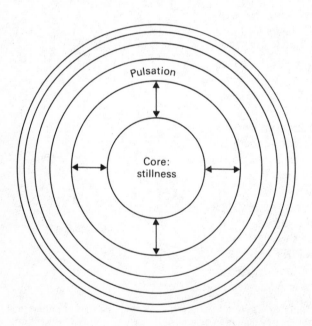

Fig. 1.6. The movement of energy by pulsation

The Hologrammatic Model of Energy Pulsation

We have seen how two Eastern traditions view the macrocosmic or universal play of energy in its involutionary phase. This interplay of energy is a vast multidimensional pulsation which can be most likened to the concept of a hologram. A hologram is a three-dimensional image within which are patterns of energy waves that interfere with each other as they cross each other's path. This interference sets up what is known as an 'interference pattern'. Within this pattern all the information of the complete interplay of the energies is stored. The interesting thing about a hologram is that every part of the hologram, no matter how small, has stored in it *all* the information of the whole interplay. Thus the microcosm has within it all the information of the macrocosmic movement. This understanding is most commonly applied photographically (see Figure 1.7).

For a hologram to be created, there must be two interacting light beams. One is called the reference beam and is a neutral, pure beam of light. The other is called the working beam. This beam has been out, so to speak, in the world of form and has encountered objects. These two beams are then recombined on a photographic plate and set up the 'interference pattern'. If the photographic plate is then illuminated by the original reference beam, a three-dimensional object will appear in space.

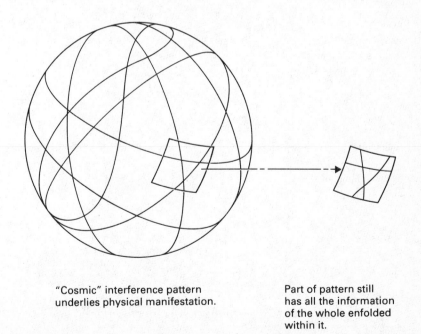

"Cosmic" interference pattern
underlies physical manifestation.

Part of pattern still
has all the information
of the whole enfolded
within it.

*Fig. 1.7. The hologrammatic concept of the macrocosmic play of energy
in its involutionary phase*

(In our example shown in Figure 1.8, this object is a pear.) This will look as 'real' as the original object. If only a small part of the photographic plate is illuminated (i.e. only a fraction of the captured interference pattern), the *whole* object will still appear, although not in such a sharp image. Thus every point on the plate has recorded *all* the information of the whole plate. This concept will become very meaningful in the next chapter when we explore the energy system of man.

The hologram, as a concept, can be a model for energy pulsation in the human being. Many different forms, patterns and qualities of energy pulsate in our mind and bodies. These patterns are all in a dynamic interference pattern which creates an 'energy body' that is the foundation for physical form. If the patterns are relating to each other in a balanced, free-flowing way, the integrity of the world pattern is kept. If blockages or imbalances occur in their relationships, disorder and dis-ease will take place.

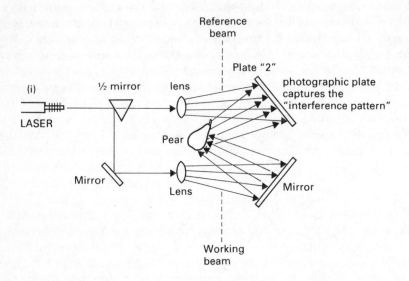

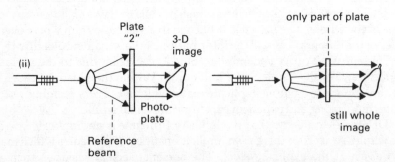

Fig. 1.8. The mechanics of the hologram

Modern Physics and the Polarity Principle

Recently a physicist named David Bohm has used the hologram to describe the nature of the universe. It is an explanation which works very well with our previous discussion of the traditional forms. He envisions the universe to be, in a sense, a vast hologram with two aspects to it. One is called the 'implicate' or enfolded aspect and the other is called the 'explicate' or unfolded aspect.

The explicate or 'unfolded' realm is the realm of the measurable, touchable world. It is the world that is available to the five senses. What we see, hear, feel, smell, taste and even think is in this explicate realm.

The tangible explicate world is governed by its own laws, which Bohm calls the 'laws of heteronomy'. These are the physical laws of our observable universe. Newtonian physics, anatomy and physiology, the senses, the sun, moon and stars all are governed by these laws. Most scientific and medical research has been carried out at this explicate level. It is the level of the material world with its measurable quantities and physical processes. There is, however, a sub-structure to this tangible world, a whole other realm that Bohm calls the 'implicate order'. This is a realm literally 'enfolded' within the more obvious explicate world. It is a realm of subtle relationships with subtle plays of energy which bind things together as a whole. This process of interrelationship creates the implicate order. This order subsumes our physical 'real' world. In the 'new physics' we are discovering that things are not as simple as Descartes' clock. A physicist named Heisenberg has shown that the consciousness of the scientist is intricately bound up in the experiment: that the observer is *part* of what is being observed. Moreover, a theorem, developed by John Bell in 1964 and subsequently experimentally proven, shows that there is a basic interconnectiveness to all things. In his theorem, Bell showed that once two subatomic particles come into contact, even if they are moved to the opposite ends of the universe they still affect each other simultaneously! If you move one in one direction the other will instantaneously respond! Time and space become meaningless concepts here. Bohm postulates that substratal to our explicate world of time, space and matter is the implicate realm. This realm has its own laws which he calls the laws of 'holonomy' or laws of the whole. The universe is likened to a vast hologram where every piece of the hologram has all the information of the whole 'enfolded' within it. This enfolded order becomes 'unfolded' or explicit due to the various implicit laws of the whole, or of holonomy. Within the blueprint of what we can observe is a whole implicate realm which ties every seemingly separate thing, being and experience into one universal whole!

Dr Stone would say that the Polarity Principle is an implicate law of the whole. At its root there is an implicit oneness or wholeness which may be unseen at the explicate level. The ancient medical sciences, such as Ayurveda and Chinese medicine, have also looked deeply, to the subtle implicate processes. A simplified two-dimensional drawing is given in Figure 1.9 to try and show some of Bohm's ideas diagrammatically. Here we have the whole 'unfolding' of information into an explicate expression of itself. When one is observing from within the explicate order, the implicate order is not seen. It is like being on the surface of the earth and not being able to perceive the core of the earth within. In the diagram, each 'bump' is an unfolded aspect of reality which, in turn, may have further inherent implicate/explicate relationships. Each unfolding may have within it further enfolded information and thus further potential for exfoliation. (See Figure 1.10.)

Here we see the seeming paradox of the implicate being within the explicate and yet the explicate being a local expression of a greater whole. Thus, as the ancient mystics said, the whole is contained within the part. This simple schema can be carried into any level of complexity with various expressions contingent on each other: worlds within worlds, and universes within universes; worlds literally enfolded and contingent on each other.

Bohm has even brought the concept of consciousness back into physics by postulating an enfoldment of consciousness within this implicate order. Every expression of physical events may be accompanied by a simultaneous expression of consciousness. This notion also concurs with traditional philosophies which see no creation possible without the play of consciousness involved.

Here, in Bohm's work, we have a new expression of traditional cosmology, where everything is seen as a whole and, depending on your

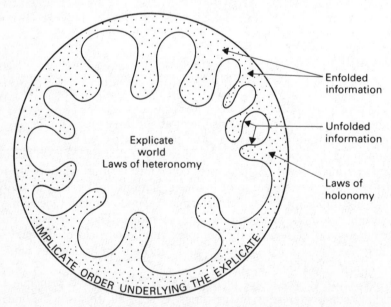

Fig. 1.9. Bohm's world-view

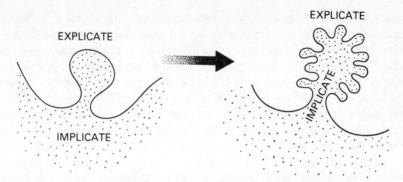

Fig. 1.10. The explicate and implicate world

perspective, we can perceive the implicate whole or the explicate part. Thus what may at first appear to be unrelated random occurrences, may actually be completely interrelated at an implicate level (see Figure 1.11).

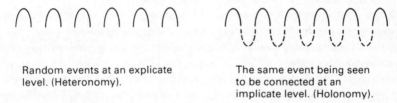

Random events at an explicate level. (Heteronomy).

The same event being seen to be connected at an implicate level. (Holonomy).

Fig. 1.11. Heteronomy and holonomy

Events in one part of the universe may simultaneously affect events in another part simply because they are actually part of the same whole. What may seem to be random events are actually following specific implicate laws of holonomy, laws of the whole. Corrolaries with traditional mysticism have not been overlooked and a debate is now raging in some part of the physics establishment about these ideas. I have oversimplified them, but hope that the basic concepts are clear.

An important aspect of this order of reality is that things need not be viewed in a linear sense. As processes come into form in relationship to each other, they may appear to be in linear relationship, but may actually be following implicate laws which determine their movement. One billiard ball hitting another causes the second to move. The sources of this movement could be seen in the complex emotional field of the player wielding the cue; a further source could include the influences which formed the player's life and so on.

If we return to our image of the Polarity Principle as a principle of unfolding, some interesting images arise. First of all, this is not a linear process, but a multidimensional one of vast complexity. If we expand the two-dimensional 'Polarity' shape into three dimensions we get a 'torus' shape, essentially a doughnut with an infinitely small hole (see Figure 1.12). In his book, *The Reflexive Universe*, Arthur Young sees this shape as the basic shape of the universe. It is a perfect holographic shape where every part of the torus is in contact with every other. If the torus is viewed as 'solid', we have the possibility of infinite 'layers'. Each layer may seem separate, but each layer is in contact with every other layer and is an organic whole; one layer cannot exist without the other. They are part of a whole, enfolded, like layers of an onion.

Eastern philosophies would claim that these relationships set up a hierarchy of consciousness and form, where the inner layers are more contracted in consciousness and denser in form. If we allow these layers the attribute of awareness, we could say that as you move outward the quality of each layer is more expansive, more aware, and of a subtler nature. As you move inward, they are more concentrated, less aware and of a denser, more physical nature. Each layer can be aware of only that which it encompasses, not of levels 'above', the more expansive layers which contain it. It is like the fish in the sea which are only aware of their layer of ocean and not of the atmosphere which surrounds it.

These relationships are the core of traditional philosophies, where the concept of hierarchy is another implicate law of the universe. The quality of the whole which we perceive is dependent on the quality of our con-sciousness and awareness. The more expansive, the more of the whole you perceive. As we have seen previously, in the concept of the enfolded and unfolded universe, the whole is enfolded in every part. Thus, if our quality of consciousness is expansive enough, the whole can be appre-hended!

This assertion is not a value judgement. The inner, more contracted layers are not 'worse' than the outer, more expansive layers. They are parts of the whole, parts of *one* movement of energy, of *one* process. As we shall see later it is the dynamic by which consciousness materialises.

The Tao and Inherent Consciousness

To return to our earlier Chinese concepts, these relationships can be conceived of as layers of an onion, with the Tao, or Source, at the centre

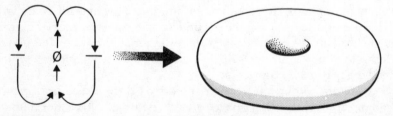

Fig. 1.12. The 'torus' shape

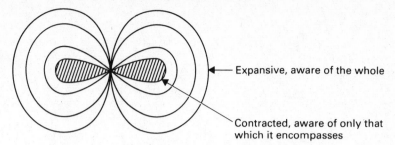

Fig. 1.13. Cross-section of 'Cosmic Doughnut'

of being. The first change into yin and yang phases is the outermost layer and subsequent changes become more and more contracted until physical form arises. The Tao is the neutral still point at the centre of things and all of the perceived world is an expression of its potentials. All of these expressions of Tao are enfolded within each other and are one (see Figure 1.14).

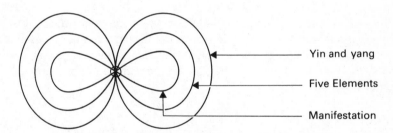

Fig. 1.14. Taoism within the 'Cosmic Doughnut'

Traditional cultures express these relationships at a level which transcends the mere physical understanding of energy. For energy, in the context of traditional wisdom, is imbued with, for want of a better term, consciousness. David Bohm envisioned this as a process of the enfolded consciousness within all processes. The traditions believe that this blueprint is due to an inherent intelligence behind the workings of the universe. This intelligence is what Dr Stone called the Source.

In the next chapter we will focus on this movement as seen within man as a reflection of the movement of energy in the universe as a whole.

Wireless Anatomy: The Microcosmic Reflection

Life is *one* even though it appears as many factors and actors. But always the same energy acts and reacts, and compounds itself . . . We draw from Nature what we need, like children of a great father and mother. The same energy which is in nature is also in us.

In the last chapter we saw how the universal or macrocosmic movement of energy is talked about both in traditional Eastern philosophies and by a modern physicist. Let us now look at these concepts in Dr Stone's terms and then see how the inner energies of man are an expression of this greater movement.

The Evolution and Involution of Energy

Dr Stone used to say, 'as above, so below'. He used this ancient saying to express the macrocosmic–microcosmic relationship. In these terms, the inner energies of man are a reflection of the greater play of energies in the universe as a whole. In David Bohm's terms, the information of the whole is enfolded within every human being. We are an explicate expression of an implicate wholeness.

Dr Stone talked about this universal play in his book *Energy*:

Polarity is the law of opposites in their finer attraction from centre to centre. Unity is the merging of these currents into one Essence. Creation brings forth opposites by its centrifugal force, like a fountain spray of manifestation flowing out to the limits of the cosmos and of each pattern unit.

He thus posits a universal law, the Polarity Principle. The movement of opposites is implicit in all of creation. To have life, to have movement, polarities must be active. They flow out of the source in an unimaginably powerful centrifugal or outgoing force. These energies interweave to form each expression of the source. That is, to form each man, each woman, each being, each blade of grass. When Dr Stone writes about the polarity movement 'from centre to centre' he is talking about the grand scheme of the universe! Traditional cultures have called the 'primal centre' various names: Tao, Godhead, Brahman, to name but a few. It is from this primal centre that all arises. From it, various step-down phases of energy occur in which polarities are drawn 'in their finer attraction' into less intense centres.

These transform higher vibrational energies into denser form. This 'fountain spray of manifestation' flows 'out to the limits of the cosmos' through a number of step-down phases and becomes denser at each successive phase. Finally, the energy becomes so dense that it 'condenses' into physical form. To describe this sequence, Dr Stone has also used the analogy of 'surface tension'.

> On the surface of these energy fields, whether large or small, they meet the resistance of space which contracts upon them and slows them down further to crystallisation. This is called surface tension . . . The surface limits the central activity . . . to confine and protect the soft and ever-expanding interior energy fields.

At the final stages of the involutionary process, when subtler energies are condensing or 'crystallising' into matter and form, the expansive outward-flowing energies meet resistance and slow down. In this process a 'surface tension' is formed where matter finds its final expression. This

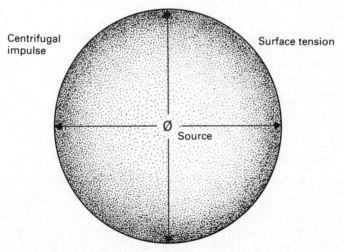

Fig. 2.1. The 'Cosmic Bubble'

occurs at the limit of the centrifugal force which originally brought forth the polarity relationship or 'pattern unit'. Each 'pattern unit' is an expression of a polarity relationship and is limited by the nature of the original impulse from the source.

This process can be visualised like a vast sphere expanding away from the source in all directions. At the point where the impulse slows down, the energy flow has lost impetus and reaches a 'point of exhaustion'. It is at this point of exhaustion of the original outgoing impulse that the surface tension forms. Physical form is at the extreme edge of this process. It is at the 'surface tension' of the cosmic bubble. The powerful thing about being at this edge, is that from here, a return to the source in an evolutionary, centripetal, receptive, phase is now possible (see Figure 2.1).

This condensing and slowing-down process into the cosmic bubble is necessary to protect the energies of the whole from being dissipated by endless expansion. As Dr Stone writes –

> Centres of energy are essential for creation of forms and their finer operation. It is essential that energy be concentrated and work according to definite patterns and designs or exhaustion would take place. If a stone is dropped in a pond of still water, waves radiate outward from the agitated area until that impulse of concentrated energy is exhausted.

Thus, the coarsening of energy into form is both an expression of a potential from within the source and a means to protect its outgoing energies from exhaustion. In modern physics it is known that no energy is ever lost or gained within the universe. It is, in a sense, a 'closed-circuit' system.

Following our earlier Polarity Principle, energy moves outward from the source to some completion and then must return back to the source both to complete the cycle and to protect its energies from dissipation. We will see later that this is a crucially important concept in Dr Stone's schema of health and disease.

In *The Wireless Anatomy of Man*, Dr Stone viewed these macro-cosmic–microcosmic relationships as a sequence of subtler energies stepping down in vibration, through various phases, until the physical realm where both mind and matter hold sway. We have previously seen this process in terms of Indian and Chinese cosmology. Let us now look at it in Dr Stone's framework. In outline form the involutionary movement of energies from the source is seen in discreet step-down phases. At each step-down, energies move through a neutral centre where, like the action of an electrical transformer, they are stepped down in vibration and intensity. At each step-down we have a coarsening of these energies and a narrowing of consciousness which is 'enfolded' within them. Figure 2.2 shows a simple map of this process.

At each phase of the step-down dynamic we have a movement of energy which mirrors the Polarity Principle. Here we have a flow of energy moving from a source in an expansive, outward yang phase of movement,

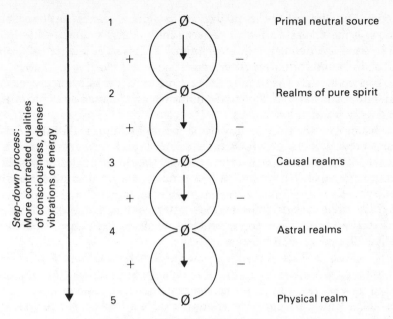

Step-down process: More contracted qualities of consciousness, denser vibrations of energy

1   Ø   Primal neutral source

+   −

2   Ø   Realms of pure spirit

+   −

3   Ø   Causal realms

+   −

4   Ø   Astral realms

+   −

5   Ø   Physical realm

Fig. 2.2. The Step-Down Process

to a point of exhaustion or completion. At that point, the energies have moved so far from their original source that they lose touch with this connection. At the point of this completion of the outward impulse, a contractive yin phase ensues. The energies, which are now of a lower vibration and of a more contracted quality of consciousness, are drawn together to form a new neutral centre which 'resonates' with the original source, but is of a coarser quality (see Figure 2.3).

At each centre, when the energies are drawn together, they merge into one neutral essence, which is a more opaque reflection of the subtle centre above.

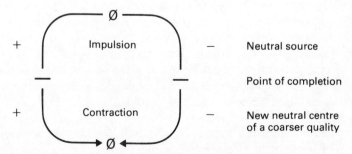

Ø

+   Impulsion   −   Neutral source

Point of completion

+   Contraction   −   New neutral centre of a coarser quality

Ø

Fig. 2.3. Impulsion and contraction

This impulse moves through various subtle realms until what is known as the 'Causal Realm' arises. The causal realm is a realm within us where consciousness crystallises as 'Mind'. This is not the physical brain, but a subtle and formative layer where movements of thought arise. At this phase, thoughts predominate and are of a neutral 'uncharged' or non-emotional state. In Tibetan Buddhism this is known as the Kun Zhi phase or 'ground of emergence'.

This movement is again slowed or crystallised into the 'Astral' realm where these thought processes take on subtle feeling tones. The Astral realm is therefore a realm where thought takes on qualities of subtle emotional charge. These energies of thought and feeling step down in quality to form the physical realm. An understanding of this configuration is crucial in understanding the patterns of health and disease. Currents of thought and emotion mould the physical body and must be dealt with in all healing relationships.

The causal and astral realms are not mystical places outside ourselves but are representations of an ongoing inner process of thought, emotion and form. We will explore this more deeply in a later chapter.

At the physical centre an energy system arises which mirrors the step-down process above. Although we are talking in linear terms of 'above' and 'below', this is really a dynamic relationship where each successive step-down realm is contained in a greater whole. So another way of picturing this model is in the image of the onion of the previous chapter. The onion is another way of visualising the 'cosmic bubble'. Here, each step-down represents a narrowing of consciousness and a crystallisation of energy and is contained, or is part of, a greater, more expansive, more conscious whole. (See Figure 2.4.)

The model describes the same movement from the source that was discussed previously in the Indian and Chinese systems. It represents a slowing of energies into physical condensation or, as Dr Stone would say, a crystallisation of energy into form. At the formation of the physical

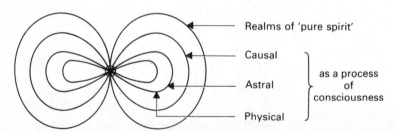

Fig. 2.4. A cross-section through the 'Cosmic Bubble'

centre, energies condense into a pattern which determines physical structure.

The realms of energy and matter below the physical centre, mirror the step-down sequence above. That which is above the physical centre is the macrocosm and that which is below is the microcosm. Again, this isn't a linear event, but a dynamic one in which the microcosm is contained within the macrocosm and, paradoxically the macrocosm is inherent in every part of the microcosm. The whole is within the part and the part is an expression of the whole. Within every cell of our body is a blueprint for the whole. indeed, the whole, which is contained in every nucleus of every cell, is necessary for the proper functioning of the part.

The Gunas

Dr Stone used the Ayurvedic and yogic model of energy relationship for his map of the subtle anatomy of man. This energy system is driven by three forces, or, as he would say, a 'triune function'. These forces, the *Gunas*, were introduced in the last chapter. They are, in Bohm's terminology, an implicate law of the universe and represent the three qualities of polarity relationship which allows all of creation to come into being.

The sattvic principle is one of neutrality. It is the principle of essence and stillness. It is a representation of the unconditioned neutral state found in all existence. It is, as the Chinese say, the stillness within motion which is at the centre of any event.

The rajasic principle is the positive yang phase of energy movement. It is the driving aspect of energy suggesting action and propulsion whose quality is the expansive, centrifugal phase of energy. It is the drive behind an event or experience. Rajas is the male aspect of our energy system, of assertion, warmth and the sun.

The tamasic principle is the negative yin phase of energy movement. It is the quality of the contractive, centripetal phase of energy. It is the phase of completion and of receptivity. It is the female aspect of our energy system, of receptivity and of crystallisation into forms.

Energy moves in these relationships. Rajas governs the positive impulsive phase of energy; sattvas governs the neutral ground which allows this movement and tamas governs its negative phase of completion:

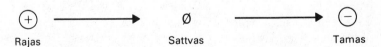

| (+) | ⟶ | ∅ | ⟶ | (−) |
| Rajas | | Sattvas | | Tamas |

The qualities of the Gunas underpin the subtle anatomy system of man which Dr Stone called the 'Wireless Anatomy of Man'.

The Three Principles

Satvas   Neutral Principle of Source: essence, stillness, neutral ground.

Rajas   Positive Principle of Action: driving force, expansion, warmth, centrifugal movement, assertive principle.

Tamas   Negative Principle of Completion: crystallisation into form, contraction, centripetal movement, receptive principle.

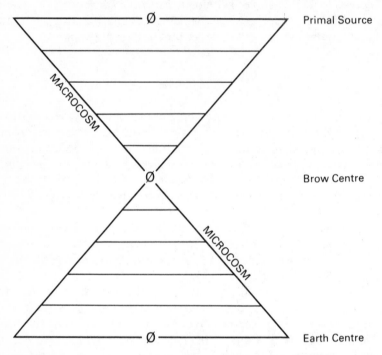

Fig. 2.5. Energy is expressed at the Brow Centre and manifests as physical form

The Physical Manifestation of Energy

As energy impulses from the Primal Source it goes through various step-down phases until it 'condenses' in the physical realm via the 'Brow Centre', sometimes called the 'Third Eye'. This, in many cultures is called the 'place of the soul'. The Chinese call it the 'upper field of elixir', which is the place of our 'original spirit'. (See Figure 2.5.)

When energy impulses from the Brow Centre, a whole chain of events is set off. From this centre, energy steps down in intensity to create our physical body. This embodiment mirrors the formation of the universe as a whole and sets the context for the creation of the individual. Thus the movement of energy from the Brow Centre mirrors the movement of energy from the source. The individual or the microcosm is alive within the context of the whole or the macrocosm. Further, as we have seen, the whole is implicate within each of its individual expressions.

The first crystallisation into physical being arises from the Brow Centre. Two waves of positive and negative energies expand outwards from the Brow Centre to form two pulsating currents. These are traditionally called the *pingala* and the *ida* currents (see Figure 2.6). These

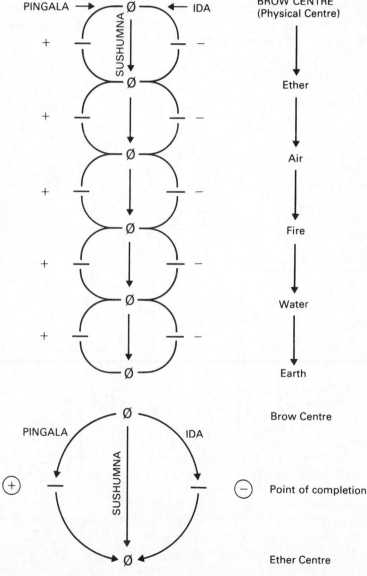

Fig. 2.6. The Three Currents: pingala, ida and sushumna

expand outward, reach their point of completion and then undergo a contractive phase. They are pulled together to form a new neutral centre in the throat, the Ether Centre.

Between the two centres, a third channel also arises. This is a neutral channel which is physically located in the spine. It is traditionally called the *sushumna*. These three currents, the pingala, ida and sushumna, represent the three phases of movement of the Gunas in their positive, negative and neutral qualities. They spiral down to form each chakra where they intersect. Where the currents are drawn together, a chakra or energy centre forms. From the Ether Centre down, a similar process occurs and four more centres are formed which are called the Air, Fire, Water and Earth Centres (see Figure 2.7).

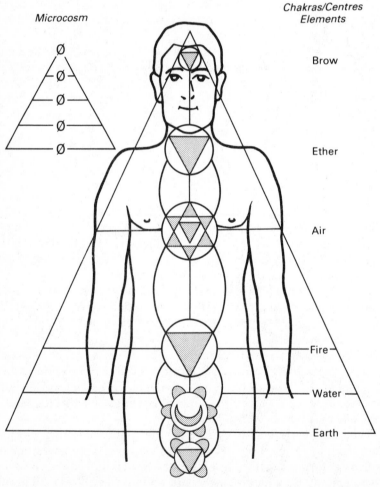

Fig. 2.7. The centres of the body

The Chakras and the Five Elements

These six centres are traditionally called *chakras* and they can be visualised as pulsating orbs which both suck energy in and push energy out of their centres. They are the source of energy flow for all the Five Element energy pulses. As energy steps down from centre to centre there is a narrowing of the field of consciousness and a lowering of energy intensity at each successive phase. Each centre acts like a two-way electrical transformer which steps down electrical voltage from a higher intensity to a lower intensity and back up again.

From the Ether Centre downwards, the five elements or energy relationships come into play and these five qualities of energy interweave to form the subtle energy patterns of man. At each chakra centre a different quality of energy arises. The quality of energy at each centre is called an 'element' and relates to the functions and processes of life which that centre governs.

The elements are also the bridge between body and mind and govern the physical expressions of emotional activity. The relationships between the elements and their energy patterns are dynamic ones and these are described in the next chapter. Health is dependent on a fluent and open relationship between them, and the polarity therapist works with these relationships on as many levels as possible.

Oval Fields

At each energy centre or chakra, fields of energy arise which Dr Stone called the 'oval fields' (see Figure 2.8). These fields arise from and surround the chakras. For energy to move, there must be a field to support its movement. These pulsating 'motor' fields provide a ground or medium which allows the movement of other energy patterns across them. The chakras may be thought of as sensory feedback fields. If more energy is required in a particular pattern, that information is 'fed' into the chakras and an appropriate response is made. The oval fields are motor fields which allow this to occur.

Although there are six chakras (the seventh or 'crown' chakra is really not a pulsating energy centre, but is rather a centre of potential expansive enlightenment), there are only five oval fields. This is because the last two chakras are of such a low vibration and low intensity that they can only drive one oval field between them.

Whereas the chakras are named for the quality of energy which emanates from them, the oval fields are named for the dominant quality of movement through them. The field in the head is named the 'fire oval' for the potentially fiery nature of thought and intellect. We've all heard the term 'a fiery intellect'. Both the Ether and Air ovals are named after their corresponding chakras as the quality of movement coincides with the quality of these centres. The oval field around the Fire chakra is named the Earth oval due to the processing and movement of food and faeces through this area. Finally, the oval field in the pelvic basin is named the Water oval due to the quality of watery elimination and sexual fluids and to the downward and outward movement of these from this area.

We now have the basis of a 'core-energy system'. The chakras, the three linking currents: ida, pingala and sushumna; and the oval fields. This can be conceived of within a two-dimensional diagram, as in Figure 2.8. However, it is important to remember that these fields and currents are not two-dimensional, but are dynamic pulsations of energy from the centre out and from the periphery in. Dr Stone called these pulsations the

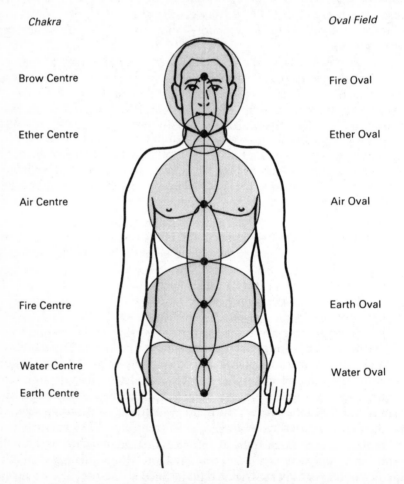

Chakra		Oval Field
Brow Centre		Fire Oval
Ether Centre		Ether Oval
Air Centre		Air Oval
Fire Centre		Earth Oval
Water Centre		Water Oval
Earth Centre		

Fig. 2.8. Core Energy Patterns: this is the Core system from which the basic energy patterns of the Five Elements arise

centrifugal and centripetal phases of energy movement. There are also many other energy patterns that relate to the elements and help weave the energy system which underpins physical form. The three major currents which emanate from the chakra system mirror the three principles of the Gunas. The first is a neutral current which Dr Stone called the East–West current. It is also called the Transverse Current and relates to the sattvic quality of neutrality. It emanates from the positive and negative poles (top and bottom) of the neutral sushumna current of the core energy system. It then spirals transversely around the body. Its function is one of intercommunication and binding. It is a neutral feedback pattern and helps to relate the periphery of the energy system to the core. It also relates to the parasympathetic nervous system, which is the system in prominence in meditative states.

The next is a Fiery current which Dr Stone called the Spiral Current. It relates to the rajasic quality of movement and expansion and emanates from the Fire Centre. It spirals from the umbilicus to encompass the whole of the energy system and it functions to provide the quality of energy for movement, warmth and healing. It governs the distribution of internal vital energy throughout the body. It also relates to the sympathetic nervous system, which is the system in prominence in activity and action.

The last pattern is formed by currents which pulsate individually from each chakra. These are collectively called the Long Line Currents and relate to the tamasic quality of completion. They emanate from each centre in specific patterns or current lines. Each current is of the quality of energy most like that of its centre. So the current which arises from the Water Centre is thus called the Water current line. They emanate from each chakra, expand outward in a vertical fashion and then return to the centre in a contractive phase. Their function is to regulate and monitor the physiology of the body. Dr Stone said that the Long Line Currents carry the energies of the mind into the body and hence govern the functioning of the five senses. It relates to the central nervous system and the

movement of energy through the cranial rhythm. We will discuss this
rhythm and this process of mind in matter in a latter chapter.

Each element governs specific organ systems and tissue responses.
These currents act as a feedback mechanism which governs the intensity
and strength of energies to related physiological processes. The three
current patterns are represented diagrammatically in Figure 2.9.

As we can see, the composite picture is a complex intermeshing of currents. This must not be visualised as a static, linear process with pencil-
thin current lines, but as a dynamic relationship where each line presents a
pulsation of wave-like energy which emanates from the core and returns
to the core. It sets up a complex interference pattern, which, like the interference pattern of light in a hologram (discussed in Chapter 1), underpins
the creation of physical form. This is the basis of the Wireless Anatomy of
Man and is the foundation for the description of other energy patterns
which relate to the Five Elements. The polarity therapist works to open
and balance blockages in these patterns and fields to encourage healing
and self-regulation in both psychological and physiological realms.

In our next chapter we will discuss the general relationships of these
pulsations which underlie physical form. They are better visualised as
pulsations of light in specific patterns than as moving energy in channels.

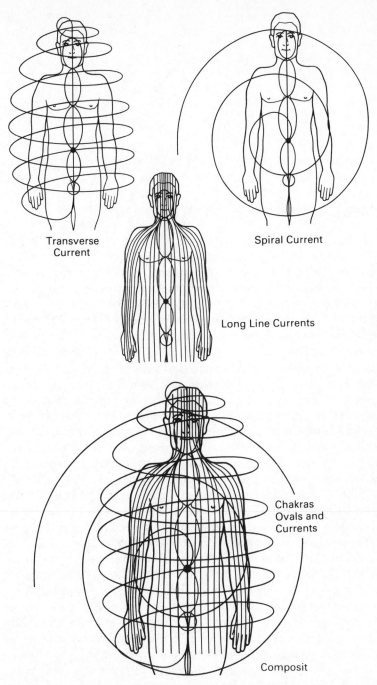

Transverse
Current

Spiral Current

Long Line Currents

Chakras
Ovals and
Currents

Composit

Fig. 2.9. The Three Currents

CHAPTER THREE

Pulsations, Fields and Transitions

The river of life's finer energy, called 'Prana' is the vital force in the body. It is the activator which flows through the five ovals of the body – the head, the neck, the chest, the abdomen and the pelvis – or five fields of matter for specific functions of sensory and motor expression.

Pulsations

All life is pulsation, movement. If there is no movement, there is no life. The difference between health and disease lies in the relative freedom and balance of the energetic and physical movement patterns in our mental, emotional and physical fields. In this chapter I'd like to explore the relationships between the general pulsation of energy in the body, the fields it both creates and flows through and the transitions it must negotiate between these fields.

As we have seen in Chapter 2, vital energy first manifests at the Brow Centre. The general flow or pulsation of energy moves from this centre downwards and from the spinal core outwards to the periphery. Dr Stone called this the centrifugal or outward-bound pulsation. It defines the general movement of energy from the core into physical form and outward in its relationships with the world.

The centrifugal phase is an expansive pattern of movement from the source of energy outward into form. In our physical patterning the source of energy is our chakra system. As we have seen in our discussion of the Polarity Principle, energy must return to its source or be dissipated. Dr Stone called this return phase the *centripetal* phase. In this phase, energy pulsates from the feet upwards and from the periphery inwards back to the core. We thus have a general pulsation of life energy in patterns of expansion and return. (See Figure 3.1.) Every subtle energy current follows this pattern of expansion and relaxation. Indeed all of our physiological relationships also follow this pattern. The expansion–contraction of the lungs and heart and the contraction–relaxation of our muscles are simple examples of this. The energy current pulsations, such as the Long Line currents, the Spiral currents and the East–West current, are not channels or meridians of energy, but are pulsations from the core outwards and back again which follows this general rule of expansion and return. They are better visualised as pulsations of light in wave-like patterns rather than as energy moving in channels.

This general movement of energy in its centrifugal and centripetal pulsation sets up general polarity relationships in the body (see Figure 3.2). The top of the body, the head, where energy arises from, is most positive. The bottom, at the feet is most negative and dense, it is where energy becomes 'grounded': these relationships are most clearly seen in Dr Stone's 'Polarity Zone Chart' (see Figure 3.3), which outlines the general polarity relationships of the body. As energy moves in its outward and inward pulsation, relative zones of polarity relationship are

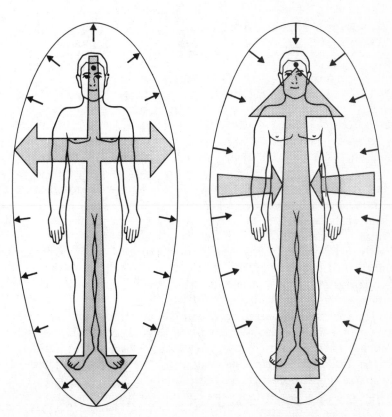

Fig. 3.1. Energy pulsates in phases of expansion and contraction

set up. These form the basic harmonics of the body and the basic polarity relationships of energy flow.

In the Zone Chart we can see these overall harmonics. As energy pulsates through the fields of the body, specific energy relationships are set up. If you think once again of our earlier discussion about energy, you will remember that energy must flow in positive–neutral–negative

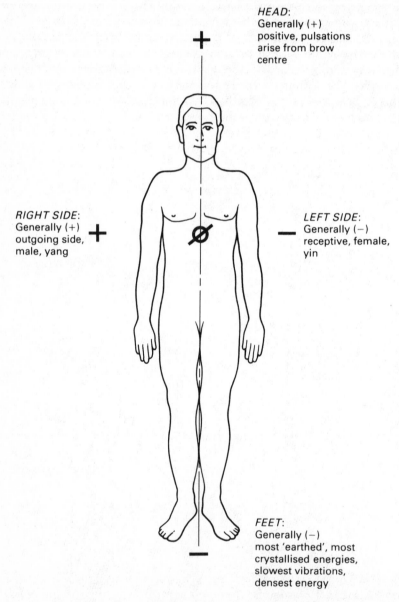

HEAD:
Generally (+)
positive, pulsations
arise from brow
centre

RIGHT SIDE:
Generally (+)
outgoing side,
male, yang

LEFT SIDE:
Generally (−)
receptive, female,
yin

FEET:
Generally (−)
most 'earthed', most
crystallised energies,
slowest vibrations,
densest energy

Fig. 3.2. General polarities of the body

relationships. When energy flows into form, zones of positive, neutral and negative relationships are set up. These relationships reflect our basic Polarity Principle of energy movement. For energy to move, these relationships must come into play. The polarity therapist can use an understanding of these zones of relationship therapeutically. A blockage in any zone of energy movement will affect the flow in all other corresponding zones. This is similar to the way in which striking middle 'C' on a piano will cause all other 'C's to vibrate. In other words, energies of like quality resonate with each other. This is a basic energetic law. Thus an energy restriction in a positive zone area will set up like restrictions in other positive zone areas. The practitioner can follow blockages and imbalances through these resonant zones and help to restore a more flowing movement of energy through its polarity relationships. We shall see that this becomes much more complex when we explore the energy patterns of the Five Elements.

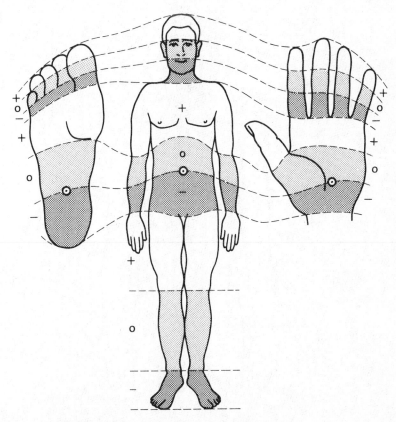

Fig. 3.3. Polarity Zone Chart: the general movement of the expansive and contractive pulsations of energy sets up zones of relative polarity relationships

The Energetic Fields and Transitions

As we know, from the Polarity Principle, energy must have fields to flow through. Dr Stone called the basic fields of the body 'oval fields' and I would now like to explore these more deeply. The positive–neutral–negative relationships of energy must be supported by fields which allow these patterns to flow. Electricity needs a field to flow through. This field could be anything which allows its flow. It could be copper wire, water or any other appropriate field. In the body's energy system these appropriate fields are the oval fields which arise around each chakra. There are, as you remember, six chakras and five oval fields. The five fields also generally define the five physical body cavities: the Fire oval relates to the head; the Ether oval to the neck; the Air oval to the chest; the Earth oval

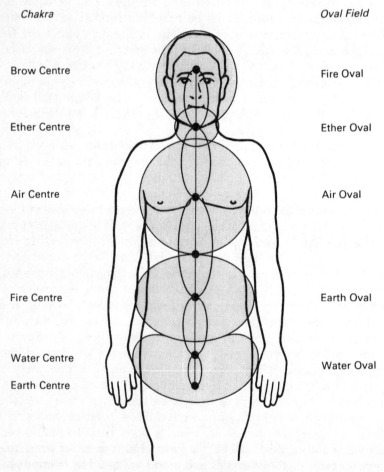

Chakra	Oval Field
Brow Centre	Fire Oval
Ether Centre	Ether Oval
Air Centre	Air Oval
Fire Centre	Earth Oval
Water Centre	Water Oval
Earth Centre	

Fig. 3.4. The Oval Fields

to the abdominal cavity; and the Water oval to the pelvic basin. The Fire oval relates to the Eye Centre, the Ether oval to the Throat Centre, the Air oval to the Heart Centre, the Earth oval to the Naval Centre and the Water oval to the pelvic centres. We thus have a picture of the chakras and the fields which surround them (see Figure 3.4).

As we have seen, each oval field manifests as a different quality of energy. The field around the Eye Centre has a different energetic vibration from the field which surrounds the Water and Earth centres. Your head has a different feel or quality to it when compared to your pelvis. They are different body parts with different qualities of energetic vibration and sensation. Each field sets the tone for the body part it underlies. As you move down the body, the fields become more condensed, more earthed. The Fire oval in the head is a lighter, more vibrant field than the Water field below. The Water field, in its position, must be heavier, denser so that grounding and movement in the world can occur. Each field has its quality and function. The Fire oval relates to the fire of energy coming into form, it is the first field formed at conception, a fusion of opposites in a fiery creation. In life it is about the fire of intelligence and the clarity of insight. The Ether field is about space and communication. The Air oval is about breath and heartfelt feelings. The Earth oval is about strength and power. It is about how we use our force, whether it be for digestion or for action. The Water oval is about grounding, flow and connection to the world. Each has its quality and function.

An important thing happens between these fields. At every place a field meets or changes into another field, there is a transition. At every transition, there is a major change of energy. So every place where the oval fields meet is a place of major change or shift in the quality of energy. Between the Fire oval in the head and the Ether oval in the neck there is a major transition at the base of the skull as energy steps down from one field to the other. The next transition is between Ether and Air at the top of the shoulders, then Air and Earth at the diaphragm, and Earth and Water at the top of the pelvis. Each transition is expressed as a transition in the body itself. We have talked about energy harmonics earlier and about how energy steps down into form. Looking at these oval fields, their transitions and relationships, we can begin to see how these fields become physical and underlie our form. The key to this understanding lies in the body's connective tissue and fascia. Fascia is tough, elastic tissue which connects, supports and integrates body structures and functions. Fascia wraps around all the muscles, organs and vessels of the body. It keeps them separate and allows them to function in relationship to each other. Connective tissue connects bones to each other and muscles to bones. It connects body parts to each other and surrounds and supports the body's functional systems. It wraps around nerve sheaths, digestive organs and blood vessels. The interesting thing about fascia and connective tissue is that it is all continuous. You cannot really say where one part starts and the other stops. Fascia is one sheet which wraps around everything and is continuous from the tips of our toes to the top of our head. On a physical level, it integrates body functions. A restriction or imbalance in one area gets transferred to other areas via this continuity. Thus tension in the pelvis can be transferred to the diaphragm and thence to the shoulders and neck. Knowing these energetic and physical relationships becomes a great tool in the process of healing and health maintenance.

The energetic oval fields take form via connective tissue. The fascial patterns of an area are underlied by these energy fields. The oval field in the head manifests via the dural membranes of the cranium. When the energy field in the head contracts or is restricted, the fascial field which manifests as cranial dural membranes also constricts and becomes imbalanced. This has important implications for the whole body and we will discuss this in a later chapter on the cranial rhythm and cranial polarity relationships.

The transition between the Fire oval of the head and the Ether oval in the neck is formed by the base of the skull and jaw. It is common to accumulate tension and strain at places of transition and I am sure many of you have experienced tightness and tension at the base of the skull and jaw. These areas also reflex down to the pelvis and sacrum as we will see later. The important point here is that a place of energy transition, in this case the interface between the Fire and Ether ovals, become a place of physical transition in the body also. Here connective tissue and muscle attachments meet and form a physical tissue pattern which mirrors the place of energy transition.

At the base of the neck, where the Ether oval meets the Air oval, another physical place of transition is formed. Here connective tissues attach to the clavicle and scapulae to form the thorax inlet. A transverse bonding of fascia results. At these places of transition, energy must negotiate its way through major step-downs. Imbalances in the fields themselves or in the relationship between the fields can manifest as imbalance or restrictions which focus at these transitions.

The transition between the Air oval, of the chest, and the Earth oval, of the abdomen, is the respiratory diaphragm. The diaphragm is the main muscle of breath and obviously an important focus for body patterns and emotion processes. Between the abdominal field and the pelvis a band of fascia is found which forms invaginations and pouches for the pelvic organs. At the bottom of the pelvis the last important fascial band is found, the perineal floor. This is the floor of the pelvis. It is comprised of muscles and fascia which form a sling which is continuous from the sacrum at the back to the pubic bone in the front. It is very important energetically and structurally. Many energy and structural patterns reflex here.

The important idea to grasp is that energy underlies physical form. Here we see a process where basic energy oval fields are mirrored in the body by connective tissue fields. Energy imbalances become physical imbalances via these fields. Dr Stone once wrote 'it's all in the connective tissues'. Our thoughts, feelings and physical processes become manifest in the fascial patterns of the body and these conditioned processes can become manifest as tension, restriction, limitation and disease. So for every energy field, there is a harmonic physical field. The oval fields form fields which allow other energies to move through. Fascia also forms fields for other things to happen in. Fascia holds everything together and creates structural and movement fields for body functions to act in.

Coming back to our discussion of transitions, the transitions between fields allow movement between the fields to occur. They are places of transition and transfer of movement. If the transitions are restricted, movement becomes restricted. Every oval field is also a fascial field. At the edge of every fascial field there is a major transition in the body. It is where fascial patterns come together and connect to body structure. Here one field meets another. (See Figure 3.5.)

These transitions are quite important. When the relationship between two fields becomes imbalanced, the transition between them becomes stressed. So we see that at every place where there is a transition between energy fields there is a physical relationship that expresses that transition. Let's say a person receives an emotional shock and their Heart Centre closes down. The oval field around it will tend to contract. The fascia which relates to this field will contract also. The areas of transition at the shoulders and diaphragm then become stressed and will also contract to protect the heart from further pain. The diaphragm restricts breathing and pulls up on pelvic fascia. The pelvis becomes involved and tension appears in the pubic and sacral areas. Fire may get bound up in anger in relationship to the heart pain. Abdominal fascia reacts, especially around the solar plexus. This places further stress on the diaphragm. Fascial fields further react; the shoulders pull forward, the chest collapses; the head drops and cervical fascia become involved. This is transferred to spinal membranes, the dural tube and the cranial membranes. A whole body pattern results which all began from an emotional shock and energetic contraction. Remember, form follows energy and our thoughts, feelings and physical form are not separate.

The five oval fields are three-dimensional. They are both sensory and motor. They are motor fields in that they are the fields which allow other energy movement through them; they allow a movement into the world. They are sensory in that they relate to the feeling tones of the front of the body and allow a return flow from the periphery back to the chakra centre. These five fields support the energy movements of the Five Elements as energy patterns arise from each chakra. They support our emotional and physiological functioning. I like to consider the five oval fields as sensory fields, because we feel things through them. When our feelings close down, our energy fields close down and the fascial fields that relate to them also close down. They are very responsive to how we

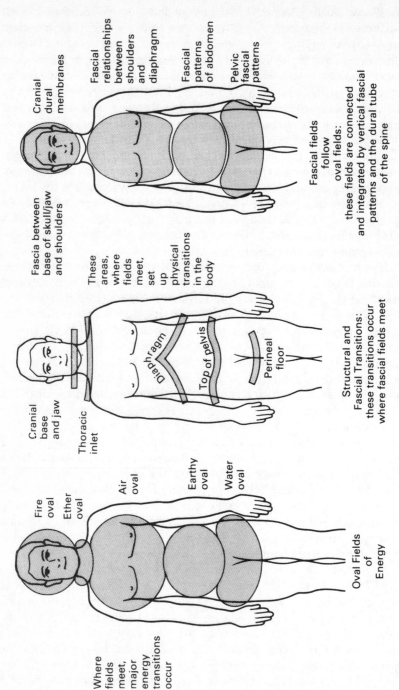

Fig. 3.5. Fields and Transitions

Left figure (Oval Fields of Energy):

Where fields meet, major energy transitions occur

Fire oval
Ether oval
Air oval
Earthy oval
Water oval

Oval Fields of Energy

Middle figure (Structural and Fascial Transitions):

Cranial base and jaw

Thoracic inlet

Diaphragm

Top of pelvis

Perineal floor

These areas, where fields meet, set up physical transitions in the body

Structural and Fascial Transitions: these transitions occur where fascial fields meet

Right figure:

Cranial dural membranes

Fascia between base of skull/jaw and shoulders

Fascial relationships between shoulders and diaphragm

Fascial patterns of abdomen

Pelvic fascial patterns

Fascial fields follow oval fields: these fields are connected and integrated by vertical fascial patterns and the dural tube of the spine feel. These oval energy pulsations support our emotional and physiological functioning. We all know that how we feel, what we hold in, manifests in our body.

The front of the body is generally considered to be sensory, as we face the world from our front, feel our feelings related to the front and take in the world from the front. The back of the body is generally considered motor. It is about support, structure and movement. The fields on the back of the body allow support and movement to occur. My ability to bend my spine and flex and move my arms and legs all relate to what is happening behind me. The fields in the back rest on the pelvis. Above the pelvis the fields form a pattern of inverted triangles. The neck sits on the upper triangle and the head sits on the neck. (See Figure 3.6.)

So we have five fields of energetic and physical functioning which relate the head, neck and shoulders to the pelvis below and underlie mobility and muscular action. The lower triangle sits on the sacrum, so as the sacrum and hip joints come into balance, everything above tends to

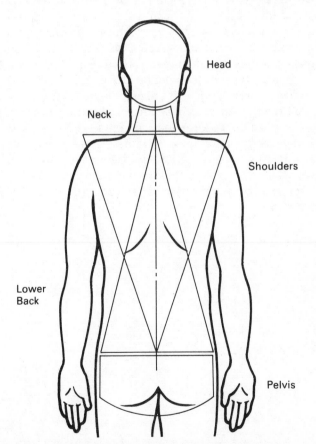

Fig. 3.6. Five posterior motor fields set up by gravity patterns and muscular/fascial patterns

move to balance. Dr Stone stressed this in his structural balancing work. If the sacrum torsions, the triangle above must compensate.

The quality of these motor fields is very different to the sensory oval fields in front. They are about balance, support and movement. These functions are reflected by fascial planes that go up and down and corner to corner. The trapezius and latissimus dorsi muscles physically mirror these patterns. Although they are about structure, they are not separate from the sensory fields in front. They support the action of the sensory fields. If you close your heart down, there will very likely be a motor response behind the heart. The shoulders may tense, the tissue may thicken in response to the sensory fields' contraction. The motor field will contract to help withhold feeling and action. A great hurt may translate into great anger. It may be inappropriate to express this anger at the time, or it may be too dangerous to express. Tense muscles and deadened feelings in the shoulders and upper back may help to hold the anger back.

A sensory feeling withheld unskilfully may give rise to a motor restriction. So we first have the energetic imbalance, then the physical response gets translated into body structure and structural imbalance results. An imbalance anywhere results in compensations elsewhere. The energetic field in the pelvis contracts as the Water chakra closes down due to sexual assault or fear, the oval field in the pelvis contracts, an imbalanced sacrum results, the spine above must compensate to maintain an upright posture. The cervical vertebrae become involved, the cranial base distorts and again a whole-body pattern of imbalance and compensation results. The sensory block takes on a motor tone. Feelings get frozen, crystallised in form. The polarity therapist works with these sensory and motor relationships with a deep whole-person integrated understanding. In our next chapter we will begin to explore the patterns of energy which move through these sensory and motor fields, the patterns of the Five Elements.

CHAPTER FOUR

The Five Elements: The Mind in Manifestation

Mind is Consciousness; Prana is Life. These two forces must be understood in all rational therapy.

In our last few chapters we saw how energy moves from the source to form the subtle energy system of man. This universal movement is mirrored or reflected in our inner energy system. The six chakra centres are a reflection of the greater movement of energy within the universe as a whole. Recently, in electron microscopy it was discovered that the helical pattern of the basic DNA molecule crosses over itself six times: we see the universal pattern expressed at even this most subtle physical phase.

In this chapter we are going to look more deeply at the Five Elements in terms of energy process. The unfolding of our thoughts, emotions and bodily relationships is an expression of this process. The Five Element relationships are very formative expressions of energy which underlies our mental, emotional and physical states. They are all, as we shall see, energy flows in dynamic relationship. All of these patterns overlap, interweave and interrelate in dynamic movement. As energies step down at the various chakra centres, qualities of energy and awareness contract and become narrowed. A kind of layering is effected where certain patterns are more expansive and encompassing than others. Thus, all that the Air element encompasses is more of the total picture than, say, the Water element and its relationships. However, the Water element is just as essential for a healthy and flowing energy system, and blockages and imbalances in any 'layer of the onion' will affect the *whole* matrix. This elemental confluence is the 'stuff' of life and the most important realm of work in Polarity Therapy. (See Figure 4.1.)

THE POLARITY PROCESS

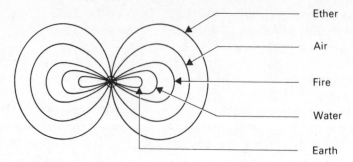

Ether

Air

Fire

Water

Earth

Fig. 4.1. The Five Element Configuration: each layer becomes more and more contracted in awareness, energy vibration and expression; each outer layer encompasses and takes in more of the whole

Dr Stone based his system of healing on a deep theoretical understanding of the Five Element interrelationship. He used the Ayurvedic system of elements as his model. He found within it a clear knowledge of both the psychological and physical ramifications of unbalanced energy and a clear presentation of the dynamics involved. As the Five Elements are names given to the qualities of energy which arise from each chakra, and as these energies govern the anatomy and physiology of the body and are also expressions of qualities of consciousness, they have vast implications in the understanding of health and disease. One's quality of consciousness and modes of behaviour are reflected in this flux.

Let us first look at our overall energy process, whereby subtler qualities of energy move through step-down phases to become more and more physical. Dr Stone worked with three major phases of energy in this overall movement: the subtle patterns of the Five Elements which directly arise from our core-energy system; the step-down qualities of these patterns as seen in the nervous system; and the most condensed form of energy, the physical body through its muscles and bony structure.

There are other phases of energy in this process whereby it is also possible to affect the energy system. The Chinese, for example, chose to focus their acupuncture system on the meridians or *ching* as they are called. These are subtle channels of energy which pass through all major organs and also have various specific functions. They are a dense form of *chi* which can be contained in subtle channels. The subtlest energies, however, are pulsations and 'streamings' which cannot be contained even in subtle channels. The meridians are a kind of 'middle ground' of energy where energies can be affected very directly via needles and other methods. They are a denser form of energy, but the *chi* within these channels is still very subtle compared to physical structure.

The Chinese also knew of the subtler pulsations of energy which Dr Stone called the 'Wireless Anatomy of Man'. To work with these they focused on what they called the three *Tan T'iens* or 'fields of elixir' and their wavelike pulsations. These reside in the Brow Centre, the Air or Heart Centre and the Water or Generative Centre. The Chinese developed various powerful meditation processes and exercises to affect these subtler pulsations of chi which are generally called *Chi Kung* exercises or 'good works on vital energy'. For our purposes we will focus on the three phases of energy used in polarity therapy as these describe the general movement of energy from the most subtle phases to the most physical.

Energy moves from the Brow Centre through the five physical chakras. We can call the incoming energy 'Primary Energy'. Energy enters each chakra from above and is then transformed and pushed out as a Five Element pattern. So, Primary Energy enters the chakra via the *pingala*, *ida* and *sushumna* currents and is transformed and pulsated outward as specific Five Element pulsations. Each chakra pulsates waves of specific vibrations in dynamic relationships and these all intermesh to form the Five Element energy orb sometimes called the 'etheric body'. These patterns, in turn, 'step down' in vibration and pulsation and take expression via the nervous system. The energies of the nervous system convey the Five Element energies into physical form and can be thought of as a middle ground where subtler energy flows become physical and subtler imbalances take physical form. (See Figure 4.2.) In the rest of this chapter we are going to explore the most formative phase of this energy process via the Five Element relationships.

The Descent of Energy

As we have seen, the general movement of energy in both man and the universe as a whole, is governed by the three *Gunas*; the *sattvic*, *rajasic* and *tamasic* phases of energy movement. All energy moves through these phases of neutral, positive and negative relationships. The Gunas, as principles of energy movement, outline its flow. The Five Elements, as expressions of the quality of this movement, define its progression. The Gunas represent the movement of energy through its positive and negative poles. The Elements are an expression of this movement in its specific patterns. The Five Elements delineate the quality, energy patterns and sphere of influence of each chakra. Each element defines and expresses an 'orb' of consciousness, energy pattern and bodily function. At each step-down phase there are corresponding differences in the quality and intensity of each energy orb. The first centre, the Ether Centre, is the subtlest; the last centre, the Earth Centre, is the densest. All five qualities of energy are found everywhere in the body, but each is in predominance in its own sphere of psychological and physiological activity. The lower the chakra, the more restricted the quality of consciousness and the slower the quality of energy vibration. The Brow Centre is most expansive and has the potential for all-encompassing perception. The Earth Centre is least

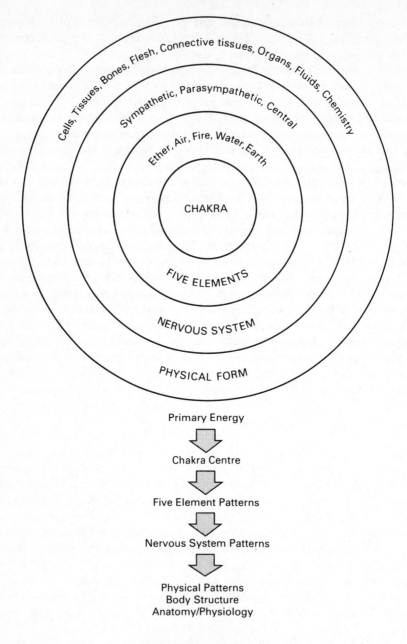

Primary Energy

Chakra Centre

Five Element Patterns

Nervous System Patterns

Physical Patterns
Body Structure
Anatomy/Physiology

BASIC ENERGY DYNAMICS
Primary energy as it pulsates
through its layers into form

*Fig. 4.2. Basic energy dynamics: primary energy as it pulsates through its
layers into form*

encompassing and most contracted, and deals with a limited realm of expression. But, as we shall see, it is just as important and vital as any other centre above.

The elements can be viewed as defining a movement of energy which creates a cycle. An outward, centrifugal phase flows from Ether to Earth and an inward centripetal phase flows from Earth to Ether. Dr Stone used to say 'That which is first becomes last and that which is last becomes first' to express this concept. Each element has its own movement and patterns and these step down or up in intensity to interrelate with every other element. This overlay creates the 'interference' pattern we mentioned earlier. Energy blockages can occur anywhere in this cyclical, interrelated pulsation. It is important to realise that these Five Element relationships are a structure for the expression of *one* energy in different ways. All energies are one (as modern physicists are discovering) and this one energy takes different forms. The chakras and elements together form a structure for the unfolding of this one energy, this one universal consciousness.

An understanding of the interrelated elemental cycles can give us a wonderful framework for understanding emotional and physical imbalance. These cycles can be viewed in very practical terms. If we take the building of a house, we have the Ether phase of a 'field of need' for the new house, the Air phase of thinking and planning, the Fire phase of putting energy into its creation, the Water phase of grounding the ideas in the nuts and bolts of building and the Earth phase of completion. We then return to Ether when we take possession of the new house and have a new 'field' for the family. Although each phase seems separate, they all actually interpenetrate each other.

The Ether field must always be present for the other phases to work in. The Air phase of thinking and planning is actualised by the Fire phase of 'putting it out' into the world, which must always be present for the Water phase of construction to complete itself in the Earth phase of the finished product. If we get stuck in any of these phases, the cycle will never reach completion. It is the same in the body; each phase of energy and its patterns must relate fluently to all other phases, or imbalance and blockages of energy flow will occur. We will explore this process more deeply in our next chapter.

The Foetal Triads

The first step in our life process is the moment of conception. This is also the moment in which the Five Elements first arise. In the cosmology of the ancient traditions referred to earlier, at the time of conception, three things must come together to form the new foetus. They are the sperm, the ovum and the soul or consciousness of the newly formed being. This again mirrors the polarity principle of energy flow and the movement of the Gunas through positive, negative and neutral poles. The sperm is considered to be the male, positive pole; the ovum, the female negative pole and the soul, the neutral pole which resonates most deeply with the source. When this occurs a great fusion of energy takes place and the subtle energy patterns of the foetus begin to form.

This is a process where the very formative phases of energy interweave to create the subtle energy 'hologram' for physical form. At the centre of this developing matrix the chakras come into being in their dynamic flux of Five Element energy pulses, working through triad relationships. There are many relationships for each element, but the most primary or formative triads are the ones that arise at this primal intermeshing and are called the 'foetal triads'. As we have described earlier, all energy moves through the three relationships of positive, negative and neutral phases. These relationships set up energy and bodily 'triads' or poles for each element. These energy relationships occur at the time of conception, interweave and overlay to form the subtle matrix which allows the physical body to form. These relationships are beautifully shown in Dr Stone's 'Foetal Chart', depicted in Figure 4.3.

The important thing here is that the various Element triads are expressions of interpenetrating relationships which pulsate as *one* process. Ether is the 'ground' element or field which allows the four active elements of Air, Fire, Water and Earth to form their relationships. This intermeshing of Elements and relationships is actually a process of vital energy moving through its various phases. The Elements are the aspects through which this universal energy moves in its various phases of steam, water vapour,

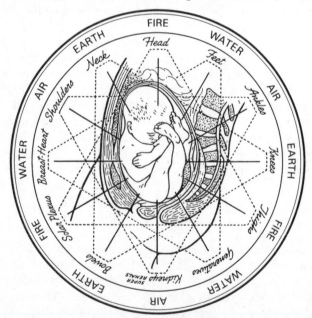

Fig. 4.3. The Foetal Chart shows the interweaving of the four active elements to create the basic energy relationships of the physical body

liquid, ice, etc. Each phase seems quite different and separate; yet it is just the same energy occurring in its different states. Let us explore these phases more closely now and start with the Brow Centre as energy pulsates from it to form the subtle anatomy of man.

The Brow Centre

As we have described in our last chapter, energy moves from subtler fields to the Brow Centre, which is the first 'chakra' or energy centre of the 'wireless anatomy' system. This centre is used in many spiritual traditions as a 'way in' to higher levels of consciousness and a reconnection with our Primal Source. In Taoism it is the place of pure spirit, in Hinduism it is the seat of the soul, in some forms of Mahayana Buddhism, the highest energy centre and the seat of intuitive wisdom, clarity and insight. It is the energy centre closest to the source and is the most encompassing of all centres. It is the pivot point between the subtler realms of energy and physical form and is a 'place' where we have a foot on either side of the door. We can use this door as a 'way-in' to cultivate subtler and more conscious energies and thus to follow the receptive pull back to the source, or we can follow our energies through the other side of the door and become immersed in our conditioning and habit patterns, caught up in our own private world of ego. From this centre our physical energies emerge and it is from here that the first of the five elemental chakras takes expression. (See Figure 4.4.)

The Ether Centre

From the Brow Centre, energies step down in vibration and intensity to create the Ether Centre. As we have seen earlier, the Ether Centre has its location in the throat area and is the first centre to be expressed as a Five Element relationship. The Five Element energies arise from the Ether Centre and the other four energy centres of Air, Fire, Water and Earth are step-downs of energy from it. The superimposed pulsations of energy from all five centres form the interference pattern sometimes called the 'etheric body'. The Ether Centre is thus the ground or field from which the other elements arise. Dr Stone called it the 'one river from which the other four rivers arise'. Ether is a basic ground element, a unified field which creates subtle space for the movement of the other elements. We recall from our previous chapters that in order for energy to flow, there must be a neutral field. Ether creates this subtle neutral field. The basic qualities of this element are stillness, harmony and balance. It is the closest element in quality to the neutral centre of the source and is the neutral ground for the manifestation of the mind–body complex. It is not a moving element but is a field which allows movement and thus has no triad polarity relationship

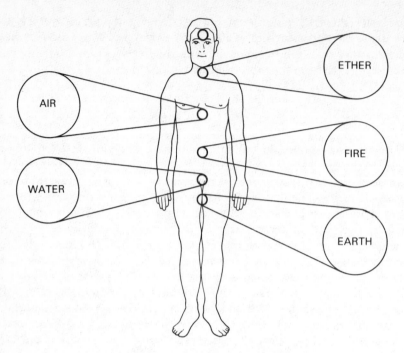

Fig. 4.4. Chakras and Elements

attributable to it. The other elements have specific 'triad' relationships in the body which are defined by their positive, neutral and negative poles of movement. Ether does not, as it is the neutral field in which the other elements move. The triads are relationships of energy movement. Ether is the quality of stillness at the heart of this movement.

Each element has attributes which relate to various qualities of consciousness. These can be thought of in a threefold framework. Thus each element governs certain qualities of mind, of emotion and of physical expression. Ether governs the qualities of mind which relate to tranquillity, peace, stillness. It is said that when one is in the presence of a great Spiritual Master, one's mind turns towards these qualities. Thus, in many traditions it is important to be in the presence of the teacher in order to experience the transmission of this subtle quality of mind. When our minds are still and our rambling thoughts are quiet, we can then truly see, hear and feel the truths within. The field of the Ether Element is the quality of energy in physical form which mirrors the harmony and balance of the Primal Source of the Tao, of Nirvana, of God.

This peaceful quality is also related to our aesthetic sensitivities. Great natural beauty, such as beautiful flowers, a peaceful forest, a sunlit field, can help us to touch this place of introspection and peace. We have all experienced the wonderfully expansive quality of Ether in a silent forest glen, or in the expanse of the desert or on the top of a mountain. Taoist recluses used to find peaceful mountain retreats to experience this expansive aspect of nature which is in harmony with the wholeness of Tao or the source of all things. All of the Five Elements can be experienced both in nature and in ourselves. Being in touch with them in nature helps us to be in touch with them within ourselves. We are truly a reflection of all that is around us.

Ether also governs the emotions in general and combines with the other elements to create various qualities of emotion. It creates the space for the emotions to flow freely, with balance and harmony. We all know what it feels like not to have 'space'. That closed-in, compressed feeling yielding either deep depression or extreme explosiveness. That's the feeling of a contracted field of Ether which yields no space for the other active emotions to move in. In polarity therapy, the therapist may want to help the person get more space or more of the Ether quality, by practical work with life-style, emotional responsibility and specific body-work technique relating to the Ether element. The Ether field can be 'opened-up' and made more expansive for energies to flow more easily and fully.

Ether governs the specific emotion of grief. Remembering that Ether has its seat in the neck and throat, those who have truly grieved know that these areas must be open and not tensed for grief to flow freely. Holding back grief can cause a blocked throat and tense neck muscles, and can effect a contraction in any of the other elements. Grief can bring about a great cleansing and can be quite positive in an existential sense. A deep sense of grief and loss can be touched in relationship to the basic separation from our true selves, from our source. Recognising this separation can reveal a positive need to raise our level of consciousness, to touch deeper places of love within us and to experience true compassion for all creation.

The Ether Centre in the throat (see Figure 4.5) is the centre from which the other chakras of Air, Fire, Water and Earth arise. As these patterns of energy form the basic personality structure, the Ether Centre is usually considered the seat of the ego in the physical body. In the Tibetan tradition the Brow Centre is the Centre of Wisdom, the Throat Centre that of ego, and the Heart Centre that of compassion. All three must be open and balanced for true compassion, insight and clarity to arise. The Ether Centre thus governs the polarity between pride and humility. Pride in the sense of self-pride and attachment to ego structures and humility in the most positive sense of openness, flexibility and a true strength of humbleness in the knowledge of the grand play of the universe within and around us.

Ether combines with other elements to create various attributes (see Tables 4.1 and 4.2). When it is in combination with Air, which governs movement, a quality called 'lengthening' occurs. Ether allows the expansion or lengthening of the qualities of energy through its space; Air governs the general quality of this movement. Ether also governs the sense of hearing. Hearing in this case is not just of external sound, but of

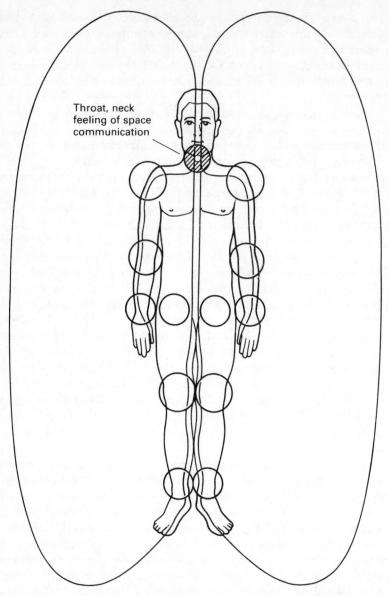

Throat, neck
feeling of space
communication

Fig. 4.5. Ether relationships. Ether creates the field for the other elements to manifest in. Shown are the Ether oval at the throat, sub-fields at each joint and the Ether Long Line current. Ether governs the expansiveness or boundaries of our 'space'. It governs communication and our emotional fields generally.

hearing in a deep sense of knowing. In some traditions hearing and subtle sound is used as an important meditational practice. In combination with Fire, Ether governs sleep; with Water it manifests physically as saliva, and with Earth its expression is seen in body hair. As the Ether element is focused in the neck and throat, it also governs communication. It is an area which relates to all other elements and is commonly congested. In the neck are diaphragm and scapula reflexes which relate to Air, digestive reflexes which relate to Fire; pelvic perineal reflexes which relate to Water and colon reflexes which relate to Earth. Blockages in the neck can further relate to nervous system and structural imbalances.

In polarity therapy there are various techniques used to unblock this area and to relate it to the other elements, to the nervous system and to body structure. Ether treatments allow patients to contact their neutral core and to create general stillness and balance. Gentle sattvic treatments can be extremely powerful, as a sattvic touch (a gentle neutral touch) will resonate with all neutral qualities of energy within us, producing relaxation, peace and balance. A student of mine expressed this very clearly when he wrote,

> . . . anyone whose elements are in balance or whose elements are being brought into balance, will feel the benefits of the etheric as its presence opens and relaxes the body, bringing feelings of harmony and tranquillity. Ether might be seen as the 'bounty' of good health, which if valued and nurtured recreates us and brings stillness and peace of mind.

The Four Active Elements

Let us now look at the four 'active' elements and explore their interplay as they create our physical world. Each element represents a quality of movement. This movement takes shape in our thoughts, our emotions and our bodies. Each element has various energy patterns and energy harmonics which arise from its chakra. Each element governs its sphere of mental, emotional and bodily patterns. Specific energy patterns and relationships create the structure for how we express our ideas, emotions and actions in the world. These patterns of energy form relationships in the body which can be used therapeutically. At the time of conception, energy patterns arise which set up polarity relationships for each element. These relationships were called 'Triads' by Dr Stone, as they relate each element to its positive, neutral and negative poles in the body (see Figure 4.6). An understanding of these triads, their interrelationships and reflexes is basic to an understanding of the therapeutic process in polarity therapy.

Every element also relates to the energy and the taste of the food we eat. Each element is in prominence in specific foods in relationship to the stratum in which it naturally grows. The closer to the earth, the more it

Table 4.1. Summary chart: Five Element interrelationships

Element	Ether governs Emotion	Air governs Movement	Fire governs Function	Water governs Liquid	Earth governs Solid	Associated sense	Food	Taste	Pulse
Ether	Grief	Lengthening	Sleep	Saliva	Hair	Hearing		Sour	Snake-like
Air	Desire	Speed	Thirst	Sweat	Skin	Touch	Fruits, nuts, seeds		Fast-irregular Feeble-faint Moving from place to place
Fire	Anger	Shaking	Hunger	Urine	Blood vessels	Sight	Grains, legumes, sesame seed, sunflower seed	Bitter	Frog-like, jumpy regular, high-volume, like beating drum
Water	Attachment	Movement	Lustre	Semen ovum	Flesh (fat)	Taste	Green vegetables, cucumber, melons, squash, marrow	Salty	Full-bounding Rolling-wave-like
Earth	Fear	Contraction	Laziness	Blood	Bone	Smell	Root vegetables, tubers, herb roots, taro, beets, potato, carrot, onion, garlic, turnip	Sweet	slow, moderate full volume

Table 4.2. Summary chart: Five Elements

Element & qualities	Attributes and functions	Harmonics	Associated centre	Associated organs and body parts	Quality and poles of mind	Quality and poles of emotion	Quality of body
Ether Stillness Harmony Balance Spaciousness Universal love	Aesthetic sense Neutrality Emptiness Core energy	Neuter field of neck Permeates body Creates field/ space	Throat C3–C5 Centre of space and communication	Neck	Tranquillity Peace Neutrality Stillness	Governs emotions Generally Creates space for Emotions Ego⟨Pride⟨Humility Grief	Light, underweight, tall, thin, under-developed, 'drawn-out' thin, wiry
Air Movement Mental activity Attention Thought	Conscious Emotions Compassion Breath Heart-felt feeling rational pole (thought)	⊕ Shoulders, chest lungs φ Kidneys, adrenals colon ⊖ Ankles	Heart T5–T8 Anahata Centre of compassion	Nervous system lungs, heart kidneys, adrenals colon Joints, circulation	Thought and ideas may dominate, detached, thinks before acting, maybe anxious, worried, fickle, cut off from feelings	Desire⟨Greed⟨Aversion Charity⟨Desirelessness⟨Compassion	Moderate weight Muscular without exercise In proportion Lean/muscular Medium build
Fire Intelligence Insight Vitality Quickness of mind	Impulse behind movement Drive Temperature Control The 'fire' of life, metabolism	⊕ Head, eyes φ Solar plexus ⊖ Thighs	Navel L2–L3 Manipura Centre of vitality	Digestive organs stomach, liver pancreas, spleen Gall bladder Heart Eyes	Enthusiastic, excitable focused, self-centred, wilful honest, direct acts before thinking, expresses, emotions quickly	Anger/resentment ——— Forgiveness/ letting go	
Water Intuition Creativity Receptivity Nurturing Generation-seed Potential	Unconscious emotions Irrational pole Grounding energy Seeks lowest level	⊕ Chest, breasts φ Pelvis, generative organs ⊖ Feet	Genital Lumbo-sacral junction Swadhishthana centre of intuition and nurturing	Generative system Breasts Lymphatics Secretory glands Bladder Heart, feet	Intuitive, sensitive, patient, fluid mind, in touch with feelings, irrational unconscious out of control of feelings, acts intuitively	Attachment 'Holding-on' Lust Letting go Flowing Moderation Chastity	Moderate-stout Fully developed 'Padded' look Overweight Padded pelvis
Earth Foundation Support Stability	Field of completion Field of crystallisation Final manifestation Inertia Heaviness Vital pivot-point	⊕ Neck φ Colon ⊖ Knees	Anal Sacro-coccygeal junction Centre of foundation, Support	Colon Rectum Neck Kness	Steady mind, in touch with physical senses practical 'down to earth', good, endurance, addiction to routine resistant, prone to inertia	Fear ——— Courage	Moderate – stout 'Block-like' Thick neck Heavy build, Muscular-out of proportion

Energy Centres   *Physical Triad Relationships*

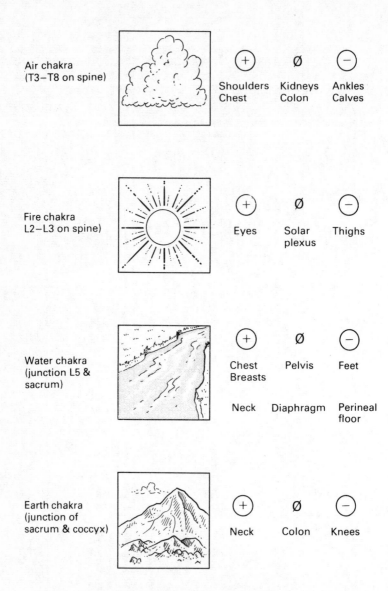

Air chakra
(T3–T8 on spine)

$+$	$\emptyset$	$-$
Shoulders	Kidneys	Ankles
Chest	Colon	Calves

Fire chakra
L2–L3 on spine)

$+$	$\emptyset$	$-$
Eyes	Solar plexus	Thighs

Water chakra
(junction L5 &
sacrum)

$+$	$\emptyset$	$-$
Chest Breasts	Pelvis	Feet
Neck	Diaphragm	Perineal floor

Earth chakra
(junction of
sacrum & coccyx)

$+$	$\emptyset$	$-$
Neck	Colon	Knees

Each of the four active elements have polarity
triad relationships. These outline the basic
energy relationships for each element.

Fig. 4.6. Centres and Triads

tends to have the denser elements prominent, the farther away from the earth, the more it tends to have the lighter, more energetic elements dominant. (See Figure 4.7.) The elemental qualities of foods are dealt with in more detail in Chapter 8.

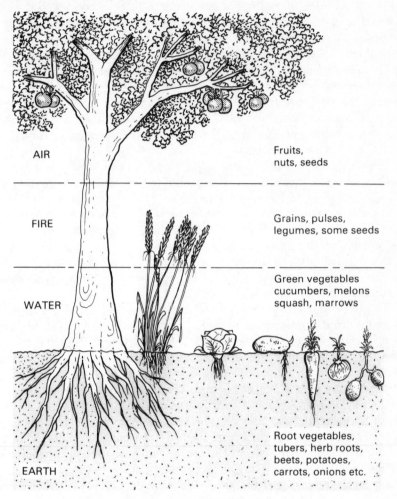

AIR — Fruits, nuts, seeds

FIRE — Grains, pulses, legumes, some seeds

WATER — Green vegetables cucumbers, melons squash, marrows

EARTH — Root vegetables, tubers, herb roots, beets, potatoes, carrots, onions etc.

Fig. 4.7. Food categories and Elements

Next we will explore the first step-down from the Ether Centre – the Air or Heart Centre and the Air Element.

Air

The Air element is the first step-down from Ether and, being the first 'moving' element to come into existence, it governs movement generally.

Air is known by its movement or by its lack of movement. When Air is not moving, stagnation results.

As Air governs movement in general, it combines with other elements to create various qualities of movement (see Table 4.1). The expression of Air in the world is that of speed and motion. It is the congested flow of this quality of energy which precedes rigidity in both mental and physical processes. A rigid person may not be able to flow with new ideas or approaches. Likewise, an imbalance in the Air element may underlie rigid, congested joints. Thought is also movement and the Air element governs mental activity in general. An 'Airy' person may be caught up in thought and detached from their emotions and their bodily sensations. Thought may dominate and an 'Airy' type usually thinks before acting. This can become extreme when the person gets caught up in thoughts, worry, anxiety and never acts.

The Air element arises from the Heart Centre and governs the qualities of desire that arise in relationship to this centre. Desire has two heads, attachment and aversion – desire to draw something towards you or to push something away. A person with a truly open heart is acting from the pole of desirelessness which can be expressed as charity and compassion. In this sense, having no desire doesn't mean stagnation or dullness, but indicates a flowering of the heart and an opening of the Air element in a positive expression of caring for other beings who share common sufferings and joys.

To get in touch with the Air element we can again look to nature. When the wind is moving in a steady balanced way, not too strong and not erratic, a feeling of freshness and relief can be found. This mirrors the cleansing processes that the Air element governs within the body, such as the removal of body wastes via the kidneys, colon, lungs and skin. When Air is not moving, a feeling of heaviness and stagnation can result as on a hot summer's day. Air can also be turbulent and unpredictable as in a stormy and blustery sky. So when the Air element is in excess our thought processes and our emotional responses become confused, disorientated and unpredictable. Air governs the *movement* of our thought processes, our emotional life and our internal physiology.

As we mentioned before, the body relationships which define the physical movements of each element are called Triads. The primary energy triads are formed at the time of conception after the core energy system. These patterns underlie the formation of the nervous system and the physical structure. The primary or foetal triad of the Air element relates to the shoulder area as its positive pole, the kidneys as its neutral pole and the ankles as its negative pole (see Figure 4.8). There are energy reflexes in each area which can be used therapeutically to open blockages in the Air element and balance its flow. Another triad which relates to the Air element is found in the front of the body and relates to the chest and lungs, the colon and the calves. Again, reflexes found here can be used with deep therapeutic effect. These will be discussed in later chapters. The

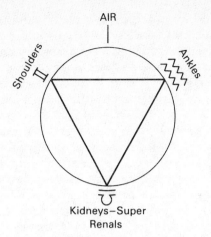

Fig. 4.8. The Air triad

positive pole of the Air element, in the chest and shoulder area, is directly governed by the Heart Centre. This centre governs emotional imbalances that occur in a situation with which we are consciously involved. So, for example, a father frightens a small girl. He may appear huge and menacing in her eyes. Anger is directed towards her, fear of violence, perhaps even of death, then arises. The father acts violently, grabs her arm and throws her into her room. In this powerfully emotive and fearful situation, the child's Heart Centre closes and perhaps certain 'life statements' arise. A life statement is something we internalise due to emotional or traumatic situations. These get fixed into a conditioned and locked way of reacting, and behaving. Here the little girl may have blocked her love and trust of men in general or may have an impossible time relating to her father in later life. These emotional reactions step down and become locked into a physical posture and a physical 'holding' pattern. In a sense, the original situation's emotional response becomes locked into the body's structure. The little girl may have had to 'swallow' her anger and sadness due to fear of violence. These become physical patterns which we grow into. They were, perhaps, useful at the time, i.e. in this particular case prevention of harm, and thus a useful defence mechanism. But they become unuseful patterns generalised into other situations, say with male authority figures or mates. The important thing here is to note that they become *physical* patterns, which are locked or held in place by unbalanced *energy* patterns at a subtler level.

When the Heart Centre closes down, giving and receiving love becomes more difficult. This is seen physically in a contracted diaphragm, tense shoulders, congested rib-cage and collapsed chest. This physical pattern is determined by the *energetic* closing of the Heart Centre. This imbalancing factor may reverberate throughout the Air element relationships. Thus, the neutral pole at the kidney and colon area may become blocked energetically as Air will now move through its relationships in an unbalanced way. Chronic kidney and colon problems may result. The kidney and colon areas may become held in chronic tension and problems such as kidney stones or spastic colon may arise. A tension band might be seen across the skin in these areas in some cases. These imbalances may be seen below in the calves and ankles at the negative pole of Air as tension and pain and result in poor circulation and varicosity. The important concept here is that all of these imbalances, at their root, are caused by habits of thought and emotion which become locked in the body in very specific way. These imbalances predispose us to disease processes and can be treated through the various energy reflexes and relationships involved. (See Figure 4.9.)

Each active element has certain body types that tend to arise when it is in precedence. An 'Airy' body type may become excessively light and underweight. The Airy person may seem tall and 'drawn-out'. They may seem underdeveloped, too thin and 'wiry'. There may be a sense of disconnection of body parts. The legs may not seem to belong to the same body, or the body may seem to be segmented with a pelvis not 'fitting' the chest, as if they were put together from different bodies. This segmentation might also be seen where modes of thought are disconnected from the emotions and physical sensations. The person's movements, may seem disjointed or uncoordinated when the Air element is not being balanced by the other three active elements.

The Air element also governs other specific bodily processes. It governs the health and balance of the nervous system, the lungs, the kidneys, adrenals, ductless glands, the colon (also governed by Earth), the circulation of blood, the health of the heart and the flexibility of the joints. Every activity that is governed by movement in the body must have an Air element aspect that is flowing freely and in balance. One of our primary physical movements is that of breath. If we stop breathing for just a few minutes, we die. As it is the first of the active elements to arise, and as it governs movement in general, it also governs this most basic physical activity. Freely flowing energy as seen in a freely moving diaphragm, open shoulder blades and clavicles and balanced relationships with the other elements, allow a freely flowing breath.

Besides these body processes, the Air element, in combination with Fire, governs thirst; with Water, it governs skin condition. It also governs the main organs in the body which remove toxic accumulations and waste products from body tissue. This includes the kidneys, colon and skin. Along with the Water element, which governs the lymphatics, the Fire element, which governs the liver and spleen, and the Earth element which also governs the colon, it helps to keep our body tissues healthy and free of toxic accumulations.

Imbalances in the Air element may affect any system or relationship it

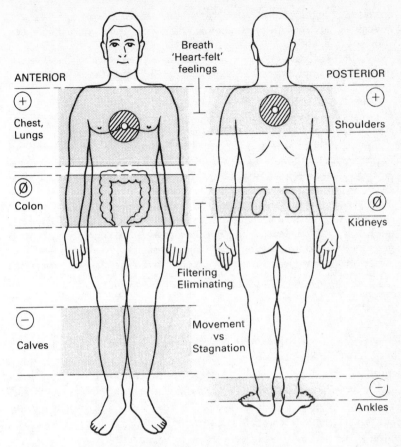

Fig. 4.9. Air Triad relationships

governs. Thus problems in the lungs, kidneys and joints, along with skin conditions and nervous disorders, may all appear in relationship to Air. As we will see in our following chapters, however, the picture isn't as clear as this, as all elements overlap and congestion in any one organ system may relate to an imbalance *between* the elements and not just within one element system. Thus a lung problem may focus in Air, but it may also relate to Water with excessive mucus formation and fluid retention, or in another example, dry skin and eczema may relate to excessive Fire *causing* an imbalance in Air.

Earlier on it was mentioned that each element relates to a particular food-growing stratum. The Air element is most abundant in fruits, nuts and seeds which grow high up in trees and relates most to lighter, airier energy. The tastes which stimulate the Air element in the body are sour tastes such as sour plums or soured milk. One of my students has summed up the Air element very clearly in the following passage:

Shakespeare's characterisation of Hamlet might be considered to be a classic portrayal of an 'Air type'. An initiator, full of ideas, quick-minded and good with words, but because of the tendency of the Air element to move rapidly in zig-zag patterns, someone who, bird-like, darts from place to place, setting many things in motion, yet unable to see things through to their completion, or consolidate his actions.

The Air oval is that of the chest, embracing the lungs and the heart (T5–T8). Contraction of this oval, perhaps through early childhood hurt, will lead to a closing down of feeling, both emotional and sensory. The word 'heartfelt' accords well with the centre concerned with feeling, and its sense: that of touch. Improving the movement of energy through this centre will enhance the more positive aspects and qualities associated with the heart: compassion, giving, expansion and space.

Physically, Air types tend to be lightly built, thin-limbed, agile and nervy, perhaps using their hands a lot when they speak and speaking often and quickly . . . it has a tendency to move upwards and one might see a reflection of this in their body structure. They may for example give the impression of 'lifting off' as if they were finding it difficult to actually remain on the ground.

Fire

The next step-down from the Air Centre is the Fire Centre (see Figure 4.10). Here the Fire element holds sway and, due to its rajasic, outgoing nature, it is possibly the easiest to feel in ourselves and others. Whereas the Air element governs movement, the Fire element governs the direction of that movement. The Fire element is the positive expansive impulse behind movement. It is the rajasic impulsive phase of energy which is the driving force behind bodily functions. It is the vital force of the body's energy system. It provides the warmth of healing, seen in its extreme as fever, and its umbilical centre is the wellspring of the body's vitality.

Air governs thought in general, but it is Fire which directs that

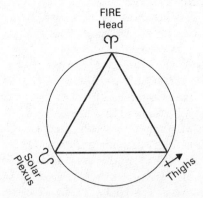

Fig. 4.10. The Fire triad

movement. Expressions such as 'a fiery intellect', or 'quickness of mind' express this quality of the Fire element. A person with a strong tendency to Fire would have a lot of enthusiasm for life and could focus that enthusiasm into activity. He might, however, be self-centred and wilful and use this strength of Fire to manipulate others. A Fiery personality type would tend to be direct and honest towards others, but an imbalance in this tendency could give rise to callousness and insensitivity to others. Fire governs the emotional qualities of anger and resentment. A person who holds back their Fire in the world may have trouble getting their needs met and may channel this Fiery energy into seething resentment or may disconnect from the Fiery feelings completely and internalise them as insecurity, self-denigration, depression or powerlessness. A person who uses their Fire in an unbalanced way may be power-orientated, manipulative and emotionally or physically violent. A person with strong and balanced Fire would have good vital energy reserves, clarity of mind and purpose and an insightful intellect capable of cutting through confusion and turmoil.

The holding back of Fiery emotions like anger, aversion and resentment is quite common in our society. These feelings can smoulder and come out 'sideways' towards others as snide remarks, negativity and hurtful speech and action. This negative undercurrent is often denied and a person may even compensate for it by 'good' actions such as charitable acts and high-minded ideals or politics. But if the Fiery negativity is not acknowledged and dealt with, even these activities will be tainted by its power. Once acknowledged with awareness, the energy of the negativity can be released in positive actions: in assertiveness and forgiveness.

The quality of Fire can be seen in nature in very clear ways. The heat of the sun is necessary for life to exist (as indeed are the qualities of all the other elements in their sphere). We all move towards the fireplace on a cold winter's day and lay in the summer sun to recharge and revitalise ourselves. Fire in excess, however, can scorch and burn. The bitterness and burning of excessive bile in our digestive system can be an expression of this and the saying 'you have a lot of gall' represents this Fiery imbalance in interpersonal relationships. Fire can erupt explosively as in volcanic eruptions. You can hold your Fire down for just so long, but sooner or later it may erupt volcanically in the most unlikely situations. Fire flowing in a balanced and open way may be perceived as personal warmth, and as caring and helpful action.

The Fire element takes physical expression in the Fire triad which relates to the head, and in particular the eyes, as its positive pole of energy movement, the solar plexus as its neutral pole, and the thighs as its negative pole (see Figure 4.11). A person with low or unbalanced Fire may have a dullness in his eyes or glassy look in them. A person using Fire in power-orientated manipulations may have what is commonly called an 'eye block'. Here their Fire is absorbed in the ego-power struggle and they don't allow their energy to make real contact with others via their eyes.

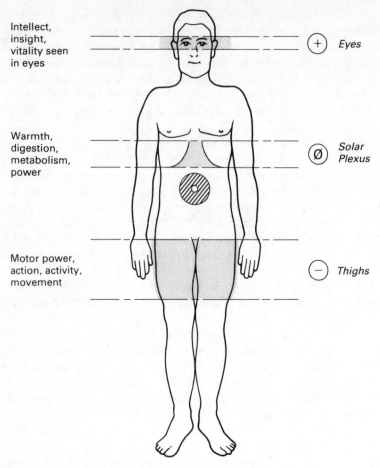

Intellect,
insight,
vitality seen
in eyes

⊕ *Eyes*

Warmth,
digestion,
metabolism,
power

⊘ *Solar*
Plexus

Motor power,
action, activity,
movement

⊖ *Thighs*

Fig. 4.11. Fire Triad relationships

Chakra: Fire Centre at umbilicus   (L3–L2)

Core pulsations: Fire Long Line current
                        Fire principle current
                        Spiral current

Triad relationship: + eyes, head ⊘ solar plexus − thighs

Organ systems: Digestive organs, liver, gall bladder, stomach, spleen, small intestine, pancreas.

The eyes, as the positive pole of our vital energy, are mirrors in which the world can see our vital state. The practice of iridology, or the reading of the physical–emotional complex in the iris, is a finely tuned art which makes use of this fact.

At the neutral pole of the Fire element is the solar plexus area. Here we have the physical centre for the Fiery energy in the body. It is the 'sun' centre which regulates warmth and digestion in the body. It is the physical energy step-down from the subtler Fire chakra in the umbilical area. In many sources there has been some confusion as to where the Fire Centre is located. It is commonly located in the solar plexus area. It must be stressed that this area, as with the other triad relationships is a *physical* manifestation of a subtler centre. To quote from a famous Sanskrit text called the *Satchakranirupana* by Purnanuda-Swami and translated by Sir John Woodroffe, himself an accomplished yogi: '. . . at the root of the navel, is the shining lotus of ten petals (the Manipura or Fire Chakra) . . . By meditation on the Navel Lotus the power to destroy and create is augured.' Here it is stressed that the Fire Centre deals with power issues. Its emotional polarity moves between anger and forgiveness. Pent-up anger may be felt at the neutral pole in the solar plexus as a seething burning or as a burning coal ready to ignite suddenly into fire. Withheld resentment may affect the whole of the Fire triad and, as the Fire element governs digestion and the digestive organs, may result in problems in these areas. As mentioned earlier, we commonly say to a person who puts their force into the world aggressively and angrily, 'You have a lot of gall!'. This expression recognises the reactions of the liver and gall bladder to pent-up or unbalanced Fire energies.

The negative poles of this triad are the thighs, which manifest Fire in the world by movement and running. It is also common to find painful Fiery tension patterns relating to the holding back of anger and resentment. A person with an issue in the Fire element, whether it is a holding back of anger or resentment or confusion about feeling power and strength, or problems in the digestion and assimilation of food, may be seen to have dull or menacing eyes, a tension block or holding in the solar plexus area and tense and painful reflexes in the thighs. Thus the eyes, the solar plexus and the thighs are reflexes in the Fire patterns which the polarity therapist can use to open, stimulate and balance a person's Fiery energies. People with a fiery block may first have to learn to discharge pent-up emotions which relate to this element and to use them in a constructive way. They may need to learn assertive behaviour so that they can start to say what they need in the world and then, from this base they can cultivate the positive aspects of acceptance and forgiveness. Until this is done, in these cases, purely working with the symptomatic aspects of this emotional holding, such as a digestive problem, will not have any long-term effect.

There are three distinct energy patterns, each with its own reflex relationships which relate to this vital element. They deal with the regulation and balance of Fire in the body, with the dispersal of vital energy through the body, and with the physiology of digestion and the function of sight. (See Figure 4.12.)

The body type which relates to the Fire element is one of moderate weight and good physical balance. The person may appear muscular and in-proportion without having to exercise. We all know people who look trim and firm, yet do not need to exercise to maintain this state. They are of lean, muscular build and radiate much vitality and physical strength. These people often need physical activity and physical work to channel their Fiery energies in skilful ways.

Fire also governs the sense of sight and the quality, on a mental and emotional level, of insight. It also governs hunger and digestion and its balance is necessary for internal temperature control, a balanced metabolism and, in conjunction with Water, a strong self-healing ability. Fire governs the digestive system and its organs and provides both the subtle and coarse centres for the production and dissemination of warmth and vital energy.

Fire governs foods that grow above the ground, but do not grow as high up as Air type foods in trees. Fire foods are foods which help maintain

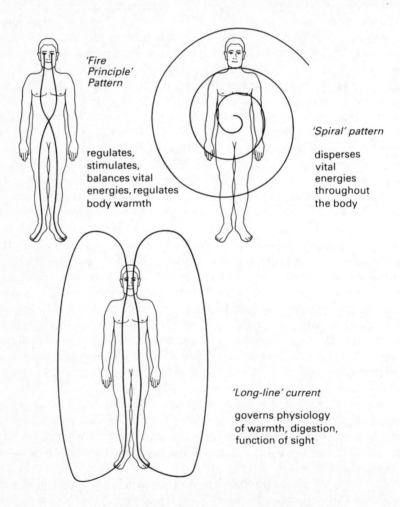

'Fire Principle' Pattern

regulates, stimulates, balances vital energies, regulates body warmth

'Spiral' pattern

disperses vital energies throughout the body

'Long-line' current

governs physiology of warmth, digestion, function of sight

Fig. 4.12. Fire energy patterns

Fire in the body and tend to be slow-burning protein foods. These include all the grains, pulses, legumes; seeds such as sesame, pumpkin and sunflower seed which stimulate Fire and some strong spices and roots which also stimulate Fire, such as chillies, cayenne pepper, ginger, garlic and onions. Generally speaking, the sprouting of grains and pulses (such as mung, aduki and lentils) make the Fire energy more available and the protein more easily assimilated. The taste which stimulates Fire in the body is bitter. Most medicinal herbs are bitter-tasting and this helps to stimulate Fire in the healing process. A student of mine nicely summarises the Fire element as follows,

> Fire is the impulse behind movement (the thighs). Its qualities are intelligence and insight (which show in the eyes) and vitality which is connected with the Fiery function of digestion and which leads to strength and energy, again expressed through the eyes as well as the overall vigour of the body. The Fire chakra lies at L2–L3 in the Earth oval. It also has a strong relationship with the sun centre of the solar plexus, hence the expression 'lion-hearted'.
>
> As an active, positive element one can expect 'Fire types' to be impulsive, and quick to act. Laertes in Hamlet is a marvellous portrayal of a Fire type: quick to anger, impulsive and always prepared to act, even on false information, yet finally learning forgiveness, that positive emotional quality associated with Fire.

Water

After the Fire Centre, vital energy again steps down in intensity to form the next centre down, the Water Centre (see Figure 4.13a). This phase of energy coarsening is quite an important event. Here the quality of energy undergoes a major change. In this phase, energies are seeking their final manifestation in form, they are becoming 'earthed'. The Air and Fire Centres are centres of light and expansive energies. They are considered yang or rajasic in quality. The Water and Earth centres, in the phase below or within, are denser and more contractive and are considered to be yin or tamasic in quality. The Water Centre is the pelvic centre and is located at the junction of the last lumbar vertebra (L5) and the sacrum. It governs the phase of energy which like water, seeks its lowest level and grounds us to earth. It is the energy which brings us in touch with the physical world in this grounding function (see Figure 4.13).

The Water element governs unconscious emotions and deep feelings and is thus sometimes called the 'irrational pole'. The Air element which governs thought and rational thinking has been called the 'rational pole' in relationship to this. The Water element is the sphere in which emotions and feelings hold sway. If the Water element is flowing freely through its energetic relationships, and if it is in balance with the Air element, a person may have a fluid and flexible mind capable of changing easily with new insights and not locked into rigid belief systems. Flexibility of mind is

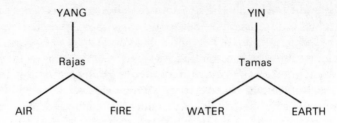

Fig. 4.13. Phases of Energy

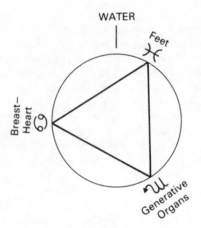

Fig. 4.13a. The Water triad

thus an important Water/Air characteristic and for this to occur a person would need to be in touch with their feelings and emotions and yet, as we shall see, not be attached to them.

The realm of Water is the unconscious and this element therefore governs the whole undercurrent of dreaming and the knowledge that dreams can bring to us. The quality of this knowledge is not that of the mind, but from a deep well of feeling and intuition, a mine of self-discovery. It is a deeper realm of knowing before things are shaped into thoughts or actions. A clear mind, free from thought, can touch this deep intuitive knowing. It is, in a sense, like a deep and still lake, where one can see clearly to its bottom and all within is revealed in the stillness of its waters.

The Water element governs attachment and 'holding on'. Deep-rooted urges and attachments have their seat here. It is the kind of attachment that has an emotional 'charge' to it, an almost life-and-death holding on to all that we have experienced. If the Water element is not freely flowing in its energetic relationships, then this attachment controls us, unconsciously motivating our activities. Sexual attachment and need is especially charged for most of us and pelvic holding and imbalance is commonly seen in relationship to it. The pelvis is, in a sense, the negative pole of our feelings and emotions. Chronic emotional tensions and fears lodge there. Energy, as it contracts, crystallises or stagnates in the pelvic floor. This area, the bottom of our pelvic basin, can become quite a focus of imbalance and the polarity therapist uses specific perineal techniques and perineal reflexes to release these patterns of emotional tension. Once the Water element starts flowing freely and pelvic energies 'ground' to earth, then patterns of attachment and need can become less compulsive and have more opportunity to be dealt with consciously. Rather than stumbling through our unconscious emotional life, the opportunity to flow with it and through it can thus become more available.

The Air element, as we have just seen, becomes unbalanced in relationship to conscious emotional trauma. The Water element, whose realm is that of the unconscious, becomes unbalanced much more in relationship to primal urges, deep unconscious needs and fears and ongoing build-up of the daily tensions of life. Sexuality and sexual issues are deeply rooted in the Water element, and fear, inhibition or excess in this area powerfully affect Water element energetic relationships. A person whose Water element is flowing freely in its relationships would be in touch with their feelings in a very grounded way. They would be able to process and work through emotional patterns as these patterns arise, whether it be patterns of strong attachment, sadness, fear or joy. They could use the strength of water – that is, the ability to flow around obstacles and seek the path of least resistance, to their emotional advantage. Rather than becoming caught up in the emotions and indulging in sadness, depression and despair, they could flow through these and let them go and not become stuck in any place. When Water is flowing freely we can flow freely through our emotional states. If Water is not flowing, if the Water element patterns are held in imbalance, we can become caught up in unconscious desires and urges.

An important quality of the Water element is *receptivity*. Water will receive and accept all things. It is the feminine quality of receptivity and nurturing within us all which allows growth and healing to occur on all levels. Whether it is self-growth and healing, family and interpersonal relationships or the deep love possible in child-rearing where all negative as well as positive aspects of our children are accepted, it is this receptive aspect of Water which is paramount. Once things, people and personalities are truly accepted on a deep emotional level, then positive change can arise and compassion and forgiveness can both hold sway. But the foundation for this is first acceptance and receptivity, change can then occur with love rather than aversion.

Water can be seen in action clearly in the natural order. The rivers and streams flow downwards, always seeking the lowest level and always flowing to and being contained by earth. The power of water is in its flexibility and non-rigidity. It flows around obstacles and wears seemingly impenetrable barriers down. It is cleansing and nourishing in its flow and lack of it causes draught and famine. Water, when clear, can cleanse all things. We can observe this when our lymphatic system, governed by the Water element, is clearing and detoxifying our system of foreign invaders, toxins and waste products. When water becomes trapped it becomes stagnant; when our lymphatics are not flowing, toxicity and infection result. On an emotional level, if Water becomes dammed up, the potential for excessive and explosive outbursts such as uncontrollable crying and self-pity occurs. Just as a dam becomes too full and bursts, excessive holding in of Watery emotions can burst through in a seemingly irrational manner. If, however, Water is flowing freely and grounding us to Earth, our emotions can become our friends as we move through them fluidly, neither holding on to them nor reacting to them.

A Water element type of person might have a moderate to stout body appearance with a 'padded' look to it. They may be overweight or have a tendency to extra padding. Their pelvis may be structurally unbalanced and they may suffer from types of sacroiliac and lumbar pain which has an emotional basis to it. The Water element triad relationships are that of the breasts, chest and shoulders, the chest at its positive pole, the feet and achilles area as its negative pole. (See Figure 4.14.) Imbalances in the Water element may commonly be seen in excess water retention, literally stagnant pools of fluid usually held at the negative pole in the feet and ankles and the various perineal reflex areas. A padded looking pelvis is a common indicator of Watery energies pooling in the pelvis and not grounding to Earth. If the issues involved also relate to withheld anger, such as in feelings of sexual violation or inadequacy or in deep urges and needs not being met, then the Fire element may also become involved and a padded, watery look may be seen in the thighs. This is a literal 'watering down' of the Fire at its negative pole in the thighs and thus much energy can become bound up in Water-related issues. This energy must be opened and released for these issues to become clearer and more conscious. The polarity therapist in tackling these imbalances, might use a combination of body-work, exercise, diet and counselling. The body-work would be used to release the energetic blockages and imbalances; the exercises to help the person work on these themselves, the diet to cleanse the Water-related tissues and organs (such as the lymphatic system) and counselling work to clarify the issues and 'de-charge' them.

As the Water element governs the movement of energy to earth, it is logical that its negative pole is located in the feet. The feet connect us to earth and our relationship to this grounding can be seen in them. The feet are the last body part in which energy is expressed in its downward, centrifugal phase. They are also where energy begins the return flow from Earth back to Ether. At this most negative pole of the body, energies tend to become 'earthed' and sluggish and the feet are an expression of this phase. The history of the whole body becomes crystallised in the feet and thus makes them an important diagnostic tool. All elements and all related organ systems have negative pole reflexes in the feet. These reflexes can show the overall pattern of chronic energy blockage in the body as a

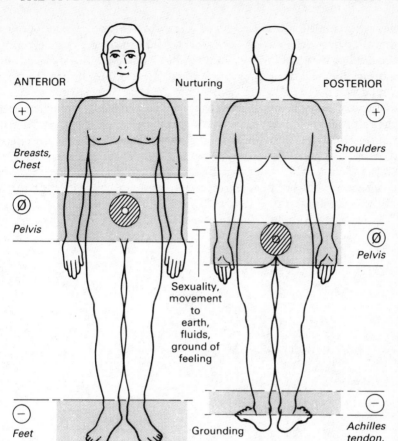

Fig. 4.14. Water Triad relationships

Chakra: Water Centre, between sacrum and 5th lumbar

Core pulsation: Water Long Line current
                Five-Pointed Star pattern
                Perineal pulsations

Triad relationships: + breasts ∅ pelvis − feet
                  + shoulders ∅ pelvis − ankles
                  + neck, occiput ∅ perineum − ankles

Organ systems: sexual organs, bladder, lymphatics, endocrine system, breasts.

whole and be used in relationship to their neutral and positive pole reflexes above. (See Figure 4.15.)

The Water element is the energy of procreation, renewal and healing. It is the nurturing aspects of Water which cleanse and renew the organism.

Combined with the healing power of Fiery vital energy it brings comfort and healing energies to areas of need. The old expression 'running water clears itself' is very apt in visualising the cleansing power of this element. Fire brings the heat of healing to the site of need, Water brings cleansing and renewal to it. The Water element governs the generative system and the organs of procreation. It governs the glands such as the mucus glands in the respiratory and digestive tracts and the lymphatic system with its job of cleansing and detoxification. It governs the sexual fluids and sperm and ovum. The solids in the body which fall under its sphere of influence are fats and flesh. The Water element also governs the function of binding and cohesion in the body, and it is, in that sense the element which maintains the integrity of physical form.

Water is in prominence in foods which grow on the surface of the earth. These include: green vegetables such as lettuce, cabbage, spinach;

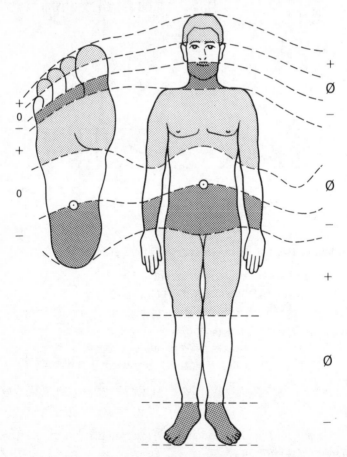

Fig. 4.15. Polarity Zone Chart – showing bottom of foot as it relates to the rest of the body

watery melons such as cantaloup; and all squashes and marrows. The Chinese acknowledge water as an important quality to emulate. Lao Tzu, the ancient Chinese philosopher wrote:

> There is nothing softer and weaker than water, And yet there is nothing better for attacking hard and strong things. For this reason there is no substitute for it. All the world knows that the weak overcomes the strong and the soft overcomes the hard. *

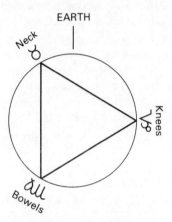

Fig. 4.16. The Earth triad

Earth

The final step-down in energy from the Brow Centre is the Earth Centre and the Earth element (see Figure 4.16). The Earth element finds its realm of action in the physical world. It is here that energies become crystallised into form. This form takes the shape of our thoughts, our actions and our speech. Things become 'grounded' in physical reality. It is the realm of anatomy and physiology and of final action and form. The Earth element deals with the physical senses and a person in touch with this realm would have a steady mind with much patience and perseverance. This steadiness is founded on the strength of Earth and the practical modes of action which are necessary in the physical world. An 'Earthy' person would be 'down to earth' and practical and could plod through whatever has to be done until it finally reaches completion. In the realm of thought, the Earth element is seen in a steady mind in touch with the senses and grounded in the physical world. The person who is bounded by Earth may, however, become addicted to routine and have limited intuition and imagination, when dealing with new problems or experiences. A person who is not

---

* Commentary on the *Lao Tzu*, translated by Ariane Rump, U. Press of Hawaii.

grounding their energies to Earth may appear spaced out or very anxious. Energies may be caught up in the Airy or Watery realms and not ground in the strength of the earth. People without this foundation of Earth may not be able to deal with practical everyday life and may become caught up in dreams or indulge in emotional excesses.

The Earth element is the energy of foundation and support, and through this function it governs the emotional qualities of fear and courage. If we feel well-grounded and solid in our dealings with the world, we would be more likely to interact with others in a direct and courageous way. Fear underlies much of the unskilful and negative patterns in the world. Fear is a contraction, a pulling in, a withdrawal from others. The Earth element is the energy of final contraction, final crystallisation. A person caught in fear may thus become immobilised, frozen – so contracted in physical form as to be unable to move. This contracting has many layers to it: from an undercurrent of fear which builds up and colours all of our activities to a paranoic cutting off from those around us, to a complete catatonia. Most of us have an undercurrent of fear and insecurity which moves its way through our decisions, our life choices and our everyday activities. It can colour our relationships, our self-esteem and our ability to experience joy and happiness in life. Most of us need to ground our energies, slow our lives down and relate to others from energies which are grounded in the physical senses and physical realities. Dr Stone used the biblical saying 'that which is last becomes first' to describe this earthing function. Earth is the great pivotal point, the great potential point of return to our subtler sources. Unless we are fully grounded, fully here, our energies get caught up in the senses and in the earthing function forever trying to be here, to complete processes and never actually doing it. It is only when we can fully be here without judgements, opinions, beliefs, without the past and future, that the Earth element becomes the great pivotal point, the springboard to Tao.

The Earth body type has a block-like look to it. The person whose constitution tends towards the Earth element may have a short, thick neck, a heavy build which appears very solid and block-like, with thick knees and 'tree-trunk' legs. This body structure usually indicates a person who may use their energies in a very practical field. Many Earth structures are attracted to the building trades, where they can see their efforts come to fruition in solid form. Others are like Dr Stone, whose body was of a very Earthy structure, and who was incredibly practical in his healing art. The Earth triad energy relationship is that of the neck at the positive pole, the colon at the neutral pole and the knees at the negative pole (see Figure 4.17). As we have seen before, the Earth element governs fear responses and a common fear response is shaky knees, uncontrollable bowels and a stiff, rigid neck. If you have ever experienced a major earthquake, where the ground is literally taken out from under you, you may have experienced some of these Earth reactions. In less extreme circumstances in everyday life, a common combination of imbalance is seen in a rigid and stiff neck with an undercurrent of tension and fear; an imbalanced colon racked with spasticity, constipation, diarrhoea or colitis and weak or painful knees mirroring a lack of grounding and stability.

Like all the other elements, Earth can clearly be seen in the natural order. We rely on Earth. We build our cities on earth and send the foundations of our constructed environment into the solidity of the earth. We live off the fruits of the earth, our crops grow from the earth, our animals eat off the

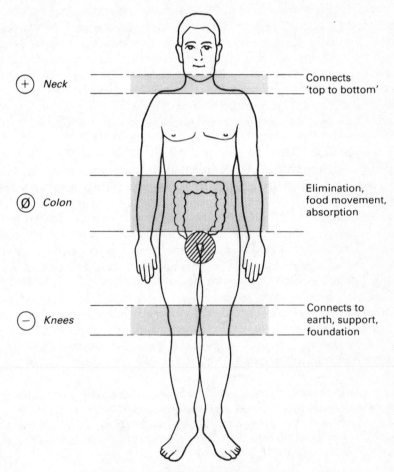

Fig. 4.17. Earth Triad relationships

Chakra: Earth Centre near rectum bottom of sacrum

Core pulsation: Earth current line

Triad relationship: + neck ∅ colon − knees

Organ systems: colon, elimination via rectum.

earth and our water supply is contained in or on the earth. Our body structure is of the earth and imbalances in our structure reverberate on all levels.
Our body depends on Earth for its solidity, support and foundation. When
we feel unsupported in the world we say we feel 'ungrounded'. When our
pelvis or spine is unbalanced, pain results and it is very hard to focus on
anything else. Our spine, our structure is our foundation and since the Earth
element governs fear and courage, a person who is perceived to be acting
from fear is commonly called 'spineless'. Because of this, the Polarity Therapist pays attention to the patients' body structure and nervous system. He
can work with the energy reflexes of the Earth element and its final manifestation, body structure. There are techniques in Polarity work which
balance the three aspects of the nervous system (the sympathetic,
parasympathetic and central) via spinal harmonics, coccyx and perineal
techniques, cranial work and structural balancing. Dr Stone was also a
trained osteopath and chiropractor. He developed sensitive techniques
which deal with this physical realm of manifestation.

The Earth element also governs the general act of contraction. Any
movement which is contractive, whether a movement of thought, emotion,
or of the physical body, is governed by Earth. Contracted and narrow
thought-patterns and ideas, rigidity of mind and the process of fear all fall
within the contractive patterns of the Earth element. Earth is a place of inertia, weight. One thing we must all struggle with at one time or another is the
resistance inherent in physical form. It takes energy to overcome this resistance, to wake up in the morning, to do exercises, to overcome negative habit
patterns. Thus to overcome laziness and inertia we have to learn to move
with the Earth and not be bogged down by it. We have to learn to use this
resistance skilfully to learn the lessons inherent in having a physical form.

The bodily fluid which Earth governs is blood, the solid is bone and the
sense that Earth relates to is smell. Earth foods are foods which grow beneath
the surface of the ground. They include root vegetables, and root herbs such
as carrots, potatoes, taro root, beets and onion. A student wrote clearly
about the Earth element when he said:

> The interdependence of strength and fear is typical of the Earth pattern. Earth
> represents completion and its corrolary, fear, is rooted in the awareness of the
> impermanence of the human form. Such a realisation can bring inner strength and
> a closeness to the peaceful energies of Ether which may hitherto have been missing
> from a purely materialistic understanding of life.

The Elements, their patterns and interrelationships, are the warp and weft
of life. Through their interweavings we create who we are; through them the
whole process of health and disease is negotiated. A helpful framework for
understanding this process is presented in our next chapter and through it we
may derive a more skilful way of being in the world. In later chapters we will
explore these Five Element patterns in a therapeutic context.

CHAPTER FIVE

The Movement to Health

Now we come to the Essence of the currents within us, by which our body operates, moves and has its being as a living human entity, in health or in dis-ease. When these four polarized energy currents flow freely, we call it health.

The healing process is the pivotal point around which all polarity procedures spin. The intention of Polarity Therapy is to stimulate and encourage it. I would like to explore this process and to see if we can arrive at an understanding of it in a polarity context. Health is not just about an absence of symptoms, but is more an attitude and way of life that can be learned and experienced. People initially come to see a polarity therapist because they are in some form of pain or discomfort. This may have physical, emotional or mental tones. I do not perceive my role as a therapist as one of curing their pain. I see my role and the role of polarity therapy at its greatest depth, as helping the client explore, tolerate, accept and finally let go of their pain or problem. It is an educative rather than a corrective role. At a deep level I believe that the body and its energies know best, if given the chance. Ill health, pain and suffering is a process, not a thing. It is a process which can be known and perceived by ourselves. Healing is also a process; it too can be known and perceived.

Energy Flow

Dr Stone understood health in terms of energy flow. He believed that the disease process began as subtle patterns of imbalanced energy. He taught that there are five interrelated energy phases which must flow freely in their relationships for health to flower. In *Energy* he writes; 'In illness and disease the energy relationship is this River of Life and its fields is [sic] disrupted and needs to be re-established.' Energy must flow freely for life to flow freely. He believed that health is based on life's finer energies and that these energies must be in harmony and balance in their relationships. He writes:

> Briefly the river of life's finer energy, called 'Prana', is the vital force in the body. It is the activator which flows through the five ovals of the body – the head, the neck, the chest, the abdomen and the pelvis – as five fields of matter for specific functions of sensory and motor expression.

When life's finer energies are flowing freely in their relationships, then health can manifest. The five phases of energy flow, the Elements, relate to the five body cavities and, as we have seen, the pulsations and transitions between them. When energies flow in harmony through these fields then vitality results. It is seen in the brightness of our eyes, the bounce in our step, the clarity of our mind and the fullness of our breath. It is not just a matter of lack of pain or symptom, but a feeling or perception of well-being. Dr Stone saw the object of treatment to be the removal of any restriction or block to the free and balanced flow of energy. He writes again in *Energy*, *'The object of treating is the removal of Energy Blocks* which are the cause of real pain in the overall sweep of wireless currents in the vital energy fields of the body.' So the object of polarity therapy is the removal of energy blocks; very clear and very precise. He further writes, 'The physiological and psychological balance of well-being in the body is maintained by the harmonious and well-balanced flow of the five rivers within our body . . . All the energies should be properly balanced and directed for the good of each individual as a soul in a body.' When there are no restrictions or blocks to the flow of energy, then well-being is maintained by the natural harmony and balance of energy as it comes into physical form. But what exactly are energy blocks and how do they arise and how are they maintained? These are critical questions and are fundamental to an understanding of the energy dynamics in polarity therapy.

Energy Blocks

Let us return to the basic process of energy flow which underlies all life patterns. In our previous discussion, we have seen that energy arises from a source, takes movement via polarity relationships, finds expression in some kind of form, and then returns to its original source. We have talked about this process as a kind of condensing or thickening of energies to create form. Dr Stone would say that energies must *complete* in some form or relationship before they can return to their source. So energies move to completion in form and then return to their source (see

Figure 5.1). No problem here: we have a free-flowing energy system of pulsation into form and pulsation back to the source. In our personal experience energies create three basic qualities of form. These are our thoughts, our emotions and our physical body. This should be free-flowing and harmonious. But something occurs which restricts and unbalances this process and I would like to look next at what it is that causes this.

Dr Stone called the process of energy moving to form *involution* and the process of movement back to the source *evolution*. Problems in this flow seem to occur at the point of completion. Somehow energies become bound up or stuck in the forms that they are creating. Something happens which causes the form to become rigid and which traps energy in the maintenance of the form. Thus thoughts can become rigid beliefs, opinions, judgements which can be held onto in a desperate fashion. Emotions, instead of flowing freely and harmoniously, become trapped in indulgence, suppression and physical tension. The physical body itself holds onto patterns of stress, tension, toxicity and rigidity, which demands a huge entrapment of energies. Energy becomes trapped in the maintenance of forms and patterns which are crystallised, rigid and counterproductive. They become trapped in the very things they become.

But what is it which causes this to happen? I would like to turn first to some ancient spiritual traditions as one approach to understanding this question. In Buddhism the answer lies in our tendency to hold onto the things we identify with. It is this holding, this attachment to things, be they ideas, feelings or objects, that binds energies into rigid forms. Problems arise when we start to identify with the forms that are being created. We create the sense of ourselves, our ego and our self-image, by this process of identification and attachment. We start to believe that we are our thoughts, we are our feelings and that we are or have a physical body. We begin to claim ownership for the forms which we create. We lock an incredible amount of energy in the maintenance of this ego structure. We become so identified with it, so attached to it, that we defend it in any way we can. In a sense, we see the world through it. Instead of perceiving our thoughts, feelings and physical body as an

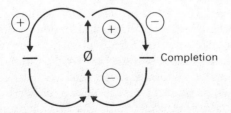

Fig. 5.1. Energy completion: energies arise from a source, take shape in some form of completion, then flow back to the source

on-going process, a flow, we try to stabilise the whole of it into a 'me' an 'I' who lives in the world as a separate entity to other 'I's' and other things. This freezes or crystallises our energies into certain forms, we accept certain aspects of ourselves and of the world and reject others. We see the world through the veils of this identification process and the weight of our conditioning. Something happens to this 'I' and it reacts in a certain way to defend itself. This then becomes part of the way the self sees and protects itself. Patterns become habit and processes become crystallised. We had trouble with our relationship with our father; this becomes a part of the self, a crystallised relationship which re-enacts itself with other male authority figures. But why do we do this? Why do we lock our energies into rigid patterns of thought, feelings and form to reinforce a self-image, a self which seems very real? This self is a learned, conditioning process. I learn how to be 'me' and become very attached to this process which I have basically constructed.

Taoists would point to a process of separation which underlies the creation of a fixed and limited ego. In Taoism, the source of all of creation is Tao. It is a deathless, changeless Essence which is the wellspring of creation. The Tao is also the Way of things, the basic harmony and oneness of the universe. When we are at one with Tao, the Way of things, all is well. But when we become blind to Tao, to the centre of existence, then our problems arise. We lose our connection to Tao. We begin to feel separate and to perceive things through the veils of separation. In the movement from the source into form, the connection is forgotten and we forget who we are. In forgetting who we are, in feeling separate, a great emptiness arises. We need to construct a new 'I' to fill this void, so we create, attach to and believe in our ego. This ego process bends and distorts our energies and traps them in the forms we create. This leads to a kind of grinding-down process, a disordering process where energies, trapped in unbalanced patterns, become disordered and sluggish! Form, instead of a divine expression of order, becomes a quagmire of confused and contradictory needs, desires and actions.

On a basic practical level, these crystallisations of energy predispose us to processes of imbalance and ill health. Energies are not allowed to complete in the form and return to the source, but are channelled into compulsively recreating the same form over and over again. Our forms, that is our thoughts, feelings and body, become a habit.

This can be seen in very basic ways. For example, Harry came into my office with a tensed and stiff neck and shoulders that were rock-like and painful. Headaches occurred frequently and there was a tendency to depression and dark moods. He also had a spastic and painful colon and 'gassy' feelings in the abdomen. Every cell of the body is constantly renewed. We have a complete 'new' body about every seven years. But somehow, the nature of that body becomes frozen. Harry's tense shoulders and neck had been an on-going problem for over twelve years. His energies had become crystallised to create this pattern of tension and holding and to recreate it continually. Even though tissue cells are continuously dividing, creating new cells and dying, the pattern and quality of that creation had already been determined. This was also the case in his spastic colon syndrome and depression. Each was a quality of energetic crystallisation which continually created the same fixed forms. So Harry had become frozen and attached to seeing and feeling himself a certain way and disorder resulted.

The Crystallisation of Thought into Physical Form

I would like to spend a little time here discussing how the mind–body process becomes so fixed and inflexible. Let us first look at the formative nature of our thinking process. Thoughts are the subtlest layer of physical manifestation. It may seem strange to think of thought as a physical form, but it is very useful to do so. In traditional philosophies, any completed pattern which energy takes is considered to be *rupa*, or form. So thought is considered to be a subtle expression of physical form. The process of thinking is a 'mental' process but the image or thought created is a 'form'. In some ways, this allows us to be a little less attached to the thought as an expression of 'me' and enables us to see the thought as a form which can be worked with. The Buddha, in the *Dhammapada*, says, 'You are what you think, having become what you thought. The mind is chief, all things are mind made.' The process of thought is considered to be a very formative one. We perceive our world through the thought processes and constructions which we have learned via past experience. In Polarity terms, thought energies become physical via our feelings and emotions. A thinking pattern becomes entrenched and part of our ego self-image. It may be driven by desire and need. This thought-pattern takes on emotional nuances and tones. Sadness, anger, joy become attached to the image. The body takes shape to express this pattern and it becomes locked into our physical body. In Harry's case above, his tense shoulders and spastic colon became an expression of his resentment and fear. Locked into this pattern he became depressed and despondent. Dr Stone comments on this process in *Health Building*: 'Our mental and emotional energies become chemistry [i.e. physical] . . . through our subtle energy system. This fact will awaken us with a shock to the truth that our condition proceeds from life and its conditioning within our selves through mental and emotional impulses.'

Jacob Needleman, in an article called 'Psychiatry and the Sacred', from the book *Awakening the Heart*, eloquently describes this movement as an 'encysting' process:

Beneath the fragile sense of personal identity, the individual is actually an innumerable swarm of disconnected impulses, thoughts, reactions, opinions, and sensations, which are triggered into activity by causes of which he is totally unaware. Yet at each moment, the individual identifies himself with whichever of this swarm of impulses and reactions happens to be active, automatically affirming each as 'himself', and then taking a stand either for or against this 'self', depending on the particular pressures that the social environment has brought to bear upon him since his childhood.

The traditions identify this affirming-and-denying process as the real source of human misery and the chief obstacle to the development of man's inherent possibilities. Through this affirmation and denial a form is constructed around each of the passing impulses originating in the different parts of the human organism. And this continuous, unconscious affirmation of identity traps a definite amount of precious psychic energy in a kind of *encysting process* that is as much chemical–biological as it is psychological.

So it is the identification and attachment to the forms which make up our psycho-physical entity which cause energetic imbalance and crystallisation. Needleman understands that this process becomes locked into our physical body and traps energy in its maintenance. Our ego process of separation, identification and attachment takes on physical expression via 'a kind of *encysting process*'.

Wilhelm Reich, a student of Freud and a well-known psychoanalyst in his own right, developed a form of psychotherapy based on this understanding. Imbalanced psychological processes become crystallised into our bodies as patterns of tension and blocked energy. Reich believed that in order to release this locked-up energy, which he termed 'orgone energy', the body had to be taken into account. This was a major departure from his teacher Freud, and he was, indeed, ostracised for it. Although he focused on repressed sexuality, this approach can be extended to all patterns of emotional armouring. His theories were expanded by Alexander Lowen and John Pierrakos into a system called Bioenergetics. It included ways of reading the emotional history of a person as expressed by their body. It uses exercises, breathing practices, body-work and counselling to release physically bound emotional patterns. In polarity therapy we also have ways of reading the emotional history of a person. Unlike Bioenergetics, which uses Reichian character analysis into schizoid, oral, masochistic, psychopathic and rigid structures, Polarity Therapy relates the individual's condition to the subtle energies of the Five Elements. The body is an expression of their movements and their relationships and imbalances can be read by observing their dynamics and structure. So thought becomes physical and we tend to become identified and attached to the process. We do not allow energies to complete in the form and return to the source, but hold onto them in the continual recreation of the form we are attached to. This sets up unbalanced and crystallised patterns of energy which become enslaved to the forms they create. It sets the stage for psychological or physical imbalance and breakdown. The process is summarised in Figure 5.2.

Source
Higher Order

Energies move, pulsate towards
form

Energies 'step down' into form via
the Five Element patterns

Processes of separation, ego structure
and attachment crystallise energies into
maintaining specific forms

Processes of thought, emotion and physical
form become crystallised into set
patterns.

This traps the energies into the
maintenance of these patterns.

Energies thus crystallised become
more and more disordered.

Processes of disease and disharmony
results.

Fig. 5.2. The path to illness

Let us take an example from my private practice to illustrate this process. When Jenny walked into my office, I saw a teenager with a young girl's body and face. Much to my surprise, I discovered that she was 32 years old. She complained of extreme hyperacidity and stomach upset. She had been put on a drug which basically knocked out the parasympathetic enervation to the stomach. This consisted in blocking vagal nerve impulses to the area. It also imbalanced other digestive and eliminative function and she was very frightened about it. An operation to cut the vagus nerve innervation to the stomach had also been talked about. During our session it became apparent that she held much frustration and anger towards her husband and felt very caged by their relationship. She was always seeking more 'space'. This was a pattern that arose in all of her previous relationships with men. We discovered that it was related to her relationship with her father and her need to be a rebellious teenager. In polarity therapy terms her Fire had become locked into a cycle of repressed anger and frustration. She placed herself in situations with men which reinforced the 'caged-in' feeling and the teenage anger and rebellion which accompanied it. If we remember that the Fire element governs anger and the digestive system, we can see a link between her hyperacidity and her repressed anger and frustration.

We tackled Jenny's condition from as holistically orientated an approach as possible. This included body-work to open her Fire and balance the related element patterns, polarity exercises to help release the emotional content and balance her energies, very specific dietary changes and a herbal remedy to help balance the acid-base relationship in her stomach. Interlaced with this was counselling work where her patterns were clarified and life choices made clearer. Within three months her hyperacidity was over and she seemed a stronger, more grounded person. She also looked more her age. Here we saw a condition where thoughts and feelings had become crystallised via the Fire element into a physical imbalance. Her relationship with her father had become a crystallised pattern and was her model for relationships with men generally. Her frustration, anger and need became entrenched patterns of thought, feeling and physical imbalance. She thought about her husband and herself in very fixed ways, she felt the same feelings again and again and her body eventually had to express the acidity of her thoughts and feelings in physical terms. Her energies had become crystallised and locked into maintaining the form of her patterns. Disorder was sure to occur.

Health Building

So how do we relax and open up this process of crystallisation? Let us now explore this in more detail. Dr Stone called the movement towards greater health and freedom 'health building'. The first components of this movement are our thoughts and attitudes. As we have seen, thought-patterns are very subtle and formative aspects of the crystallisation process. Negative thinking patterns which are based on fear and contraction, will yield physical processes in the body which express the mental pattern. Dr Stone stressed that the foundation of our health rests on our thoughts and attitudes. He wrote in *Health Building*:

We become what we contemplate. Negative thoughts and fears make grooves in the mind as negative energy waves of despondency and hopelessness. We cannot think negative thoughts and reap positive results, and therefore we must assert the positive, and maintain a positive pattern of thinking and acting as our ideal.

The assertion of the positive is a means to an end; it is not the end itself. It can lay fertile soil for positive life directions, positive responses to life situations and a foundation for seeking after deeper truths, it sets a 'tone' for health building. One important attitude that a therapist can help a client perceive is that everything changes and that potential for change is ever-present. Many people come to see me entrenched in a belief that nothing will really change and that they will be like 'this' the rest of their lives. Positive attitudes such as openness to change can start off a whole process of self-exploration and health building. It is important for us to see how much we take for granted; how we believe the thoughts we think. In a sense we need to gain a little space from our thoughts so that we can see them for what they are, and realise that we don't have to 'become' the thought over and over again. In one sense, thinking itself is not the problem, it is the grasping onto the thought and the identification with it that creates crystallisation and disorder. In my private practice I help people explore their beliefs and 'life statements' and support them in the process of clarifying and letting go of ones that limit their potential and unbalance their energies.

Body-Work

The main focus of much of polarity work is body-work. As we have seen, processes of thought and emotion when held by attachment and need become physically manifest in the body. This process is underpinned by the patterns of the Five Elements. These interweave to form the energy matrix that underlies our body. Patterns of thought and emotion are also patterns of the Five Elements. When these become crystallised in the physical body, the energy reflexes that relate to the currents affected will also become unbalanced. The polarity therapist uses this understanding of the energy patterns and their physical manifestations as a way into the client's energy and life process.

In the body-work the imbalances are literally 'touched on' and the therapist's hands are used to reflect these patterns back to the client so that they can become aware of them. When energy begins to move, the client can become aware of how they tend to hold themselves in certain patterns and how they have crystallised and locked their energies in the maintenance of these patterns. The body-work is a potent mirror which can show us how we 'do ourselves' and how, if we choose, we can soften these boundaries, let go of the fear which tends to hold them in place and explore the greater potentials which may arise in this process. This may mean letting go of physical pain, such as a low back pain, and taking on the responsibility of greater mobility. It may mean letting go of negative life-patterns which tend to define us in narrow or painful limits. The potential is truly great. We can discover that what has been made can be unmade and that our beliefs, fears, emotional patterns and physical form can be a much more open and fluid process than we might at first think.

Fear

The things which cause our energy system to rigidify and become unbalanced arise from our feelings of separation, of ego structure and from identification with this structure. A major factor which supports this identification process is fear. If we think back to our discussions about the elements, we will remember that fear relates to the Earth phase of energy movement. The process of energies becoming trapped and crystallised in order to maintain a form or process is basically an earthing process. The Earth element relates to contraction and fear. Basically *any* process where energies are locked into the maintenance of a form, be it a thought-pattern, emotional pattern or physical imbalance, is a process of contraction and is based on fear.

Let us explore this movement of fear. We have said that energy crystallisations arise due to attachment and ego process. This is based on a feeling of insecurity and emptiness which is in turn an expression of our separation, our feelings of aloneness and autonomy. This is all founded on a loss of awareness of and contact to our deeper source and essence. We have forgotten who we are and what we are and feel separate from everything and everyone. In this movement fear arises, we are separate, alone. We grasp at form to create continuity, to create a belief, a certainty that 'I am'. So energies become trapped in this creation. The process of letting go, of moving from this fixed position, is very much a process of letting go of fear. There is no 'I' to be hurt and no 'I' who dies, there is indeed no 'I' to cling to, yet we cling so fiercely and strongly. Allowing energies to flow more freely means at its essence, letting go of the rigidity of our self and releasing energies which have become locked in fear and attachment.

'Whew!' you may say – 'I just came to see you for a pain in my back!' That's fair enough. When a client comes in to see me, the first step is to determine a clear 'contract'. This may be an agreement to see me for a short term of sessions to help alleviate that back pain or it may be an intention to work for a longer period of time and to embark on a mutual exploration of the dynamics which underlie the pain. This may take the form of bodywork, counselling, dietary routines, exercises, anything in fact, which helps the client become aware of their own energy process.

The Individual's Responsibility

The bottom line of all of this discussion is that of energy flow and its relationship to health and disease. When energies are not allowed to complete and return to their source, then restriction and imbalance can result. Dr Stone wrote:

> Now we come to the *Essence* of these currents *within us,* by which our body operates, moves and has its being as a living human entity, in health or in dis-ease. When these four polarized energy currents flow freely, we call it health because it is unperceived and natural. But when there are obstructions as cross-currents or short circuits and blocks in its energy lines then these register as pain or limitation of motion and function in that particular area. This is the real picture of dis-ease in our *wireless energy field,* before it becomes physical energy and gross phenomenon where it can be seen externally and by means of X-ray.

Here Dr Stone says that health is the free flow of energy. The four active currents or elements must relate to each other in an open and free-flowing way. When obstructions arise then ill health and pain result. These energetic obstructions underlie what are usually perceived as 'gross phenomena'. We tend to perceive only the physical effects and not to acknowledge the subtler play which underpins them. In some sense, this is very comforting. We then have only to deal with the symptom and the physical relationships. We do not have to deal with our thought processes, our attitudes, our emotional life, our eating patterns and most important of all, we do not have to learn about ourselves. Moreover the doctor or therapist can also take refuge in the physical realm and take comfort as changes are perceived in it. These changes, however, are more superficial than we like to admit as the deeper energetic imbalances may still predispose us to similar physical or psychological imbalances.

Health-building and the healing process is based on becoming aware of the factors and tendencies which tend to trap our energies into maintaining thoughts, feelings and physical forms which are basically unhealthy and disordered. It means taking responsibility for our own process. During a session, the therapist is only a guide, a facilitator in this work. He or she becomes a clear mirror for the client to perceive their own polarity energy process.

Cleansing and health-building diets are one way that people can start to get a handle on their life process. Our relationship to food is very emotive and habitual and working with food not only helps clean the body of toxicity and waste products but is also a chance to explore our relationship to food and nourishment. Polarity exercises are another aid in this movement to greater responsibility and a more open energy system. They give people tools to use to work with their physical contractions and patterns without a dependency on the therapist. In this work greater energy becomes available as the energy restrictions and blocks are released This increased vitality can become available for healing to occur. The basis for all of this is an acceptance of responsibility for our own thoughts, attitudes and feelings. This can be most difficult as these are commonly bound up with fear and insecurity. But it is the most important part of the healing process. Without it imbalances return or take on new forms and we are in the end, just fooling ourselves.

Illness and the Five Elements

I would like to finish by using the Five Elements to explore the disease and healing processes. The cycle of the Elements can be used to describe any process, so let us apply them here. We will take the example of a physical illness and follow it via the framework of the elements. The Ether phase can be thought of as a state of balanced and open energy flow. Energy pulsates and condenses in form, is expressed and then returns to its source. At the Air phase the process of attachment and the movement of the ego has crystallised energies into set patterns of thought, feeling and physical form. This sets the stage for physical imbalance to arise. Due to this 'field of imbalance', disorder occurs and disease processes can arise. At the Fire phase an acute illness does arise. The body tries to purge itself. Fever, chills and pain will occur as the body tries to move back to balance. If the body's vitality is too low or if the acute symptoms are suppressed by drugs, then the symptoms 'go underground'. The imbalance will then enter a chronic 'Watery' phase where the symptoms become an underlying tendency. There is not enough vitality in the system for the body to purge itself, but things have not broken down completely. Here the mind–body system moves to greater and greater disorder as its energies become more and more congested. At the Earth phase this process results in stagnation and tissue death. This describes the movement from balance to disorder.

In the health-building process we start a movement back to health. We place attention in the chronic Watery phase of the process and get energies moving via tissue cleansing, health-building diets and exercise. Body-work starts to allow energies to flow and balance. At the Fire phase the body-work and exercises increase vitality to the point that a healing process is possible. This is a movement from processes of disorder to greater order where vitality is raised and energies are freed. A healing crisis might occur here as the energy is now available for the body to purge and heal itself. In a healing crisis some of the original symptoms in the acute phase may again arise as part of the healing process. We then move into an Airy phase, where insights into the process have occurred, lessons have been learned and processes of thought and attitude have shifted into healthier, more positive patterns. We arrive at Ether again as a feeling of great space can occur here as we move back to a more balanced state. The whole cycle is depicted in Figure 5.3.

Health-building is about this movement from confusion and pain to greater balance and harmony in life. It is important to remember that the foundation for this process rests in our state of mind, thoughts and attitudes. This is the realm where we create the fields for either health or disease. As Dr Stone used to say, 'As you think, so you are.' To finish this chapter, I'd like to share this final quote from Dr Stone which is perhaps the best definition of health I have discovered:

> Health is not merely of the body. It is the natural expression of the body, mind and soul when they are in rhythm with the One Life. True Health is the harmony of life within us, consisting of peace of mind, happiness and well-being. It is not merely a question of physical fitness, but is rather a result of the soul finding free expression through the mind and body of that individual. Such a person radiates peace and happiness and everyone in his presence automatically feels happy and contented.

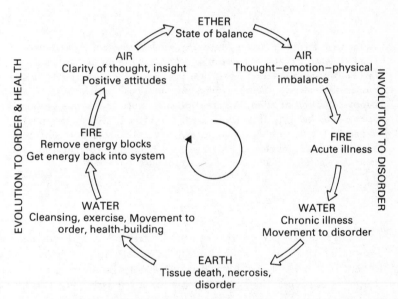

Fig. 5.3. Involution – evolution in the disease process

CHAPTER SIX

Health and the Elements

At the very core of the search for true health lies the essential question of what life is for. What is our personal goal, in terms of the use we make of this body and mind – and what is the purpose of the divine gift of this human life? Merely having no physical pain does not always mean a happy condition of mind. We are entitled to more and have a greater purpose for being in this world. Each one of us is seeking the inner happiness that comes not from outward accomplishments but from the harmony of our inner being. What is life for, if it is not to make an effort to achieve a higher realization of consciousness?

Therapist and Client

Dr Stone approached the question of health from a viewpoint that few doctors or therapists take. He asked questions that are very basic to the unfoldment of our lives. Health is not just about the absence of pain or symptoms, it is about 'the harmony of our inner being' and 'a higher realization of consciousness'. This is critically important in the under-standing of polarity therapy. When making a commitment to healing, we are making a deep commitment to ourselves. It is an exploration, a deep learning. This has many repercussions for both therapist and client. On a basic level, it is about trust. Trust must be earned; for the client to feel trust in both the therapist and his procedures, the quality of contact between the two must be very deep. The only way this can occur is for the therapist to take the lead and to be truly present for the client. Being present means being with that other person with *attention, intention* and *effort*. Dr Stone wrote that these three qualities are essential in the healing relationship. When I am with a client he or she is my world. All of my 'stuff': my fear, anger, anxiety, pain, worry are all put to the side. I become receptive and let the other person in. I 'listen' with all of my senses and am as truly there for the person as I can possibly be. This means that the therapist must be working to contact a deep place in themselves, before they can deeply contact another. I have to confront, and make friends with, my own thoughts, feelings and emotions, recognise them for what they are and put them aside as they come up in this very special client/therapist relationship. In polarity therapy terms it is called 'finding your neutral ground' or your 'Ether space' while treating another. Being neutral with a mind clear of opinions, judgements and 'shoulds' is essential for this to occur and requires the therapist to be mindful of their thoughts and feelings in a session so that they do not 'colour' the relationship. This doesn't mean repressing them, but acknowledging them as they arise and putting them aside as you maintain your attention and contact with the other person. In simple terms, for me, presence implies being with the client in a fully attentive and receptive space with as quiet a mind and as open a heart as possible.

This quality of contact creates a situation which encourages the client also to make contact and to let down his or her defences, allow themselves to be vulnerable and to trust. This is a great responsibility for the therapist. The client is allowing him or herself to be open and vulnerable, entrusting you with their process. Whether it is a dis-ease process, a thought process, an emotional process or a psychological process, they are entrusting its unfolding to this therapist in this therapeutic encounter. In polarity therapy we believe that no matter what process is occurring it is an expression of that person's consciousness. It is a reflection of their 'way of being' coming into form. All of the seemingly different processes are just aspects of *one energy* and *one consciousness* and this ultimately derives from the Source itself.

The healing relationship is about presence, compassion, love and oneness at the deepest level.

The Polarity Therapist's Method of Working

Let us explore the various levels that the polarity therapist deals with. As mentioned earlier, Dr Stone worked with the three major phases of energy process as our energies move from subtle spheres to physical form. These phases are the Five Element relationships, the nervous system and body structure and form. The most formative and important phase is that of the Five Elements. The therapist picks up information about the client's energy system through an understanding of how these relationships dynamically coalesce or 'mesh'. We gather clues from posture and body reading; from the way the client expresses thoughts and emotions; and most important of all, through our ability to perceive blocks in the Five Element system, by touch. When we 'read' a person's body, we see that their imbalances take shape from deeper processes within. Our thoughts, attitudes and emotional life shape our body. How we think and feel literally takes form in our physical body. Blockages and imbalances in any element can be seen physically as body structure, tension patterns, areas of excess flesh or fat, skin texture, colour and temperature, and in the elasticity or flaccidity of tissue in various parts of the body. Nothing is arbitrary. Everything is a reflection of who we are. There are two aspects to what the body tells us. The first is a general sense of how that person's energies are being used. You can look at the general symmetry of the body and note areas of tension or obvious imbalance. One quick way of doing this is to compare the top of the body with the bottom, one side to the other and the front with the back. Does chest area 'fit' the pelvis? Is the chest too narrow or the pelvis too wide? Does one side of the body have a collapsed look? Is the back of the body telling a different story from the front? Does the body take a shape that tells you something? (See Figure 6.1.)

Allan came into my office complaining of low back pain, shoulder tension and a general feeling of depression, felt as low energy, irritability and a sense of having a 'black cloud' hovering over him. His body told a clear story. His chest seemed to be excessively padded. There seemed to be an excessive amount of flesh between him and the world. His pelvis seemed small in comparison. His arms were reasonably proportioned, but his legs were very narrow and slight compared with his upper body. It was as if all of his energy was caught in his chest area and not much was reaching the ground. His back was also 'pulled back'. Although padded it looked like his chest had caved-in and his shoulder area had pulled back. There was also a 'side-to-side' difference, with his body seeming collapsed on the right side. It was like his shoulder and pelvis had contracted towards each other.

In subsequent sessions we explored his chest and shoulder area and found it to be a very protected area, full of sadness and withheld anger. He weighted himself down with everyday life, and his right side – which is the outgoing, more aggressive side of the body – had literally contracted in response to this stance. His excessive padding in the chest area helped him protect his heart from further hurt. The tension in his shoulder area was his way of literally pulling back from the world and anger and resentment were also held back there. His low back pain occurred at the bottom of this tensed area as excess physical stress was placed here. There was also a band of tension across this area just above the navel. Little energy was reaching his pelvis and his legs seemed hardly able to support him. He tended to be a very 'heady' person, much caught up in thoughts and worry and had a very hard time 'grounding' himself, in being in the world, was not very practical in his approach to life, and was not a good communicator.

The second aspect of body reading is, after a general appraisal, to look at the Five Element relationships as seen in the body. This is done by looking at the triad body relationships for each element. If we remember that each element has a positive, neutral and negative polarity triad area in physical form, then we can start looking at these areas to see how these energies have become unbalanced.

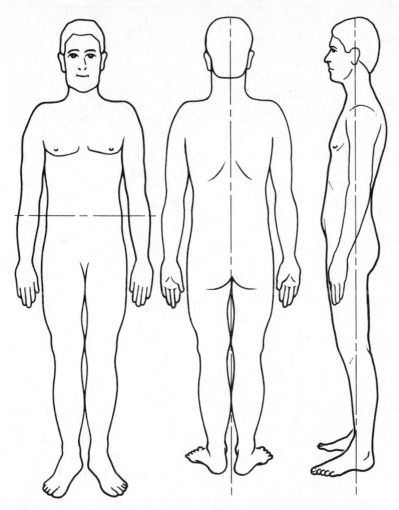

Fig. 6.1. General body reading. Comparing relative aspects of the whole body. Does the chest 'fit' the pelvis. Is one side different from the other? Are there obvious areas of tension or imbalance?

In Allan, our example above, the Air element was the focus of his imbalance with an overlay of withheld Fire. His chest had become withdrawn and padded to protect his heart. The Heart Centre governs the Air element and the sadness and suffering held there affected all Air relationships. The 'motor' area of the Air element in the shoulder area also pulled back and held back the anger which overlaid the heart-felt hurt. The withheld Fire was also seen as a band of tension across the solar plexus area going right around the body to the upper lumbars where back pain was felt. His diaphragm, an Air-related muscle, was very tight, and little energy was felt in the pelvis, the neutral pole of the Water element.

CONSTITUTIONAL TYPES

AIR   FIRE

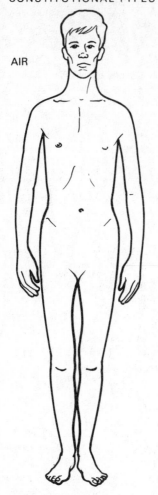
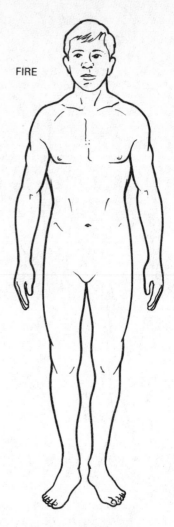

Underdeveloped, light build slim, thin, drawn-out/ thin-boned/light weight, narrow lumbar area

Moderate/medium build balanced look, muscular without exercising, in proportion, moderate weight, medium lumbar area

Ectomorph

Mesomorph

Look for: Basic body type or combination of types.
Tells you general element tendencies of person
which may be strengths or weaknesses

Fig. 6.2. Constitutional types

WATER 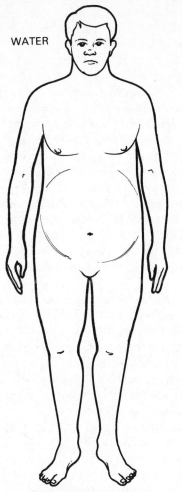 EARTH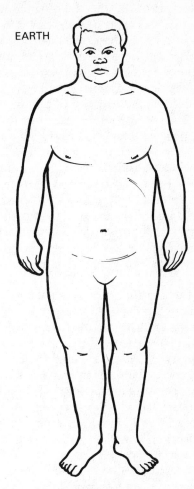

Moderate-stout build
stout-padded look,
excess fat, full
buttocks, full breasts,
overweight, wide
lumbar area

Endomorph

Block-like build
thick, short neck,
thick arms and legs,
'tree-trunk' like,
looks very 'earthed'

Endomorph

His pelvis was like unknown territory to him. His calves and ankles, negative pole areas of Air, were thin and deprived as most of the energy was held in his chest, shoulders and diaphragm. From this a 'picture' of the Element imbalances in Allan could be built up. Along with information from him, from how he is in relationship to me and others, from his emotional processes and physical problems, a picture emerges. Coupled with sensitivity of an experienced therapist to energy flow via touch work, the session can start to unfold and the therapist can follow that person's unique expression of the wireless energy system of man.

Body reading with the Five Elements has two aspects: 'constitutional type' and elemental triad relationships. The constitutional type relates to the overall body structure and its tendencies. The constitutional type is set at conception but it can become clouded by overlaid imbalances and compensation in the energy triads. Thus a Fire body type, which is usually well-proportioned and muscular (without exercising) may be covered up by a Water element imbalance seen by excessive padding in the hips and thighs. The constitutional relationships can be seen in Figure 6.2.

The constitutional type tells you the general tendencies of a person. You can see the overall structure, its tendency to one or more elements and the tendency of the energy system to express itself in one or more particular elements. This can show either strengths or weaknesses. Thus a 'fire-type' structure would indicate a person with a tendency to good vital energy but *how* they use this energy is completely up to them. Is it used openly and *heartfully* to help others and gain insight into life or is it held-back and repressed only to come out as power-games and manipulation? No constitutional type is good or bad, they just indicate tendencies. How that person learns their lessons within that structure is the crucial issue. Dr Stone was a very 'earthy' structure. He could have tended to crystallisation and laziness, but instead chose to use the positive aspects of earth to benefit himself and others. He learned his lessons at a very deep level.

The constitutional types also tie into the orthodox medical categories of ectomorph, mesomorph and endomorph. The ectomorph has a body structure built predominantly of tissues which derive from the ectoderm of the embryo. Thus this is an embryonic or foetal type. The ectoderm is a germ layer from which the nervous system, skin, hair and external organs such as ears and eyes derive. In an ectoderm type or ectomorph, the body tends to be thin and linear and has a quality of fragility to it. It is our Air constitutional type. The mesomorph has tissues derived from the mesoderm of the embryo and from it are derived primarily the muscles, connective tissue and bone. The mesomorphic body type has a predominance of muscle with a solid physique with good proportions; our fire constitutional type. Finally, the endomorph has tissue derived from the endoderm of the embryo. From it are derived fatty tissues, the respiratory tract, the digestive tract and bladder. The endormorph has a body structure with soft roundness, accumulations of fat and typically a large trunk and thighs. This is our water constitutional type. The Earth type is also an endomorphic type with an aspect of the mesomorph if the muscles predominate. I have gone into this to show how the same observations have been made by the orthodox medical profession.

The triads tell more of a specific story. They show the development of the elements after birth due to conditioned processes of mind and emotion. These take physical shape in the body and can be read like an open book. Is there excessive tension seen as tight bands or tense muscles in any area? Is there lack of movement or mobility in any area? Is there excessive 'padding' or flesh in any area? Do the parts of a triad fit? In our previous example, Allan, there was excessive padding in the chest area, combined with thin calves and ankles. The positive and negative poles of Air didn't 'fit'. Energy was trapped in the core around the heart. The shoulder area was pulled back. The pelvis was seemingly small compared to the chest. There was an Air/Water imbalance overlaid on the original pattern. Energy and awareness wasn't getting down into the pelvis and certainly wasn't grounding to Earth as seen by overly thin legs and ankles. The holding back of anger in the shoulder area related to a holding back of Fire in the core and a tension band was seen in the solar plexus area. The triad relationships can tell you a clear story if you tune into them.

The body reading can give you an overall impression of a person. You must then fill in the picture by seeing how the client is in relationship to yourself, to others, to their friends, family, work situations, etc. How are their ways of being in the world an expression of their energies? What elements seem in prominence? One example I can give is of an older woman who saw me for an extended period of time. She came into my office one day and my first impressions were of slow, Watery movements, much show of pain/depression in her manner and feeling of great neediness. Her Water element called out to me. Her body was very padded, very sluggish, like muddy water deposits. When she sat down she gave an impression of low vitality and low Fire. Then the torrent opened, she opened her mouth and couldn't stop talking; complaining and moaning. She generally discharged a lot of energy verbally. There was a lack of order to her words and thought-patterns – a very imbalanced Airiness to her words. Much was said, but very little had deep meaning. It was her way to 'unload' and to control the situation. There was much suffering behind the words, but the words themselves were not important.

As we progressed through the sessions a clear Air/Water imbalance came through. Much energy was caught up in erratic thought and worry and many issues arose from the past in relationship to sexuality, love and relationship. She bottled up her Water energy in her pelvis and could not ground herself to Earth. Air, which is in a dynamic relationship to Water, became imbalanced and the energy system released its pressure via thought and erratic speech. So much vitality was locked up in this cycle that her vital reserves, her fire, were always low. Much information can be gained via body reading, but this is only one of many tools available. In the previous example I took in information through all my senses. I saw her body language; how she sat and moved in my presence, her body structure and form and also her general appearance and demeanour. I heard her words, her quality of speech and felt what was behind the words. I tried to become clear about her thoughts and attitudes and watched, felt, heard, the unfolding of her emotional life. Sometimes you can smell changes in a person as their body produces smells which react to their changing states. During the sessions, most of all, I felt via touch the energy patterns of her body and followed her unique expression of subtle energy patterning.

The polarity therapist thus takes in information about a person and translates this into information about their energies. It is a process of building up a picture of a person gradually over a number of sessions. It is important to separate what you are actually seeing or hearing from your opinions, projections, hunches and intuitions until a complete impression is gathered. Thus in Allan, our example above, I saw his shoulders and chest pulled back and seemingly caved-in. I projected that there was much hurt involved and a pulling back from relationships which might also be hurtful. I saw his tense and knotted shoulders and projected that much anger was held there. This was borne out later, but, at first, I could not be sure if my projection was his reality. The more the therapist is in that neutral or Ether space we talked about earlier, the clearer the information about the person is. It is more likely to be free from the therapist's own imbalances – from projections, fears, worry, insecurities, power trips, etc. This again implies that the therapist must be working on himself to clarify his own issues, to become friends with himself and to avoid projecting his 'stuff' onto the client. The relationships become a mutual learning, a true dance.

We are going to approach the body-work from a framework of following the three major phases of energy as they take form in the physical body. These three are the Five Element patterns, the nervous system patterns and the physical patterns of the body structure and form. Foremost are the Five Element patterns. The polarity therapist knows the various relationships of the elements as they occur in physical form. The Five Element patterns are patterns of energy pulsation which interlace and overlap to form an intricate energy hologram. It is this pulsating interwoven 'egg' of energy which underlies physical manifestation. I am going to talk about these patterns in a rather artificial way. We are going to isolate the various major patterns and talk about their reflexes and repercussions of blocked and imbalanced energies in their flow. We must, however, realise that we are really talking about the aspects of *one* energy system and that an imbalance in one aspect will unbalance related patterns.

Before we do this, let us review some basic concepts. We live in an ordered universe where energy relationships are a reflection of this order. The energy patterns of human beings take one pattern of order, while that of a dog takes another. This order or patterning is not just about quantity or position but is also about quality – quality of awareness, consciousness and life mode. The energies in our bodies take on very specific patterns in relationship to this ordered movement. These patterns and flows of energy relate to each other in what may be called 'harmonic' relationships. Thus, patterns of energy of like quality resonate with each other. It is like hitting 'middle C' on a piano: all the other 'C's will also vibrate. They have what is called a resonance with each other. If you look at Figure 6.3, you will see what is known as the Polarity Zone Chart.

The three zones, positive–negative–neutral, outline the general harmonics of energy, as energy pulsates outwards in its centrifugal phase and inwards in its centripetal phase.

This general pulsation sets up zones of energy relationship which are in a harmonic or resonant pattern. Thus all positive zones resonate with

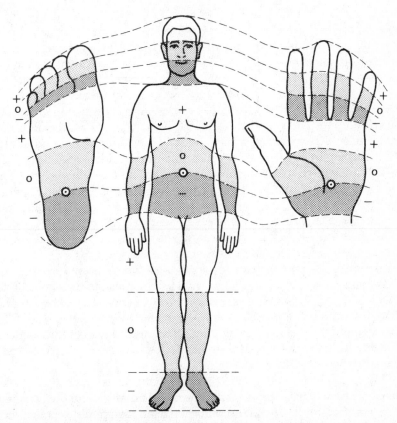

Fig. 6.3. Polarity Zone Chart: pain, blockage, contraction in any zone has similar harmonic blockages in proportion in like zones.

each other, all negative zones resonate with each other and neutral zones resonate with each other. A block in any zone yields blocks in other, like zones. The feet, the most yin, negative area of the body, reflect the longer-standing chronic imbalances in the core of the body above. The hands, which are generally neutral, reflect the more recent acute imbalances in these same areas. Blocks in any zone can be located in like zones and released with bi-polar hand contacts in two zones at a time. These relationships become much more complex as we start to overlay the Five Element patterns over them.

Ether Element Relationships

Let us look at the Ether element relationships again and see how these relationships can be affected via the therapist's knowing touch. In Chapter 4 we talked about the quality of the Ether element. It is the first of the physical elements to manifest and is closest to the quality of neutrality and peace, qualities in resonance with the Source itself. On a practical level, Ether is space; it is the field element. As we have seen, it creates space for the other elements to unfold – the matrix which allows movement on a subtle level. When its field is contracted, usually due to the reactions of mental and emotional stress, we feel closed in, almost like a box or cage has formed around us. As our energy fields contract we may find ourselves stuck in either a pole of explosiveness or depression.

An Ether treatment can help open our energy fields up and give more space for things to work through. Although there is a specific touch procedure which encourages this, we all know how the sensitive and sattvic touch of a close friend or relative can calm and open things up for us. This caring, heartfelt quality must be brought to all sessions. The object of the Ether treatment is to open the Ether field and create more 'space' for the person. As Ether governs the emotions generally, this can give more space for emotional crisis to work in. It is especially useful when things seem 'boxed in', suffocating and explosive. It is also useful to open things up in exhausted or depressed states.

The intent of the Ether session is to calm the client and expand the energy fields generally. This is done by working through the sub-fields at each joint. There is a neutral cross-over point of energy at each joint and the fields around the joints resonate with the general Ether field. The fields around the joints are worked first and then general chakra-balancing techniques are applied to gently balance the field around each major energy centre. (See Figure 6.4.)

One client came to me recently in a very contracted, frustrated space. Her job was becoming oppressive as she could not deal with the demands that seemed to be heaped upon her. Her relationship also seemed very demanding and she generally felt weighed down and laden with the world's worry. After an Ether session, she felt much lighter. 'It was like

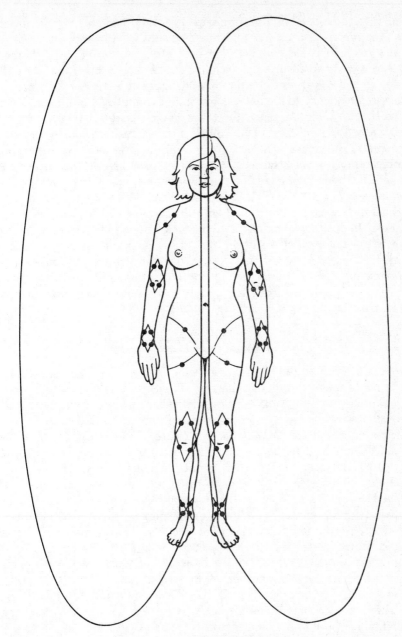

Fig. 6.4. The Ether treatment relationships showing contact areas for Ether treatment

being filled up like a balloon,' she said. We were then able to talk about her situation from a clearer and more spacious vantage point. Feeling more space, she could deal with her own process at work and at home. She could see how she drew the demands to her and realised that she had a need to make everyone else happy and secure at her own expense. She also had a tendency to see her self-worth in the approval of others. Thus at work she took on more than she could handle and tried to be everyone's 'earth-mother'. This spilled into her relationship, where she took on all the housework, shopping, and cooking along with general responsibility for her boyfriend's well-being. She literally had no space for herself. From having created space in the session, we then worked on creating space in her life. The Ether session can be a powerful movement to spaciousness and calm. It can, with the support of a skilled therapist, be useful in creating space and taking stock of one's life. Any treatment done with what is called a 'sattvic' or neutral touch can also help a person touch their inner core. Cranial work, which we will talk about later, is also very powerful in this sense. The unique thing about the Ether treatment is that it works directly to open up the general Ether field which is the matrix that supports the other elements.

Types of Touch in Polarity Therapy

Before talking about the four 'active' elements, I would like to talk about the types of touch in polarity therapy. The three qualities of touch are named after the three Gunas. If you remember that the Gunas represent three phases of energy movement, positive, neutral and negative, then their relationship to touch may become clearer. The first type of touch is the sattvic touch. It relates to the neutral *sattvas* guna, and is a firm yet gentle touch. It is a touch which does not challenge the client's resistance. It is gentle and calming and tends to bring the energy system to a more balanced state. This being said, I have seen very powerful emotional releases with sattvic work as the client's energy field is expanded and allowed room for emotional cleansing to occur. The second touch is the *rajasic* touch. It relates to the positive, yang, *rajas* guna and is a stimulating, directive touch. It is used to stimulate the flow of energy and direct it from one area to another. It can be shallow or deep and tends to be a vibrating or rocking touch. It may elicit a moderate response from the client if pain or emotional patterns are felt. It is not as deep or potentially painful as the *tamasic* touch. The tamasic touch relates to the negative, yin, *tamas* Guna. It is a deep touch which is used to disperse cold energy blocks. The tissues may be felt to be deeply contracted and knotted and the energy locked in that area needs to be dispersed and then directed through its polar relationships (more of this later). The tamasic touch can be quite painful if much congestion is locked into the connective tissues. All three types of touch can be used together at any point depending on the intent of the practitioner. They are depicted in Figure 6.5.

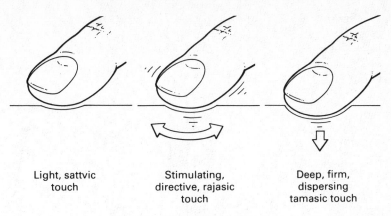

<table>
<tr><td>Light, sattvic
touch</td><td>Stimulating,
directive, rajasic
touch</td><td>Deep, firm,
dispersing
tamasic touch</td></tr>
</table>

Fig. 6.5. Three types of touch

Air Element Relationships

Let us now go on to explore the Air element, its relationships and techniques. The Air element is the most formative of the elements. It governs movement and when energy blocks arise, movement stagnates. It is very common, for instance, to have 'Airy blocks' of stagnant gas deposits in the connective tissues. If the colon is congested, gases can build up and collect in the connective tissues around it. Similar deposits are found in any area where the Air element and the movement it governs has stagnated. The body is very intelligent. It moves excessive toxins and wastes away from vital organs into the periphery. Thus Airy blocks and gaseous wastes can be commonly found in connective tissues and in the peripheral Airy reflexes in the forearms and calves. Dr Stone talks about this in his book *Polarity Therapy*:

> As the airy principle is the essential essence in the life currents in the body, it is also the one most frequently involved in pains as a negative effect. Gas pressure may diffuse and manifest as painful symptoms in muscle tissues, the bowels, or even in the head, very much like a gas bubble in a hot water pipe.

The Air element is closely connected to the Heart Centre, and heartfelt feelings strongly affect its relationships. I have seen so many clients open up their feelings, especially sadness and hurt, when the energies of the Heart Centre and the Air oval open. These can rapidly change to great joy and a wonderful quality of selfless love as the heart opens and lets go of years of accumulated hurt and aversion. This love, not attached to any object and without neurotic expectations and need, allows us deeply to touch a universal quality of joy and receptivity. It is said that love is what holds the universe together; it is the order which moulds chaos into

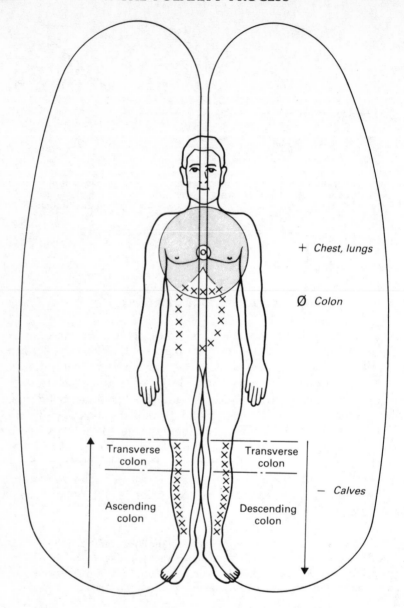

+ *Chest, lungs*

Ø *Colon*

Transverse colon   Transverse colon

— *Calves*

Ascending colon   Descending colon

Fig. 6.6. Anterior Air treatment relationships

- One can work generally around Air oval – top to bottom, side to side, corner to corner, front to back – in proportion.
- One can reflex colon points to calf points and to similar points in reflex colon areas between shoulder blades and on the feet (see zone chart) and ankles, arms and hands.

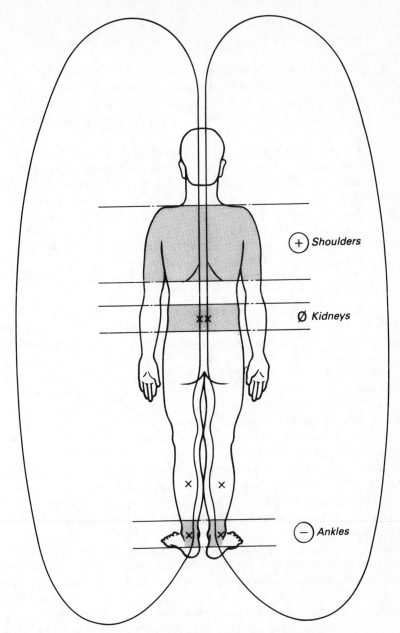

Fig. 6.7. Posterior Air treatment relationships

- One can work through blocks in the Air current line via the zone chart.
- There is also general work to release the Air-related areas of the diaphragm, shoulder blades and specific colon techniques.

form; it is the energy of Tao; the love of God. Such are the potential depths of allowing the free flow of the Air element to seek its deeper sources.

Figures 6.6 and 6.7 show some of the major reflex areas for the Air element and show some commonly used contact points. The two charts shown focus on the two main Air element triads. One deals with the lung/chest–colon–calves relationship and the other with the foetal triad of shoulders–kidneys–ankles.

Since this is not a book on polarity technique, but much more about concepts and relationships, I will not go into specifics about the different techniques and treatments. Polarity technique, in its simplest form, is to release the congestion or blockage locally and direct energy through its triune (positive, negative and neutral) relationships. The therapist must become sensitive to the feelings of flow and the feeling of stagnation in the energy system. It then becomes a matter of following and releasing the energy blockages through its interweaving pulses.

The Air element work has many levels to it. From implications on the organ level with relationships through the lungs and heart, the colon, kidney and skin, to formative relationships in the nervous system and heart chakra. Although the Air element governs the nervous system generally, we will explore the nervous system relationships in another section. Many of the cleansing organs of the body, such as the lungs, kidneys, colon and skin are governed by the Air element and thus the Air work has many implications in the cleansing of internal gases, and toxic wastes. The Air element patterns commonly become unbalanced with emotional upset and holdings in relationship to the Heart Centre.

I remember one beautiful session with a man who needed to present a 'macho' attitude to the world. He had come to me because of gas pains in his colon area and a general tendency to spastic colon. He also had a lot of tension in his chest, diaphragm and shoulder areas. In previous sessions we had worked with his colon and shoulders in what is known as 'gas releasing' techniques and worked to release his diaphragm. He had also been diligently working with some specific polarity exercises to open his shoulders, chest, spine and pelvis. In this session we were working with his colon reflexes and then began working around his heart area and Air oval area. Suddenly, it was as if his heart had sucked my fingers in. I was drawn to do deep work around the heart and direct energy through it. He then went into deep breathing and deep sighs started coming out. These were blocked by tensing his neck and throat muscles. I then linked his heart to the Ether field, one hand over his heart and gently stretched his neck. With one seemingly vast deep breath, waves of sadness and grief streamed out. Tears of relief and joy washed down his face. He ended by embracing me in a joyful and tearful hug. It was the first time, he said, that he could ever remember feeling his heart open with trust and joy. When he stood up his whole body shape had changed. His shoulders were much more open, his chest relaxed and his whole body seemed to sink to earth. It was a joyful experience for us both. The Air element is about open-hearted living, giving and receiving and moving through life; it can be a wonderful experience to feel its relationships open and flow.

Fire Element Relationships

Fire is the next step down in the dynamic movement of energy towards form. Fire, as we have seen, is the vital driving force within us. It is felt in the warmth of our hearts and bodies and in the heat of the healing process. It is the heat of digestion and the energies behind anger and forgiveness. It provides vital energy to all parts of the body via its spiral energy patterns. Dr Stone talks about the Fiery relationships in *Polarity Therapy*:

> The superior pole is manifested in the light of the eyes and descends over the region of the heart and chest as respiration and the fiery warmth in the blood, to supply every cell of the body. It crosses over in the abdomen in the region of the umbilicus, where it becomes the fire of digestion in the splanchnic area and in the solar plexus. It centres especially in the duodenum as an *emotional seat of the fire principle*; also in the gall bladder and duct as the organ of anger, jealousy, envy, hatred and bitterness. Its third function is action and motion which are expressed through the skill of the hands in the neuter pole and as running through the action of the thighs.

Fire imbalances can affect the digestive organs and cause imbalanced digestion of food, leading to fermentation and gaseous release. The organs themselves can become energetically blocked and this is quite common as many people in our culture have a hard time dealing with their anger. Another common problem affecting our Fire is that of over-stimulation and exhaustion. We live in a society where there is constant stimulation and input on many levels. Radios, TV's, computers, all spray information at us. Our jobs tend to be sedentary and stressful. We tend to exhaust our Fire just coping with it all. Most of us need to learn ways of relaxation to conserve Fire, proper diet to augment and fuel Fire and exercises which balance and stimulate the release of Fire. Most of all we need to look at our relationship to anger, how we deal with our anger and how we process resentment and anger energetically within our bodies. It basically means becoming more aware of our feelings, how they arise, and how we either suppress, repress or express them. Anger, like any other emotion, is energy. When we are in touch with its energetic impulse, it can then be worked with. But if we identify completely with it, become it, then there is no possibility for change.

The Fire patterns are shown in Figures 6.8, 6.9 and 6.10. Figure 6.8 shows the general Fire triad areas and contact points. Figure 6.9 shows the Fire Principle Current which stimulates and balances blocked Fire with its contact points. Figure 6.10 shows the Spiral Current which disperses Fire throughout the energy system with its contact points.

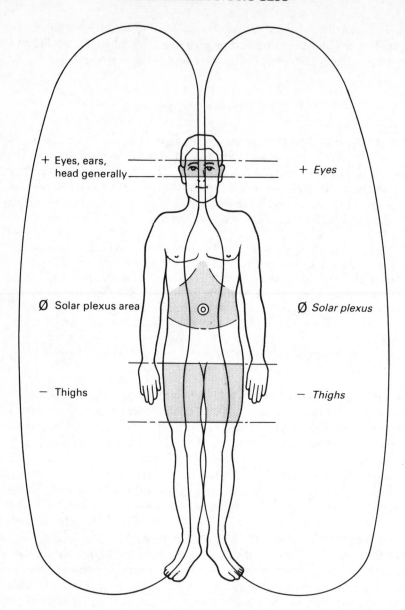

+ Eyes, ears,
head generally

+ *Eyes*

Ø Solar plexus area

Ø *Solar plexus*

− Thighs

− *Thighs*

Fig. 6.8. General Fire Triad relationships

To generally open up Fire relationships
*   one can work generally around the Fire oval in the head and with Fire
    reflexes at the occiput, eyes and ears.
*   one can work generally to release the solar plexus area and thighs.
*   one can reflex fire areas and organs to foot reflexes through the Polar-
    ity Zone Chart.

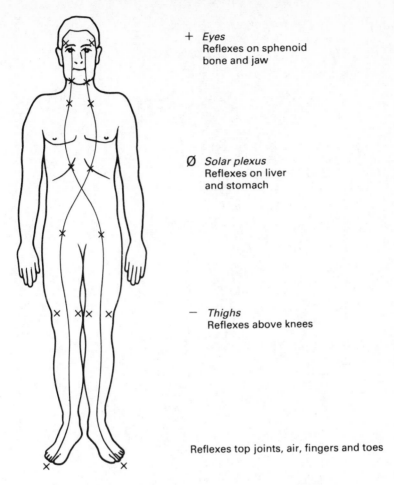

+ *Eyes*
   Reflexes on sphenoid
   bone and jaw

Ø *Solar plexus*
   Reflexes on liver
   and stomach

— *Thighs*
   Reflexes above knees

Reflexes top joints, air, fingers and toes

Fig. 6.9. Fire principle treatment relationships

To stimulate and balance Fire relationships in body
• one can work through the various reflexes to stimulate and balance Fire; major reflex areas are shown.

Due to their rajasic, stimulating nature, the Fire element patterns are some of the easiest to experience for both practitioner and client. When they flow in a harmonious, open way, it seems like boundless warmth and energy is available. When blocked or repressed, exhaustion and illness result. In a session a release of Fire may be felt by the client as heat, shooting warmth, tingling, shaking and a general feeling of 'glow'. Fire governs the digestive system and its free flow is necessary for full and healthy digestion to occur. Fire is the element of purification. It governs the liver, which is a key organ both in digestion and in detoxification. When Fire is flowing well the liver and gall bladder are able to fulfil their roles. The

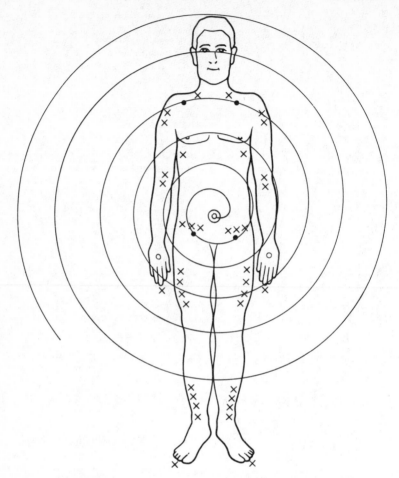

Fig. 6.10. Spiral current treatment relationships

Disperses Fire throughout the system
• one can work from the umbilicus outwards to disperse blocked Fire.

stomach, spleen, small intestine and pancreas (in its digestive functions) are also governed by the Fire element. Holding or repressing Fire via mental or emotional processes strongly affects the Fire-related organs.

I had been seeing a client for over a year. He had come to me for his low back pain and considered the pain and the sessions to be 'physical' work. We talked about the connection between mental/emotional processes and the body, but it was not a 'felt' reality for him. His back greatly improved and we agreed to bring the sessions to an end. Over a year later he returned to see me for sessions but this time his intent was very different. Changes were happening in his life. A move to the country, less stressful work and most of all, a deepening relationship with his wife allowed him 'space' to look more closely at his life. He was more aware of the feeling in his body and much more open to deeper work. One subsequent session dramatically demonstrated a deep Fiery release.

We started the session by talking about his boarding school days, which had been very unhappy years for him. I started working generally on the Fire triad areas. We worked to release the solar plexus area and the reflex points on the thighs. It was as if the solar plexus was tied into a knot and he found it very difficult to let me into this area. We spent a lot of time with touch and breath to encourage his letting go. I then came up to the Fire reflexes on the ears. These were exceedingly painful. Suddenly, his face turned red and a wave of screams, accompanied by pounding fists and kicking feet, spontaneously exploded. Welts of anger streamed through his body. This soon changed to the sadness and hurt underlying the anger. Sobs, accompanied by flowing tears, then racked his body. We spoke after about his early years, the isolation, the hurt and loneliness of being away from his home and his parents for so long. The feeling of powerlessness and deprivation had long coloured the rest of his life. He felt that ages of pain had been released. When Fire moves, much can happen. He felt strength, his power, perhaps for the first time in his life and this allowed him to feel his softness and be comfortable with his gentleness. He had found the power to be a gentle-man.

Water Element Relationships

In its movement into form, Water is a step-down from Fire. Water is a beautiful element. When it flows, we flow. It represents the ability to move fluidly through life without contention and with minimum resistance. It is an element of deep intuition and vast receptivity. It represents the well of our knowing and the huge range of our 'unconscious'. Memory and dreams are under its sway and it can give us a clear reflection of our life situation and deep intuition into skilful living. Dr Stone talks of the Water element and the importance of its neutral pole, the pelvis, in his book *Health Building*:

> The vital force of our being is located in the pelvic area, as the water principle. It has the eternal aspect of the seed power in itself, by which it can be used to create outside for *generation* or by drawing on that force for body rebuilding, it can be used for regeneration of cells and structures inside. As a motor force, it is asleep in the space of the sacrum and has been spoken of as the 'kundalini' force, coiled like a serpent. Latent within the physical aspect of it are many mysteries of man's being.

The nature of Water is transformation, cleansing and 'mystery'. The ancient Chinese sages said that the wise person acted like water in its various attributes and transformations. It is the energy of healing and regeneration, while Fire is that of purification. The Water patterns are key patterns for most of us and many Water-related issues, such as grounding, sexuality, memory, dreams, intuition, come up in Polarity sessions.

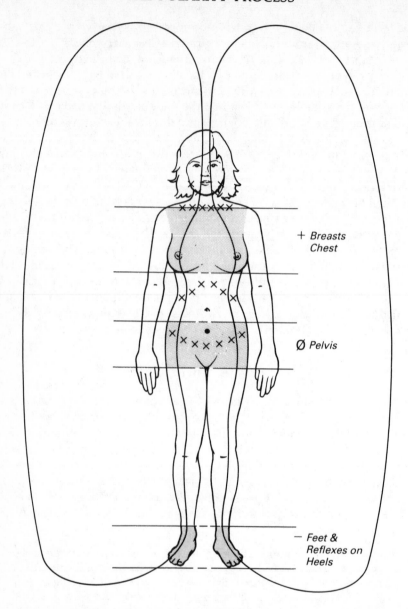

Fig. 6.11. Anterior Water treatment relationships-work to generally release blockage in Water Element relationships

- One can generally release the pelvis with various rocking and stretch–release techiques.
- One can release the inguinal ligament (Pouparts ligament) and the psoas muscle.
- One can work through blocks in Water poles via the Polarity Zone Chart.

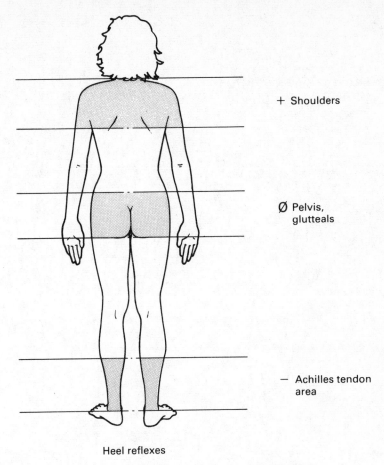

+ Shoulders

Ø Pelvis,
  glutteals

− Achilles tendon
  area

Heel reflexes

Fig. 6.12. Posterior Water treatment relationships

To release the patterns of blockage in the poles of the Water triad.
• One can do general release work on the shoulders and glutteals.
• Once can release with double (bipolar) contacts in proportion from one zone to another.

Figures 6.11 and 6.12 show general Water element relationships. They can be used by the therapist to start a release pattern through Water element related imbalances. A few years ago I had a client who came to see me with a general feeling of depression, or 'murkiness' as she put it. It was as though her world had become murky, confused and untrustworthy. She also complained of back pain in the sacroiliac area. Both her murkiness and her back pain seemed to have arisen simultaneously after an especially severe argument with her husband a few months earlier. She also seemed overly anxious and both moved and

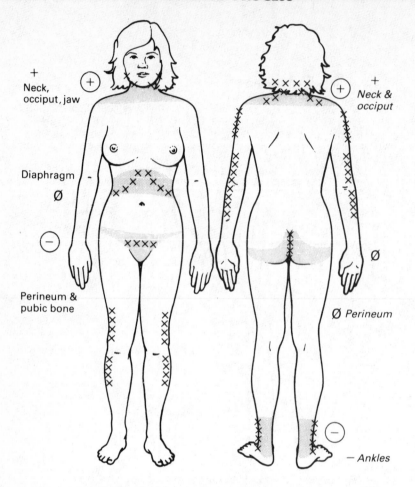

Fig. 6.13. Major perineal relationships

To release negative energy and emotional states locked into the perineal floor.

- one can work perineal points to related neck and ankle points (see Dr Stone's charts).
- one can work perineal points to related points on the pubic bone, diaphragm, jaw and occiput.
- one can work any related points to each other (i.e. pubic bone to diaphragm to jaw to occiput).

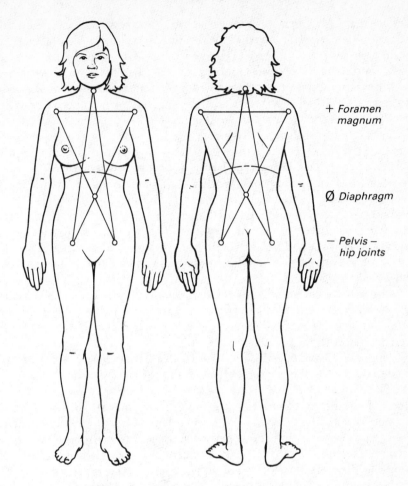

+ *Foramen*
   magnum

Ø *Diaphragm*

— *Pelvis* —
   hip joints

Fig. 6.14. Five-Pointed Star patterns

General Water element sensory and motor pattern connects Water strongly to Air at shoulders, Fire at umbilicus and Ether at the neck.

- One can release base of star at hips and pelvis with general hip work, inguinal ligament (Pouparts) release work, psoas release work and stretching.
- One can release diagonally across the Star by stretching shoulder to opposite hip.
- One can release the diaphragm and clavicle generally.
- One can work with double contacts at hips to shoulders and hips to top of star at neck/foramen magnum.

talked in an 'Airy' nervous fashion. After a few sessions we focused our attention on her pelvic area and the tensions and tightness held there. We started the session with some breath work. I asked her to breathe into her pelvis and to hold her attention there; to bring her attention, through the breath into the pelvic area. I then started working on some general release patterns for the pelvis, as well as the inguinal ligament and psoas muscle, both of which tend to get tense and contracted in pelvic imbalance. The psoas is a powerful muscle which runs from the lower six vertebrae through the pelvis to the femur. It tends to react strongly to emotions related to the Water element by becoming chronically tensed. We worked to release her pelvis and psoas and then did some bipolar (double contact) work from the pelvis to the shoulder area. Her breathing became deeper and deeper, and gentle sobs began to move through her body. Afterwards she felt a feeling of peace and stillness. We talked after the session to integrate what she had felt into her conscious life. It was as though a deep tension had been released and there was more 'space' inside than she had previously realised.

She felt she could work with her feelings towards her husband with more clarity and less 'charge'. Her back pain had completely gone. Later work revolved around grounding her energies through Water and Earth and dealing with the practical things of life.

Figures 6.13 and 6.14 deal with two other extremely important Water-related patterns – the perineal reflexes and the Five-Pointed Star pattern.

The perineum is the most negative pole of the trunk. It is literally the floor of the pelvic basin. The pull of gravity causes toxins and waste products which the body has not been able to eliminate to collect there. Even more importantly, the negative charges of unprocessed emotional tension also collect there, either in the form of tense spastic muscles or an opposite form, in flaccid tissues which cannot hold an energy charge. Perineal work is almost always critical in clearing old emotional holdings and in helping the energy system learn to process emotional charges in a more constructive way. The Five-Pointed Star pattern, although a separate energy pattern, is intimately tied into pelvic and perineal relationships.

The Star pattern rests, so to speak on the pelvic basin. If you can imagine that every point of the Star is a 'hinge' then you can see that if the pelvis is energetically or structurally imbalanced, then the energy pattern of the Star above will also distort. The Five-Pointed Star is intimately related to the Fire element as it crosses over at the umbilicus and to Air in its relationship to the shoulders and the heart. Any emotional charge related to any of these three elements (Air, Fire, Water) could result in a pattern of contraction in the Star pattern. It is quite common to see, where the pelvis is imbalanced and tense, that the diaphragm will be tense and contracted and the shoulders pulled forward and hunched forward to protect and close down the feelings in the heart (see Figure 6.15). It is a classic example of 'collapse' where a person has given up trying to feel love, due to too much past hurt and pain. It sometimes looks like the person is almost 'dragged down by it all'.

A few years ago, George came to me complaining of feeling generally listless, weak and tired. The afternoon was especially hard for him. He always felt exhausted after lunch and found it difficult to do his job in the accountancy firm where he worked. He obviously had low vitality and weak 'Fire'. In his body reading we saw a general collapsed look to his shoulders and a band of tension across the navel area. His gluteal area also seemed de-energised, appearing to hang loosely off his bones. There was no strength there and the tissues felt flaccid and the muscles lacked tone. Over a few sessions George had learned a number of polarity exercises to help balance his energies and release and increase his Fire. We had worked with his diet to eliminate foods which tended to drain his energies and to use food to balance his energies and build his Fire. We had had sessions where we talked about his life, past and present, and re-experienced aspects of his sadness and his past and present resentments. It became clear that George was carrying around a lot of old hurt focused around the woman in his life. This extended from his childhood in relationship to his mother and sisters through all stages of his life involvement with women. Intimacy on a deep level was difficult for him and sexual contact was about power and temporary release of resentment and hurt. His boss at work was a woman and his load of hurt and resentment coloured their working relationship.

We used body-work to start to release his emotional tension patterns, or crystallisations as Dr Stone would call these physical holdings. A lot of

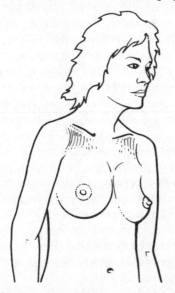

Fig. 6.15. Five-Pointed Star contraction: shoulders hunched forward chest hollow – a collapsed look to shoulders, chest

work focused around Fire and the Fire patterns to make more energy and vitality available to him. We used perineal work to help release some of the more deeply held emotional patterns. In one session we had cleared some congestion through the perineal reflexes and turned our attention to the Five-Pointed Star. I worked deeply at the base of the Star over the inguinal ligament and the soft tissue above. We then worked diagonally from shoulders to hip joints over the pubic area. These areas were very tender for George and we worked very slowly with contact, pressure and breath so that George could stay with his feelings and feel the release of energy through the pattern. I stayed on these points with pressure which just met his resistance, not going past what Goerge would accept, yet using a pressure which firmly met both his emotional and his tissue resistance. Slowly, George became able to 'let me in'.

We were both able to stay with the sensations of his body letting go of deeply held tensions. It was as if his deep connective tissues were 'unwinding' their contractions and tensions. George experienced deep warmth and a glowing sensation throughout his body. For the first time in a long while, George felt energised and expansive. The imbalanced Watery pattern had opened and released its locked energies. When George stood up, his shoulders were less collapsed and his heart area more open and relaxed. In subsequent sessions this was followed up and integrated into his life by making constructive use of his newly felt energies in both his home and work environment.

Working with the Water element, like any element, has many levels and the quality of the work depends on the consciousness of the prac- titioner and client, the relationship of the two and the contract between them. The Water element energy patterns are critical in the functioning of the lymphatics and glands, the sexual organs, the bladder, the breasts and in woman's monthly cycles. The Water element governs the balance of the endocrine system at the subtle level. Its balance is thus very critical in the key hormonal relationships in the body. Water-related work, es- pecially perineal work, is very useful during pregnancy and coupled with proper exercise, such as squatting, can be extremely beneficial in the birthing process. Releasing blocked Water patterns can have rever- berations throughout the mental–emotional system. Old patterns of emotional tension and crystallisation can be released, freeing our more nurturing, intuitive energies. When our Water energies are flowing freely we have the opportunity to be grounded and to flow through life's ups and downs.

Earth Element Relationships

The final step-down phase of energy is the Earth element. Earth, as we have seen, is the final step-down of energy into matter. It is the realm of energy where things become formed and energies become crystallised. It is the field of surface tension where energies slow down and the physical realm results. Earth energy is about 'being here'. It is about being in the senses and doing the necessary practical things of life. On a deeper level, it is about meeting the resistance of the physical world and learning the critically important lessons inherent in our life process. Figure 6.16 illustrates the Earth treatment reflexes.

The Earth element triad is the neck, the colon and the knees. If we remember that Earth governs the relationship between fear and courage then we can see some interesting interrelationships here. I have seen a very common triad physical imbalance time and time again; a tense and stiff neck, spastic and constipated colon and tense, weak or painful knees. In our culture we are constantly being judged. It starts with our parents at a very early age and continues powerfully in school with competitive exams and great pressure to 'succeed'. Education loses its qualities of inquisitiveness and wonder, to memory and exams. We are constantly judged at work, by friends, by family, husbands, wives and worst of all, by ourselves. Inherent in this life pressure with all of its survival needs – money, shelter, food, clothes, etc., which are Earth-related needs – is a movement of fear. Not a reasonable animal fear of an immediate danger, but an ongoing undercurrent of psychological fear, anxiety and neurosis. Underlying this movement is an even deeper layer of fear. It is the fear of loss, of losing all that we have created as security to buffer us from the movement of impermanence and the certainty of death. Many of us get so locked into this undercurrent that the fear matrix becomes very physical. We 'space out', become anxious or cut off from our feelings and senses and our Earth triad relationships become congested. Neck and colon problems are the most common manifestation of this.

I had been working with a client for some time. She had originally come to see me feeling depressed and imbalanced. She had bouts of lower abdominal pain, tension in the shoulder and neck areas and a heart murmur. One interesting pattern that came up one session was that she hated to have her knees touched. When we talked about this she was surprised that not everyone shared this feeling. We spent the whole session with one of my hands gently on her knee and the other on either the colon area or under the neck. Her tendency was to 'go away' from what she was feeling and to cut off from the feelings which were coming up. I had her concentrate on her breath and to try and follow her breath right down into her knees. I then asked her to try and keep her awareness in her knees. When she could do this, she experienced two things; the first was an amazing feeling of energy flow, especially between her neck and knees; the second was a wave of fear and shaking throughout her body. Every time her awareness left her knees, her energy stopped flowing. I gently encouraged her to come back to feeling her knees and staying with my touch. We spent a whole hour like this, gently experiencing and working with the fear which had become locked into this pattern. Childhood memories flooded through and many issues arose which had to be dealt

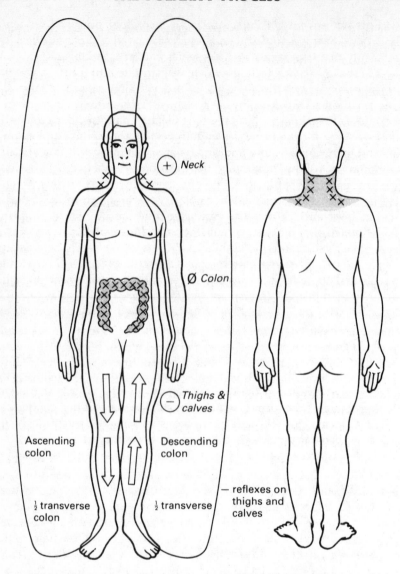

Fig. 6.16. Earth pattern treatment relationships

To open and release blockages in the Earth pattern of energy flow
- one could use techniques to generally release the neck and colon areas,
- one could reflex areas in the neck, colon and thighs/calves in proportion to release energy blocks,
- one could work the Earth current line via the Polarity Zone Chart.

with in subsequent sessions. It was an incredibly powerful session for both of us. Fear is a powerful undercurrent in us all and must be dealt with by gently making friends with ourselves and maintaining a keen awareness of the underlying feelings which we translate into fear.

In talking about the Elements, in order to illustrate the relationships and possibilities inherent in each element I have used some dramatic examples of working with some single Element patterns. But I must stress that releasing blocked energies and processing the feelings and emotions around them can be quite undramatic and very peaceful. It is also more common to follow intuitively the relationships between the various Element patterns than to lock into one single element. Our energy system is a dynamic whole and the art of polarity therapy is to follow a person's unique imbalance through its various manifestations. Thus, to release a Five-Pointed Star imbalance which is a Water-related pattern, I might also have to stimulate the umbilicus and use some Fire pattern relationships, as Fire and Water patterns cross at the umbilicus. All the elements have overlaid reflexes with each other and the excitement of being a polarity therapist is in seeing and feeling all these patterns as *one*. Then the client and his or her energies are also one and the possibility for a healing relationship is truly there.

The next step-down phase of energy that Dr Stone worked with is that of the nervous system. Dr Stone was both an osteopath and a chiropractor and deeply understood these relationships. The nervous system is, in a sense, a huge transformer which transforms our subtler energies into physical form. It is through the nervous system that our thoughts and emotions become physical occurrences and our anatomy and physiology is enlivened and controlled. We will explore these relationships in our next chapter.

CHAPTER SEVEN

Energy and Form

The life-breath or *prana* current moves in the cerebrospinal fluid con-
ductor to all tissue cells and communicates with other internal secretions
and body fluids, like a living cosmic breath.

In this chapter I would like to explore the relationship between energy
and form. Dr Stone worked with three basic layers of the energy process:
the Five Element patterns; the nervous system; and the physical body
structure. He perceived these layers as a functioning whole. Imbalances
in any layer are reflected in the others. We have spent a lot of time on
Five Element energy relationships. Let us now explore the layers where
energy takes shape via the nervous system and body structure. I would
first like to investigate a subtle life rhythm called the cranial rhythm. Dr
Stone believed that this rhythm is the means by which subtle energy is
conveyed into physical form.

The Three Life Breaths

There are three physical life pulsations, or life breaths (see Figure 7.1).
These are the cranial rhythm, the respiratory rhythm and the cardiac
rhythm. I am sure all of you are very familiar with your respiratory and
cardiac rhythms. But many of you may not be aware of the cranial
rhythm, so let me explain its importance. The cranial rhythm is a
wave-like pulsation which arises in the brain. It is an expansion and
relaxation of the brain and its ventricles. It pulsates in a frequency which
can be anywhere from 6–12 cycles per minute and averages 8 cycles per
minute. It is a very stable rhythm. A person's cranial rhythm changes
only over a period of time. If a person's rhythm is cycling at 8 per minute,
then it will be stable at that rate no matter what their present activity. It is

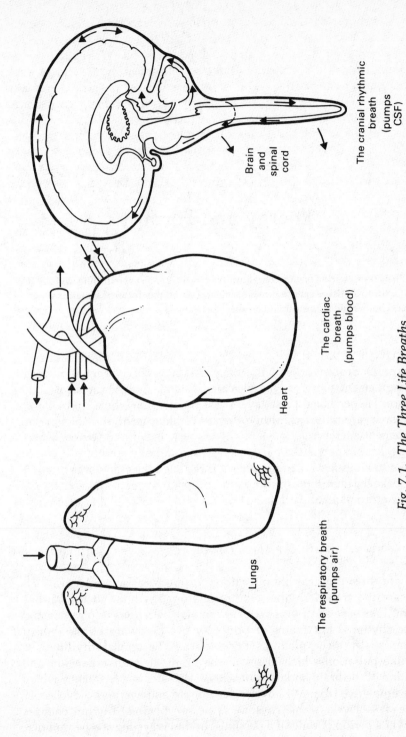

The cranial rhythmic
breath
(pumps CSF)

Brain
and
spinal
cord

The cardiac
breath
(pumps blood)

Heart

The respiratory breath
(pumps air)

Lungs

Fig. 7.1. The Three Life Breaths

not like the respiratory or cardiac rhythms, which will speed up during exercise or in strong emotional situations. For that reason it is considered a very primary pattern. It was first discovered and talked about by an osteopath named Dr William Sutherland. He developed a form of work called cranial osteopathy. It works to release any physical, especially bony sutural, restrictions to the cranial rhythm. A newer approach, called craniosacral therapy, developed and taught by another osteopath, Dr John Upledger, works with the manifestation of the cranial rhythm in the body as a whole and focuses more on the release of membraneous and fascial restrictions. It acknowledges the importance of emotional patterns in these restrictions. Dr Stone also knew about and worked with the cranial rhythm.

Dr Stone perceived the cranial rhythmic impulse to be a very important piece in the energy jigsaw puzzle. Each life breath pumps a fluid through the body. The respiratory rhythm via the lungs pumps air and facilitates the exchange between oxygen and carbon dioxide. The cardiac rhythm, via the heart, pumps blood and facilitates oxygen and gaseous exchange at a cellular level. It also facilitates the exchange of nutrients and cellular waste products. The cranial rhythm pumps cerebrospinal fluid. Dr Stone believed that this fluid was involved in energy exchange and conveyed subtle etheric energy to all the tissues and cells of the body. In *Polarity Therapy* he writes:

> The cerebrospinal fluid seems to act as a storage field and a conveyor for the ultrasonic and the light energies. It bathes the spinal cord and is a reservoir for these finer energies, conducted by this fluidic media through all the fine nerve fibres as the first airy mind and life principle in the human body. Through this neuter essence mind functions in and through matter as the light of intelligence.

Cerebrospinal fluid is produced in the ventricles of the brain and is pumped throughout the body via the cranial rhythmic impulse. It bathes the brain and spinal cord and also flows in the middle of the spinal cord where the sushumna traditionally resides. Dr Stone believed that the cerebrospinal fluid (CSF) conveyed the 'ultrasonic and the light energies' throughout the body. The two aspects or poles of etheric energy are represented by sound vibration and light energy. Sound or vibration is the formative aspect of etheric energy and light is the positive, manifest pole of it. So etheric energy is expressed as vibration and light and is conveyed throughout the body via cerebrospinal fluid. Modern research concurs with Dr Stone in his belief that the CSF is pumped throughout the body via the nerve roots of the spine. He also believed that the etheric energies, which are conducted by the CSF, conveyed the 'first airy mind and life principle' throughout the body. Via the 'neuter essence' of CSF, the mind functions in the body as 'the light of intelligence'.

This is mind-blowing stuff! What Dr Stone is claiming is truly extraordinary. He is saying that the cerebrospinal fluid conveys the energies of the mind throughout the body! Mind energy is considered to be the first principle of life. The mind, or causal realm, contains the pattern energies of life within it. It 'steps down' into physical form and brings the blue-prints of that form with it. He is saying that this primary pattern energy is conveyed throughout the body via cerebrospinal fluid. He goes on to say that, through the CSF, mind functions in the body as 'the light of intel-ligence'. Thus the essences of awareness and intelligence are conveyed into form by this process! The corollary to this is that where this flow is impeded, then intelligence breaks down and darkness and disorder pre-vail. If the flow of CSF is impeded, the flow of etheric energy is impeded and the tendency to disorder and ill-health arise. On 'Health Building' Dr Stone writes,

> The cerebrospinal fluid is the liquid medium for this life energy radiation, expansion and contraction. Where this is present, there is life and healing with normal function. Where this primary and essential life force is not acting in the body, there is obstruction, spasm, or stagnation and pain, like gears which clash instead of meshing in their operation.'

The expansion and contraction of the cranial rhythm, which arises in the brain, is a harmonic of the expansion and contraction of the energy system as a whole. Where this movement is impeded and the flow of CSF is also impeded then stagnation and ill-health will occur. Dr Andrew Taylor Still, founder of Osteopathy, called the cerebrospinal fluid the 'highest element' in the human body. Dr William Sutterland, the founder of Cranial Osteopathy, believed that CSF contained innate healing energies which are essential for the health of the body. Dr Stone was not alone in his perception of the importance of cranial mechanism, but, I believe, he saw its deepest implications.

The role of connective tissue is very important in relationship to the cranial rhythm and the flow of CSF. In Chapter 3 we saw how the energies of the oval fields took physical expression as connective tissue or fascial fields. We also saw how the transitions between the fields took physical expression as places of transition in these fascial fields. The important places of transitions are the perineal floor, the top of the sacrum and pelvis, the diaphragm, the thoracic inlet and the base of the skull. These are well known to be essential focus points by polarity therapists, craniosacral therapists, osteopaths and chiropractors. The important thing to note here is that restrictions in these areas impede the strength of the cranial rhythm and impede the flow of CSF throughout the body. In Chapter 4, we saw how the patterns of the Elements flow through these fields. Restrictions in these primary patterns cause restrictions in the five oval fields of the body and their physical counter-parts. This then also becomes restriction in the flow of CSF.

We, perhaps, now can see how these systems begin to overlap. Some-one has a great emotional shock. The first energetic response might be a contraction of the Air oval around the heart. This may take physical expression as a tight diaphragm and collapsed, tense shoulders. The physical transitions at the thoracic inlet and diaphragm become contracted and tensed. Airy patterns arising from the heart chakra may become impeded. This may manifest as heart, colon or kidney imbalances. Fire energies may become involved as Fire, in the form of anger and resentment, is 'drawn up' to maintain the contraction around the heart. The physical pumping of the CSF becomes impeded as the contraction becomes chronic. The Etheric energy conveyed by the CSF cannot flow freely and the ordering energy of the mind becomes less available. The healing energies carried by the CSF also become less available and the whole system moves closer to a final breakdown. This also usually takes on a physical structural form as the chronic imbalances manifest through body structure. The body literally takes the shape of the mental, emotional and physical contractions which act through it. Here the Airy block at the Heart Centre may manifest as restricted and tensed thoracic vertebrae, lumbar imbalances behind the Fire chakra and sacral and pelvic distortions as structure compensates to this process 'from the bottom up'. The genius of Dr Stone was that he saw the whole play of this movement and could follow the unique pattern of it in his healing work.

The Nervous System

From here I would like to discuss the nervous system in general and describe some ways in which Dr Stone developed the work with imbalances in this layer of energy movement. There are three aspects to the nervous system. They are the central, or cerebrospinal nervous system, the sympathetic nervous system and the parasympathetic nervous system. These three aspects of the nervous system are the three poles of energy expression in the human body. The positive, rajasic pole of the Fire principle radiates from the umbilicus and is stepped down into the body via the sympathetic nervous system. Thus the spiral current of the Fire element and the sympathetic nervous system are intimately related. The sympathetic system is the system which stimulates the body and prepares it for action. It is the 'flight or fright' system. It brings blood to the periphery for muscular action. It causes vasoconstriction of blood vessels in the core of the body and its digestive organs and vasodilation in the periphery which brings blood to the muscles for activity. It is the system of action and doing. It speeds up metabolism, heart and respiratory rates. It literally gets the body prepared for flight, fight and muscular action. The parasympathetic nervous system balances this. It is intimately related to the Airy East–West currents. These currents tie the periphery to the central core and manifest as a neutral pattern of balance and interrelationship. It is expressed via the parasympathetic nervous system. This system balances the action of the sympathetic system. It brings blood to the core and away from the periphery. It encourages digestion and brings blood to these inner organs. It slows down the respiratory and cardiac rhythms and is in ascendance in meditative states. The central nervous system is the body's master computer and system of voluntary action. It is the system that the conscious mind functions through and this function is to bring patterns of thought and emotion into form and action. It is thus considered the negative or tamasic pole of the nervous system. It brings the mental realm into voluntary processes in the world. We think and then we do. The doing is the completion or Watery phase of the movement and governed by the central nervous system. It is intimately related to the Long Line currents which are an expression of the mind as it comes into form via the chakras. The cranial rhythm and the movement of cerebrospinal fluid is also intimately related to the movement and balance of the Long Line currents. These currents can be traced and freed via the polarity zone chart and the flow of cerebrospinal fluid is thus encouraged.

All three aspects of the nervous system generally relate to a subtle pattern of energy called the 'inverted triangles'. In Chinese terminology these triangles govern the yang and yin or positive and negative relationships in the body as a whole. These relationships, in polarity terms, manifest via the three poles of the nervous system. The upper yang triangle has its base in the cranium and medulla oblongata of the brain. It governs yang or positive energy relationships and relates to our qualities of consciousness and awareness. The lower yin triangle has its base in the pelvis and sacrum. It governs yin or negative energy relationships and relates to our reserve of vitality and seed potential, it is the receptive pole of the energy system. The interrelationship between the two (see Figure 7.2) governs the balance and flow of energies in the nervous system as their energies move through their positive and negative relationships. The inverted triangle has one pole which focuses in the brain and nervous system and the other pole in the pelvis and its Watery systems. Due to this relationship, it governs the balance between the nervous system and the endocrine glands. It gives physical expression to the relationship between the Air and Water elements and ties the two systems into an interrelated neuro-endocrine system. This in turn governs the balance of neuro-endocrine hormonal secretions. The neutral pole of this relationship is found in the spine and the sushumna and at the diaphragm which divides the upper 'yang' aspects of the triangle from the lower 'yin' aspects. The diaphragm becomes a vital pivotal point which must be functioning freely for a balance of energies to occur. Thus imbalances between the energies of these triangles are expressed as spinal restrictions, imbalances in the nervous and endocrine systems and rigidity in the diaphragm. On a psychological and emotional level our rational mind must be balanced by our receptive, intuitive 'unconscious' life process.

Dr Stone developed ways of working with all three aspects of the nervous system. The foundation of this is an understanding of its intimate relationships to the oval fields, Long Line currents, spiral current and East–West currents of the subtle energy system. Imbalances will arise first

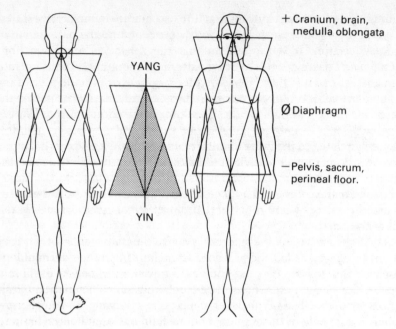

Fig. 7.2. The 'Interlaced Triangles'

here and must be traced and released in relationship to the work on the nervous system. The oval fields around the chakra centres and the physical transitions between them must be freed energetically and physically to encourage movement and balance of life energy. In releasing restrictions that relate to these fields, we are encouraging the flow of the Five Elements in their energy relationships and the movement of cerebrospinal fluid.

Dr Stone said that mind energy (i.e. formative or primary energies in the mental sphere) flows first energetically via the Long Line currents as they arise from the chakras and then are physically conveyed via the cranial rhythm as it pumps cerebrospinal fluid throughout the body. Thus mind energy steps down into the body via the central nervous system and the pumping action of the cranial system. Restrictions to the flow of the Long Line currents can be traced and released via the Polarity Zone Chart. This in turn encourages the flow of cerebrospinal fluid and can be further traced via polarity cranial relationships and technique and craniosacral therapy.

The Fiery spiral current and the sympathetic nervous system are intimately related in their functioning. The spiral current disperses vital energy throughout the system and makes this energy available for action. If we are over-active, or if our senses become overstimulated, this current can become unbalanced and depleted. Restrictions to the spiral current can be traced, released and balanced via its umbilical relationships and this can be further traced and released through the energy relationships of the sympathetic nervous system. This system can become overactive in the everyday stress of work and the sensory stimulation of modern life. We then need to balance this by cultivating a quieter mind, relaxation and exercise.

The Airy East–West currents are intimately related to the parasympathetic nervous system. The East–West currents integrate and harmonise the subtle energy system. They connect the top to the bottom and the periphery to the core. They are about an Airy movement towards balance. Likewise, the parasympathetic system is about a movement from the periphery to the core and an integration and harmonisation of body functions. It is the system most prominent in meditative states where there is a movement towards tranquillity and balance. It encourages the natural healing potential of the body and mental states related to it seem to strengthen the immune system. Restrictions to the East–West currents can be traced to restrictions in the Airy relationships to the chest, shoulders and diaphragm and to Airy gaseous blocks seen especially in the colon and shoulders. When these are released imbalances can be further traced through the spine and its parasympathetic relationships. We thus see almost the whole of polarity therapy bound up in the intimate relationship between subtle energy patterns and the nervous system. Let us explore Dr Stone's work with the energy relationships of the nervous system as seen in its triad relationship of Central, Parasympathetic and Sympathetic poles.

Figures 7.3 and 7.4 show the major parasympathetic and sympathetic reflex relationships. In both cases, we are working with the balance of the positive pole at the cranium, neck and shoulders to the negative pole at the pelvis below. Sympathetic relationships have their most negative pole at the ganglion of impar, located behind the coccyx. This is the last ganglion of the sympathetic nervous system as its energies move down the spine. The sympathetic ganglion lie on either side of the spine at each vertebral level and Dr Stone believed they were a physical harmonic of the caduceus currents as their energies criss-cross either side of the spine. The energy in this system is balanced by releasing the negative pole at the coccyx in relationship to the reflexes above. Critical relationships are found along the spine in the spinal grooves, at the foramen magnum and at the sphenoid bone above. The parasympathetic relationships have their most negative pole in the perineum. This is the end point of the parasympathetic nerves as they flow into the pelvis and the perineum becomes their negative pole. The energy in this system is balanced by releasing the negative pole at the perineum to the relationships above. Critical relationships are found along the spine at the erector spinae muscle mass, perineal neck relationships and the perineal ankle reflexes which help 'ground' the Watery energies to Earth. Working both the sympathetic and parasympathetic systems helps to bring their relationship to balance and to balance the relationship of positive yang and negative yin energies as they are expressed via these two poles of the nervous system.

The Watery pole of the nervous system, the central or cerebrospinal nervous system, is opened and balanced via the relationships of the cranial rhythm and the craniosacral system. The craniosacral system is composed of the physical relationships in the body that provide a mechanism for the pumping of CSF. In traditional cranial osteopathy there are five aspects to this system:

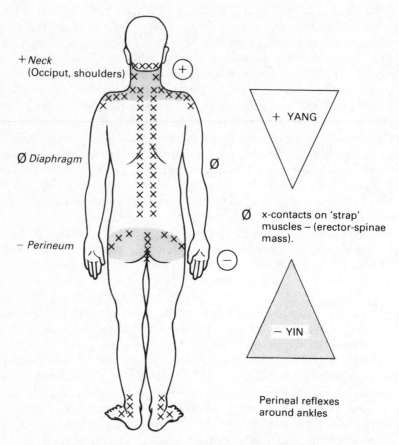

Fig. 7.3. Parasympathetic contact areas

To release blockages and balance the parasympathetic nervous system
• One can reflex the perineal points at the negative pole to:
  – neutral pole points of the sacrum, the upper gluteal area, tender points on the 'strap' muscles (erector spinae mass)
  – positive pole points on shoulders, neck and occiput
  – perineal reflex points on ankles.

1. *the motility of the brain* – the inherent expansion and contraction of the brain which sets up the cranial rhythm;
2. *the mobility of the cranial sutures* – the freedom of the cranial bones to move in relationship to each other and hence not restrict the motility of the brain;
3. *the reciprocal tension membranes* – the deep dural membranes (the falx cerebri and cerebelli and the tentorium cerebelli) which stretch and relax in relationship to the cranial rhythm and transfer the rhythm to the bones and tissues of the body;

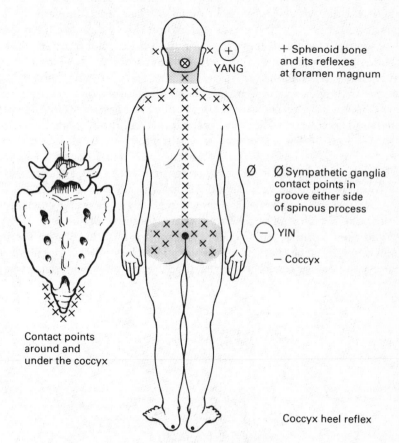

+ Sphenoid bone and its reflexes at foramen magnum

YANG

Ø Sympathetic ganglia contact points in groove either side of spinous process

YIN

– Coccyx

Contact points around and under the coccyx

Coccyx heel reflex

Fig. 7.4. Sympathetic contact areas

To release blockages and balance the sympathetic nervous system
• one can reflex the negative pole at the coccyx to:
  – congested points on the gluteals
  – tense and/or tender points in the groove next to the spinous processes (over the transverse processes) and at the shoulders
  – positive pole at sphenoid and foramen magnum
  – heel reflex to coccyx

4. *the fluctuation of cerebrospinal fluid,* this tide-like fluctuation is driven by the energetic pulse of the cranial system, its 'inherent healing potency'

5. *the sacrum,* which is attached to the dural tube and which transfers the cranial movement to the pelvis and legs below.

These relationships are gone into in great depth by cranial osteopathy. In its original form much focus was placed on the relationships of the cranial bones. In craniosacral therapy, a newer approach, attention is more focused on the membrane and connective tissues which relate to the system and the whole-body implications of the cranial movement are understood deeply. Dr Stone also understood this and, as we have seen above, appreciated the deepest implications of the cranial rhythm and the movement of cerebrospinal fluid. He developed numerous cranial holds (see Figure. 7.5) which work to release the energy blocks held in the cranium as the positive pole of the body. They also work to encourage general 'unwinding' or release of cranial bones and tissues when used and understood properly. They are very powerful and many polarity responses occur in the rest of the body when they are used. When combined with polarity work as outlined above, they encourage the flow of cerebrospinal fluid and the etheric energies that it conveys. He also wrote about numerous cranial–pelvic relationships which, when used therapeutically, balance the energies of the central nervous system and encourage the flow of CSF. The major relationships are shown in Figure 7.6.

I had been working with a client for about six months. She had come to me complaining of 'fits' of depression and a lack of order in her life. We were at a point in the sessions where she had created physical order around

Fig. 7.5. A Cranial hold

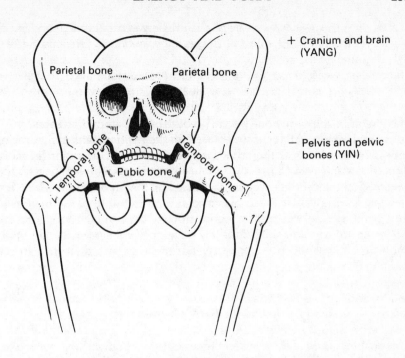

+ Cranium and brain
  (YANG)

– Pelvis and pelvic
  bones (YIN)

Parietal bone   Parietal bone

Temporal bone   Temporal bone

Pubic bone

The skull showing its relationships in the pelvis

Fig. 7.6. Central nervous system relationships

Polarity Balance

Cranial bones		Pelvic Relationships
$\oplus$		$\ominus$
occiput	–	sacrum
sphenoid bone	–	coccyx
parietal bone	–	iliac crest
temporal bone	–	acetabulum (hip joint)
temporal–mandibular joint (jaw joint)	–	hip joint
frontal bone	–	pubic bone
maxilla	–	inguinal ligament
	General Balance	
nasal bone	–	foramen magnum

- contacts are made at each relationship to bring the Central Nervous System to a balance.

her. Her shelves and cupboards were organised, her old unused clothes disposed of, drawers cleaned out and the house kept tidy. As the outer disorder in her home had been an expression of her inner disorder, the very fact that outer order became possible was very crucial for her. We had worked a lot on her Fire and Water patterns and I now turned to the central nervous system as the vital link between her inner and outer worlds. While holding her head in a specific cranial hold (see Figure 7.6), I felt an imbalanced movement or rhythm which 'pulled' parts of her cranium to the right. It was a sensation of expansion and contraction which felt 'lop-sided' on the right side of her head. We followed this movement very gently into its imbalance and held it there. Her cranium began subtly to pulsate and seemed to 'pull' and expand back to a more balanced rhythm. Along with this new movement came deep, cleansing sobs. A deep well of feelings had been unearthed as the energies locked into this subtle imbalance opened. Memories of a miscarriage over-whelmed her and the deep grief that she had not allowed herself to feel was finally able to be voiced. She cried for the rest of the session and was then truly able to let go of her unborn child and to wish it well on its further journeys. Balancing work via the nervous system can be quite important as it is the intermediary between subtle Five Element patterns and physical form.

The Physical Body Structure

This chapter is about how energy comes into form. So far we have looked at the vital relationship of subtle energy patterns to the nervous system. We now must turn our attention to the structural patterns of the body and see how energy relates to its final physical expression. Energies, in their final step-down, manifest as physical form and it is in body structure and form where the final manifestation of energy is expressed. Dr Stone, through his osteopathic and chiropractic background and years of experi-ence, deeply understood the physical and structural relationships of the body. He wrote in *Wireless Anatomy* that body structure 'as a final balancing factor' must never be overlooked. Dr Stone believed that imbalanced body structure, such as spinal rotations, subluxations and 'lesions' had deeper roots in the body's energy system. He had found over the course of his early career that spinal adjustments did not 'hold' over a period of time and that in many instances only temporary relief was given. He later realised that this was because the deeper root of the problem, the energy blockage itself, had not been properly dealt with. He discovered that both energy release and structural release were necessary to unlock a chronically painful situation.

In his work, Dr Stone thought of our body structure (bones, liga-ments, tendons, muscles and connective tissues) as a system that reacted reflexively to imbalances in the subtle energy patterns which underlie it. He expressed it thus: 'Energy impulses are from above downward. Struc-tural reflexes are from below upward.' The structural system is governed by the 'wireless anatomy' system which underlie it. Subtle energy is pri-mary. It arises from the Brow Centre and impulses 'from the above down-ward' throughout the energetic and physical system. Structure, however, in its response to subtle energy imbalances and to gravity forces, must reflex or respond from 'below upward'. Gravity energies must be responded to from the earth upwards. We stand on the foundation of the earth and our structure is an expression of this foundation in response to gravity. Dr Stone in his structural work, focused on the foundation of the sacrum and pelvis. Balance is critical here in relationship to how we meet the earth and how the spine above responds: structure above is dependent on the foundation and balance of the structure below.

The focal point of the balancing work in polarity therapy is the sacrum, the wedge-shaped 'upside-down' pyramid at the base of the spine (see Figure 7.7). It was called the 'mysterious sacrum' by Dr Stone due to

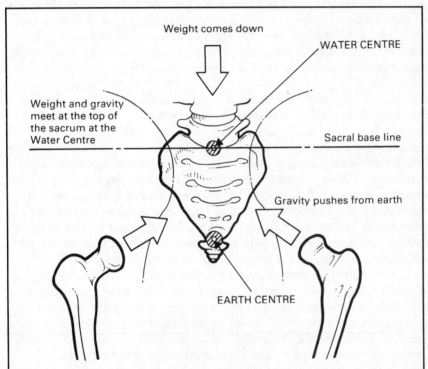

Fig. 7.7. The sacral keystone

The sacrum is the negative pole of both the subtle energy system as a whole and the nervous system as its physical expression. Much energy can become sluggish and crystallised here. The sacrum is 'sandwiched' between the Water and Earth chakras whose energies move towards greatest condensation. It is also the focal point of balance for physical weight from above and gravity counterweight from the earth below. Physical and structural energies have their vital pivot point of balance at the base of the sacrum, at the Water chakra. It is a place of great compression. Strain and back pain, sacroiliac imbalance and disc problems are common here.

the complex energy patterns and the structural variations found within it. Sacrum literally means 'sacred bone'. It is traditionally the place of stored 'kundalini' energy. The serpent energy ready to uncoil and release in the enlightenment experience. The sacrum is the negative pole of the subtle energy system. The Water and Earth chakras are located above and below it and the sushumna has its end point in it. It is also the negative pole of the nervous system and the structural system of the spine. It thus becomes a critical focus for all three energy layers Dr Stone worked with – subtle energy patterns, nervous system patterns and physical structure. Energy imbalance tends to become most chronically seen at the negative pole of the relationship when energies become most condensed. It is thus a critical place of potential crystallisation and imbalance. Dr Stone developed techniques which gently open both the energies and the structural relationships of the sacrum and pelvis. Once the foundation of body structure is balanced and stabilised, the spine above can be mobilised and a new balance in relationship to the sacrum and pelvis below can be established.

In order to encourage mobility, energy flow and balance above the sacrum, Dr Stone also developed various processes which focus on the vertebrae themselves. These include local vertebral releases, vertebral oscillation techniques and stretch release techniques. He used these in relationship to a deep understanding of spinal relationships called 'spinal harmonics'. These are presented in Book V of Dr Stone's collected works, 'Vitality Balancing', in a remarkable section called 'Chart 2, Structural Balance'. As in all other life functions, the spine must function as a triad relationship. Energy, as it flows through the spine, must move through its positive, neutral and negative pole relationships. He traced these relationships and called them 'spinal harmonics' and they are shown in Figure 7.8.

Dr Stone would apply release procedures to the vertebrae in relationship to the spinal harmonics of these triads. He noticed, not just lasting structural results when applying these triad relationships to the spine, but extraordinary functional responses in the related organs. A whole system of spinal harmonics and related organ energetics can easily be traced and used with powerful response. Some triads that he mentions are C6, T8 and T12 as a liver relationship; C7, T9, T11 for a stimulation of circulation and cellular oxygenation and waste exchange; and T1, T2, T10 for the heart and circulation and for the diaphragm and adrenal glands: any disease process will have corresponding vertebral relationships. Dr Stone writes that these can all be traced. He instructs the therapist: 'Find the active sore area or vertebrae and balance them with double contacts, according to the areas shown in the chart.' He presents in Book V, Chart Two, a wonderful and precise method of working with spinal imbalance. Once the sacrum is balanced, then the work above can proceed with amazing results. My experience over the years confirms the powerful results that his spinal balancing procedures can have, both structurally and functionally in the vertebrae and their related organs.

SPINAL HARMONICS

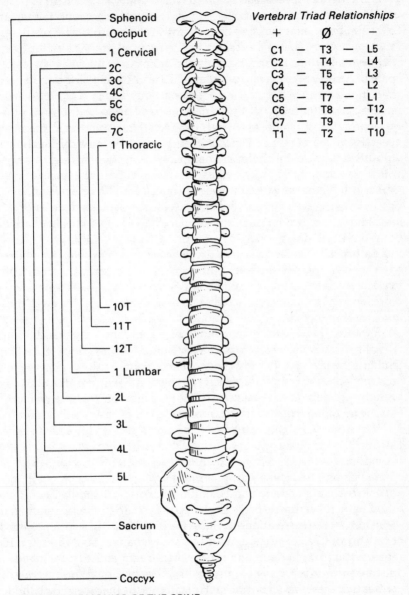

Sphenoid
Occiput
1 Cervical
2C
3C
4C
5C
6C
7C
1 Thoracic

10 T
11 T
12 T
1 Lumbar
2L
3L
4L
5L
Sacrum
Coccyx

Vertebral Triad Relationships

+	Ø	−
C1 —	T3 —	L5
C2 —	T4 —	L4
C3 —	T5 —	L3
C4 —	T6 —	L2
C5 —	T7 —	L1
C6 —	T8 —	T12
C7 —	T9 —	T11
T1 —	T2 —	T10

ENERGY HARMONICS OF THE SPINE

Energy and structural imbalances can be released via contacts at the poles of the above triads. A common imbalance can be seen at C3-T5-L3, the Ether, Air and Fire Centres.

Fig. 7.8. Spinal harmonics

We must not forget that the structural system and its harmonics are governed by the subtle energy system which underlies it. Energies become unbalanced at a subtler phase first and can appear as structural imbalance later. Tensions and blockages in the Heart Centre can, for instance, result in thoracic imbalance. Blockages in the solar plexus and navel centres may result in lumbar imbalance and blockages in the Water and Earth centres can express themselves as lumbar, sacral and pelvic imbalances.

A number of years ago a man came hobbling into my office complaining of acute low back pain. He had sciatic nerve pressure pain down his left side and a dull ache over the sacroiliac area. His life seemed generally tedious to him. He had a boring job and felt that his relationship with his wife was unfulfilling. I prescribed a series of polarity exercises which would help to balance his pelvic area physically, stretch tight muscles and increase energy flow generally. This at least gave him a way of working on his pain and some 'power' in a depressed situation. The sessions were a combination of counselling work, exercises and polarity body-work. At first the pain became more acute and his life seemed even more stressful. As energy started moving through his blocked and unbalanced pelvis, the pain became more acute and the stressful relationships in his life became more prominent and harder to avoid. When you place more energy into a chronically blocked situation, things get stirred up.

As we worked with his energy system it became obvious that much energy had become locked into an imbalanced sacrum which had its main lesion in the left sacroiliac joint. Through a combination of energy work and very specific yet gentle structural work, balance was restored to his sacrum and hip bones. Along with the exercises, this opened up his chronic pain pattern and for the first time in three years he felt pain-free.

The deeper changes, however, were really seen in his life as a whole. Having more available energy, he was able to make clear decisions about his job and his relationship. He decided to 'take the plunge': he left his secure but depressing job and went into business on his own. I helped him look at his life situation and how his patterns of fear, belief and conditioning had become expressed as a physical pain, which literally made him stop all of his activities. He saw how he had been avoiding his commitment to his marriage and had viewed his wife as a mother figure, far removed from the realities of their relationship. I referred them both to a marriage counsellor, whom they worked with for a period of time. He continued his sessions with me and rediscovered his Fire and found new strength as his sense of personal power grew. With this new sense also came a new clarity of responsibility and commitment in marriage and great energy for his new business venture. It is vitally important to see how all of this became focused as a low back pain which literally made him stop all of his activities. It was as if a deeper knowing had said 'Stop! Look what you are doing to yourself and your family.' Fortunately he did stop, and look, and learn.

Working with energy as it manifests in all of its relationships is incredibly fulfilling. In our last two chapters, we will explore the use of diet and exercise in this work and discuss the vital role of our thoughts and attitudes in the movement to health and well-being.

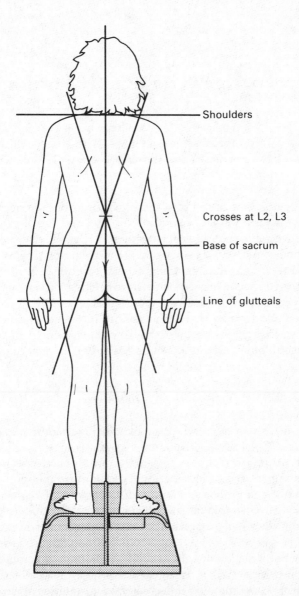

Shoulders

Crosses at L2, L3

Base of sacrum

Line of glutteals

Fig. 7.9. Perfect body polarity and gravity lines

CHAPTER EIGHT

Food, Exercise and Harmony

The problem of healing involves the harmonious relationships of man's inner energies to those of the without. The struggle is as old as mankind.

An important area of polarity therapy work involves helping clients to help themselves. In our explorations into the process of health and disease, we have seen that a movement to health and well-being is an evolutionary one. This observation is not just a theoretical construct but is eminently practical. Everything in physical form is energy; the food we eat and the movements we perform can either hinder or aid our evolutionary direction. In polarity work, diet is used both to cleanse our bodies and to support the deeper energy functions that food relates to. Movement is used in specific forms and ways to help release emotional and physical blocks and to promote a free flow of energy.

Diet

How we feel about the food we eat can tell us a lot about our relationship to the world in general. The way we use food has generally very little to do with our physical needs but much more to do with our conditioning and our psycho-emotional condition. Many of us use food to fill needs that are not being filled elsewhere. Gaining knowledge about our food patterns is also gaining knowledge about part of our way of being.

I would first like to explore our relationship to food in a very broad cultural and ethical context. Then we will hone down more specifically into our own personal attitudes. Most of us, in our early years, are conditioned to a way of eating which reflects a way of looking at the world around us and also reflects a way of treating the world and the creatures in it. I was raised in New York City. My family was very

meat-orientated. New York abounds with Jewish and Italian deli-
catessens in every neighbourhood. I was encouraged to eat – indeed,
almost force-fed – roast beef, pastrami, corned beef, tongue and chicken
in the form of sandwiches, roasts, stews and pies. I really did not have the
slightest connection with the fact that all of this meat was once living and
breathing just as I was. Roast beef came in slices, steaks in slabs and
salami in rolls. I never really thought of them as once alive. Frances
Moore Lappé, in her book *Diet for a Small Planet*, makes a beautiful
ethical argument for vegetarianism. Her basic premise is that meat
production is an inefficient, wasteful way of using our resources and our
land. In America half of all agricultural land is used to feed animals
rather than people. These animals, beef cattle, pigs and chickens are then
used to feed humans. This, in terms of protein use, is very inefficient. It
takes 21 pounds of vegetable protein to produce *one* pound of beef
protein. Cattle are very inefficient protein factories. Taking all domestic
animals into account, on average for every eight pounds of vegetable
protein, one pound of animal protein is produced.

Another factor is how land is used. According to Lappé,

> Another way of assessing the relative inefficiency of livestock is by compari-
> son with plants in the amount of protein produced per acre. An acre of cereals
> can produce *five times* more protein than an acre devoted to meat production;
> legumes (peas, beans, lentils) can produce *ten times* more; and leafy vegetables
> *fifteen times* more. Spinach, for instance, can produce up to twenty-six times
> more protein per acre than beef.

On average only 10 per cent of the vegetable protein fed to animals is
retrieved as usable protein a year in our diets! This, according to Lappé,
means that 18 million tons of protein a year is lost in this process. It also
equates to 90 per cent of the yearly world protein deficit! Meat production does rape the land in this way and with famine and starvation
abounding in the world, seems immoral and unethical. Much usable
vegetable protein could be used to feed and aid the starving of this world.

A further and perhaps even more emotive issue for me, is the actual
act of killing animals. According to many religious traditions, animals
are sentient beings (i.e. have consciousness) with their own feelings,
forms of consciousness and needs. The killing of a sentient being is
considered to be a very extreme and ignorant act. It causes pain and
suffering in order to satiate our own desires and prevents the animal from
living out its life. Whether or not you believe in past and future lives, the
present suffering caused to animals is plain enough. There was a wonderful film called *The Animal Film* made a few years ago. In a beautifully
non-biased way, it takes people into the meat-growing industry, shows
the deprivation and suffering caused to animals by the industry, and
clearly shows the suffering caused to animals during both the growing
and the slaughtering process. Enough said on the moral and 'ethical'

aspects of vegetarianism. This is something we all must decide for ourselves. Suffice it to say that I have become a vegetarian as a more helpful and harmless way of being in the world. I also have discovered a whole new world of wonderful cooking, tastes and enjoyment.

Polarity therapy uses the knowledge of both the cleansing and energetic properties of food as a therapeutic tool. Energy takes expression in our mental, emotional and physical forms and can become unbalanced at any stage. Energy can become imbalanced at its subtler phases in the Five Element Energy System or in the physical manifestations of this system. Food fulfils the need to take in physical energy to keep our very physical bodies working. The quality of food we take in relates directly to the quality of internal physical environment. The quality of the food source also relates directly to the quality of the energy it contains. I use food and diet in my private practice as a way of giving people another opportunity to look at a facet of their lives. On one hand, the food we eat affects our health on a physical level; on the other, the way we eat is also an expression of who we are and how we make our way through the world.

In orthodox nutrition food is looked at in purely biochemical terms. It is a reductionist philosophy. Food sources are reduced to their quantifiable components. So much carbohydrate, so much protein, so many minerals, so many vitamins, etc.; the key here lies in the questions What? and How much? The quantity of the component factors are the key. How the body uses these are important only from a biochemical outlook. In polarity therapy we are not so much interested in the 'how much', but in the 'how'; not so much in the quantity, but in the quality. We also look at the quality in a very specific way. It is not only the quality of the food source, its freshness, its growing technique, etc., but also the quality and the relationships of the energy it contains.

In relation to diet, the first thing I have a client do is to fill out a diet form for five days. This form divides the day into periods and clients can write on it whatever they are eating and drinking during the day. I also ask them to note down times of the day and any symptoms they may be experiencing. From this I receive a general overview of their eating habits and possible symptom relationships. This is the first stage, the 'what' stage. I then look closely at the filled-in charts and see what element categories the food sources are from. If you think back to our discussion of the Elements, you will remember that different food types relate predominantly to specific elements. When reading a person's food chart you can see how they are balancing their energies in their food, where deficiencies may be and what types of food they are energetically drawn to.

A person may be attacted to one elemental type of food because they are using that form of energy most or because there is a deficiency in it. Likewise, you may be attracted to foods which help maintain the energetic imbalance you are caught up in. It is quite common, for instance, for tired, exhausted people to have insufficient Fire foods in their diet, or for people with much resentment and anger to eat a surplus of Fire foods to feed their energy imbalance. It is only by knowing the person on a deeper level and by helping a person to know themselves that true relationships become clear.

You might want to try this for yourself. Make copies of the chart in Figure 8.1 and write in all of your food and drink for five days. Also write in any symptoms you may be experiencing (tiredness is a symptom!). Then note which elemental categories the food belong to and see your own tendencies and imbalances on the energetic level. Aim for a generally balanced diet in relationship to the Four Elements and see which elements seem to be especially needed by you in your food sources. Is nervous tension draining your Air element energies? Does anger imbalance your Fire? Do you do heavy physical work and need more Earth food? The right balance of foods energetically can only really be found by trial and error, and by being truthful with yourself about yourself.

The real baseline of our diet is how we use the energy of our food and how our pattern of eating feeds into a movement towards or away from balance. It comes back to the whole pattern of involution and evolution. We can follow the pattern of our past conditioning, eat foods in a way that unbalances us and get caught up in the involutionary cycle. Most of our diet in the West consists of meat food, processed chemicals and a mixture of foods which are overly heavy and have a 'tamasic' or heavy effect on the body. The body takes a long time to process these foods and to eliminate them. Toxic waste products have a greater opportunity to build up in body tissues due to the slowness and heaviness of processing these foods. Most meat products are adulterated with growth hormones, antibiotics and the residues of the fear the animal experienced before being killed. This includes adrenalin and other chemicals released at the time of death and the *energy* of the whole process of killing. So when you eat a hamburger, you also eat all of this too. Foods which are tamasic in nature tend to support the tamasic or crystallisation phase of energy movement. They increase our tendency to get 'stuck' and crystallised at the 'surface tension' of things and help cause a grinding-down process in our bodies and minds. It is no surprise that most cleansing diets involve the use of lighter plant foods such as fruit and vegetables and their juices. These foods tend to support a cleansing and health-building process and are more balanced and easy for the body to use.

Overlaid on this is a deep tendency in us all to use food to fulfil other needs which may have nothing to do with food as nutrition. Thus, people eat to 'fill' themselves not just with nutrients but with good feelings, love, enjoyment and to fill all the 'empty spaces' they may be experiencing emotionally. The task involved in looking at diet is not just to look at the kinds of food we are eating, but to also look at the impulses behind our eating patterns. I had the good fortune to spend a short period of my life

Date:	List main meals here everything eaten and drunk		List everything eaten and drunk list all symptoms and pains here too	
Time	Morning Meal:	Time	In between meals:	
Time	Lunch:	Time		
Time	Dinner:	Time		

Fig. 8.1. Diet chart

1. Fill in chart for five days.
2. Note elemental categories.
3. Note imbalances and tendencies in the foods you are drawn to.
4. Seek greater balance energetically in your diet.
5. Become aware of how you use these foods either to help maintain an imbalance or to 'top up' energies which you tend to drain.

Air –   fruits and nuts, cultured dairy products fermented foods.
Fire –   cereal, grains, legumes, pulses (beans peas, lentils), seeds; bitter foods – endive, escarole, dandelion, watercress; also ginger, garlic, onions, leeks.
Water – leafy greens, squash, melons, milk, vegetables grown near and on the ground.
Earth –   roots, tubers, herb roots, bulbs, honey, hard cheeses.

---

as an ordained Buddhist monk. Part of the practice was to accept whatever food was offered to me from the goodness of another's heart. Into my bowl were placed all sorts of offending foods and my main practice was to watch my judgements, opinions and needs around the whole process of eating. I was taught a specific awareness teaching to use while accepting and eating food. The purpose behind this was to open my own conditional attitudes with its 'mental-set' around food. As a monk, living a cloistered life, this was a very powerful and transformative practice. It was not a licence to eat any and everything that was placed in my bowl, but a practice to watch my conditioned reactions to it. As a lay person I have had to look at food and determine what is the best personal use of food to encourage both health and a harmless way of living in the world. What fashion of eating reduces suffering, supports balance and encourages vitality? That was my quest and polarity therapy has helped me greatly in this respect.

A process which supports changing our relationship to the food we eat is that of internal cleansing. Due to a diet rich in animal products, food additives, processed food, salt and sugar, toxic accumulations of waste products build up in body tissue. The liver is our main organ of detoxification. It can stand just so much abuse. It first stores the toxic waste overload in its own tissues and then, when it becomes overloaded, the toxicity is stored in body tissues, especially in connective tissue and fascia. This creates an internal environment which is toxic and can lead to the physical breakdown of affected organs and systems. Dr Stone developed a specific cleansing routine which has become known as the 'Polarity Purifying Diet' (see page 185). This consists of a drink taken in the morning known as the 'liver flush' which clears and flushes old waste products from the liver and gall bladder.

Along with the liver flush a specific herbal cleansing tea is taken which aids elimination of these wastes via the kidneys and colon. Fruit juice may be taken later in the morning. Lunch and dinner consists of either raw vegetables or fruit, although cooked vegetables can be used also to good effect. The cleansing tea is drunk throughout the day. After period of cleansing a 'health building' diet is started where the person slowly adds other foods to see their effect on their system. With a knowledge of the energy dynamics within the food, and experience of reactions to food, a health diet for that particular person can be built up. See the appendix for both purifying and healthbuilding diets. Dr Stone's book 'Health Building' is a wealth of information in this area and I highly recommend it.

The main focus of this discussion is developing an awareness of our relationship to food. Thought and attitude are important factors here and an awareness of our urges and needs around food is critical. Food is just another part of our way of living in the world. In the process of becoming clearer about our food, we also become clearer about ourselves. The way we eat can either support an involutionary downward spiral into imbalance and ill-health; it can be an unconscious act, hiding our true needs and entrapping us in conditioning; or it can be a process where we bring awareness to our mode of being in the world and allow a movement to true health to occur.

Another way we support energy imbalance is through inactivity. The physical world is a realm of resistance. We are always moving against or contrary to some physical force. To stand up and walk we must counter gravity and our own dead weight. To allow a thought to become an action we need to exert physical energy. We have a tendency to follow the downward pull of resistance in our lives. It is easier for many of us to space out and sit and watch TV rather than to do something active or creative. It is easy to fall prey to what Buddhists call 'sloth and torpor' or physical and mental heaviness. Dr Stone simply calls it laziness, but it is a laziness with many subtleties and many layers. At the heart of it are patterns of blocked and unbalanced energy. When energy is not moving in a fluid and balanced way our vitality is low. Our perception and our capacity to feel is dulled. We can feel heavy, tired, lazy and exhausted at various times of the day. The more unbalanced and congested our energy system is, the more tendency we will have to feel this way. Blocked energy is a disordering process, the more blocked and congested the system, the more disordered it becomes. As we have seen, the more disordered our energy system becomes, the greater the tendency to mental, emotional and physical imbalance. On a practical level we have a tendency to let things run down. As we get older we let our energies and our bodies grind down towards greater and greater crystallisation. Our thought-patterns become inflexible, our emotional states frozen into suppression or indulgence and our physical bodies rigidify with stiff joints and toxic tissues. There is a tendency for all energy systems in the physical world to run down and become disordered as energy gets caught in its physical phase. This process is called entropy.

In the body, as we have seen, Dr Stone called this process 'crystal-lisation'. Wilhelm Reich called it 'armouring' and there is a Chinese word for it which roughly translates as 'frozen Chi' (i.e. frozen energy!). Traditionally many forms of movement have been developed to counter this crystallisation process. In India the well-known postures and move-ments of Hatha Yoga were developed. In China the huge array of Chi Kung practices developed to open, circulate and balance patterns of blocked Chi. In Tibet the incredibly subtle and powerful Kum Nye practices arose within a Buddhist framework. These practices open the subtle energetic processes which underlie our pain and discomfort and open up deep-seated patterns of conditioned behaviour. In Buddhist terms it opens up the process of ego crystallisation and releases physically held karmic patterns.

In the West most of our physical exercise has been just that, per-formed to strengthen or flex the physical body. Very little work has been done with exercise on a more energetic basis. The best-known work involves the exercises of Reichian and neo-Reichian therapy, especially the exercises of Bioenergetics. These use both movement and stress positions to force open patterns of blocked life energy. The stress posture is held until the habitual armouring pattern literally has to give up. Dr Stone also saw a need to give a person tools to counter this crystallisation process. He drew from his knowledge of both Indian and Chinese forms and developed quite an eloquent exercise form. He called it 'Polarity Yoga'. Over the years many variations to the basic exercises have been developed and they have become a potent self-help aid. Polarity exercises are structured to help a person work deeply with their own patterns of energy blockage and imbalance. They help a person raise their vitality and release patterns of emotional and physical crystallisation.

The basic exercise form is based on the squatting posture. This posture is, in a way, a return to the foetal position where energies were at a formative stage. It brings all the major energy relationships and reflexes into closer proximity. It encourages energy flow when used properly. The squat helps release tensions in the pelvis and perineal floor and allows us to 'ground' our energies to earth. In it a gentle stretch can be given to all of the major muscles of the body. It is very opening and relaxing and uses gentle rocking and circling movements to start the opening process going. Many variations on the squat have been devel-oped by Dr Stone and others, which stretch the spine, release the neck and open the chest and heart. (See Figures 8.2 and 8.3.)

Dr Stone also developed various exercises done from an upright posi-tion which generally open energy in the core-spinal system. The best-known of these are the 'pyramid postures' (see Figure 8.4). These open the pelvis, stretch the spine and open the shoulders and neck. Sound can also be used with all of these exercises to help release tension and energy blockage.

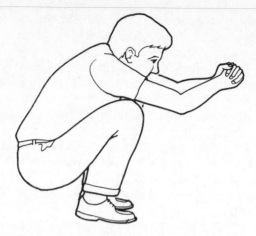

Fig. 8.2. Basic polarity squat (wide 'youth' squat)
Slowly lower yourself into the squat, heel supports such as books or pillows may be used if necessary. Circle and rock to gently open and stretch the body.

Fig. 8.3. Some variations on the squat
Hands at back of neck, elbows in between knees. Stretch spine by letting arms get heavy. Second position: lift chest up open elbows, pinch shoulder blades together, take deep breaths. Use sound, groans, etc., to help release tensions.

I had a very powerful experience with the pyramid in a session a few years ago. I had been working with a patient, Gregory, for a while and we had been doing a lot of work with the various polarity exercises. The focal point for Gregory was a blockage in his shoulder and heart areas.

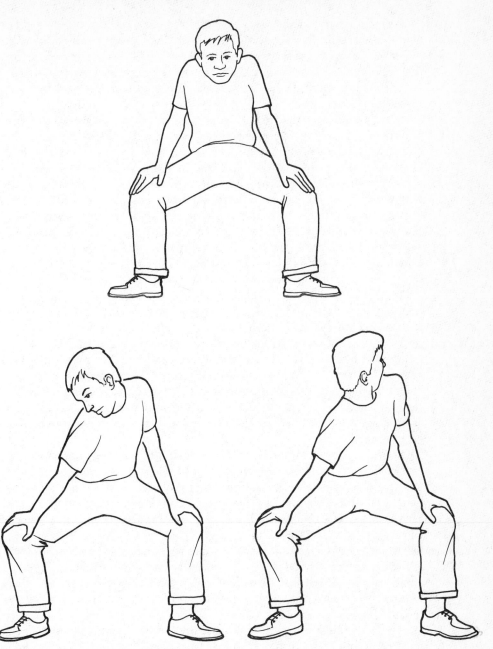

Fig. 8.4. Variations on the pyramid
Feet should be wide apart and pointing at a 45° angle. Elbows locked,
arms support upper body to transfer weight to legs. Head nestles down
between shoulders. A bouncing movement in this posture helps to stretch
and exercise the whole spine.

This was seen physically by a 'caved-in' chest and incredible tension across his scapula. He also stood in a tilted-back posture which literally pulled him away from the world in front of him. We started working on the table with chest and pelvic release work and Gregory began experiencing a block in his chest area. He described it as a 'big hand pressing my chest in'.

After a while, we reached an impasse: Gregory pulled away from the sensation and said it was because he felt fearful and powerless. This was a clear 'core statement' about the emotional holding in his chest. I had Gregory come off the table and start to work with exercises. In the upright position he could feel less vulnerable and it helped him to move with what he was feeling more easily. We both took the pyramid position opposite each other and made eye contact. His breath became very shallow and I brought his attention to this and asked him to keep his awareness in his chest. His breath deepened. I could see the pain he was experiencing reflected in his eyes. We stayed like this for what seemed to be hours but what must have been only minutes. Suddenly Gregory unleashed a piercing, grief-stricken wail that he had been desperately holding onto deep in his heart. His body shook and shook and the cleansing of grief overtook him.

Later we did some balancing work and Gregory talked about his father who had died when he was only five and his great love and great sadness for him. He had never allowed his grief to cleanse his heart and had carried it with him all these years. Allowing this movement of grief really opened up his energies generally. Remembering that Ether governs grief, we can see that his whole field expanded and this was, indeed, his experience of it.

Sound is a potent force. It can be a great aid in releasing tension and energy blockage. Dr Stone developed a whole series of exercises which use sound to help release emotional and physical blocks. The sound he used was a loud Ha! sound and these exercises have become generally known as the 'Ha! Breath Exercises'. They use movement of various kinds with a loud or prolonged Ha! sound. These quickly move energy and help start a release in blocked energy patterns. They also heighten vitality and the felt sense of vital energy flow. A few variations are shown below. I find the 'Squatting Ha!' (see Figure 8.5) especially useful in releasing blocked Fire energy, increasing vitality and moving feelings of anger or resentment.

These exercises are quite energetic and, as in all movement forms, must be followed by a period of rest and balancing. Dr Stone devised many sitting and lying forms which generally balance energy in the body. These are quite important as they allow the body to integrate the new energy flows and to consolidate the gains made in the exercise forms. Again, awareness must be brought to all the forms for maximum effect and a still mind aids the process of energy balance.

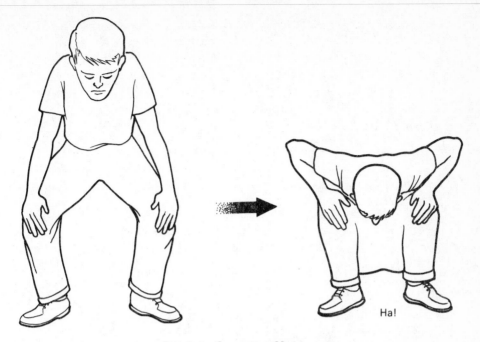

Ha!

Fig. 8.5. Squatting Ha!
Take a hip-width stance, hands above and over knees. Keep knees bent
the whole time. Sink to squatting position with a loud Ha! Immediately
push yourself up to starting position and repeat in a 'pumping' fashion as
many times as possible without straining.

The main intent in all of these exercises is to have a tool which allows us to be active in our health-building process. They give us ways to take back responsibility for our own process. Taking responsibility for our current state and *doing* something about it is the most beneficial first step we can take. With these forms we have a tool for working on our own unique energy imbalances in a very active way. They help move us from a downward slide into inactivity and disorder to an evolutionary movement where energy blockages are being opened and greater vitality is felt. The exercise forms can also help us get out of our heads and into our bodies. Through them we can become acquainted with our patterns of blockage and imbalance as we experience them in our bodies. We can use them to help open these patterns and to experience the flow of energy and feel more vital and alive. By bringing awareness to this process, as in all other processes, we gain greater freedom from the imbalanced patterns which we discover. Energy *is* movement and in these forms we are encouraging that movement.

Ha!

Fig. 8.6. Woodcutter Ha!
Feet hip width or wider. Knees bent, pelvis cocked back. Sink into
'woodcutter' action with loud Ha! Repeat as many times as possible
without straining. Keep knees bent the whole time.

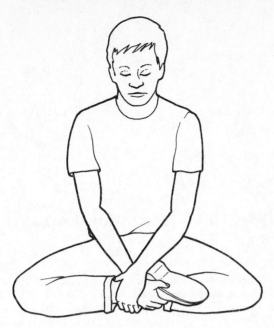

Fig. 8.7. Neutral sitting
Sit with legs flat on the floor in front of you. Cross hands and hold
opposite ankles (i.e. left hand on right ankle). Allow mind to be quiet.

CHAPTER NINE

Finishings and Final Thoughts

Life does not tolerate disease. Then why should we? If we do not struggle with our negative qualities of mind and emotions like a fish caught in a net, we never can escape those loops and 'bonds'.

In our lives we veil ourselves with layers and layers of conditioning, beliefs, feelings, thoughts and forms and sometimes it may feel like it is an impossible task to find our way through it all. We all would like to find some kind of peace in our lives and I would like to talk a bit about this potential or possibility we all have. In order to do this, I would like to use a model developed by Ken Wilber. He calls it the 'Spectrum of Consciousness'. It is based on the diagram shown in Figure 9.1.

In this diagram we have Wilber's schema of a spectrum of qualities of consciousness as we move from states of universal Mind to states of separation and duality. Each phase in the spectrum marks a shift in consciousness either towards greater Unity or towards greater separations. As we move away from 'universal consciousness of Mind' as Wilber calls it, we move through bands of greater separation and alienation. The 'Primal Change' or Great Separation occurs at a very subtle level. It is the greater split into polarities, into Yin and Yang. Subject, object, 'I' and 'other', mine and yours arise.

At the transpersonal level, this separation of consciousness into parts is very subtle. There is still a feeling of 'wholeness' or 'oneness' without a splitting into an 'organism vs environment' consciousness. But the identification with the Source has been lost and a very subtle level of separation arises. At what Wilber calls the Existential level, the split goes deeper and the organism, the being, experiences itself as separate from the environment. But the being itself still experiences itself as 'whole' in the sense that it identifies with its whole psychophysical being. It experiences the oneness between mind and body yet feels separate from its environ-

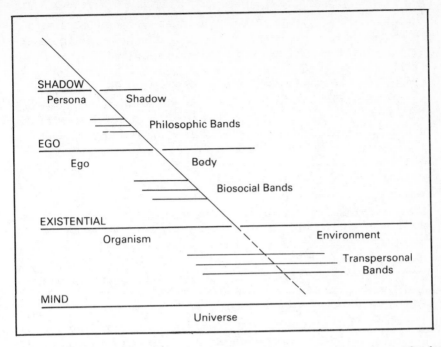

Fig. 9.1. The spectrum of consciousness. (Taken from the Journal of Transpersonal Psychology, *Number 2, 1975. The Spectrum of Consciousness.)*

ment. It is here that a very subtle level of thought arises and the organism begins to take on a deeper veil of ego. At the Ego phase this process has gone further and the being identifies with a mental construct of himself. He identifies, according to Wilber with his conditioned self-image. His organism is split into the psyche, in the form of ego and the body, as something separate from it. Thus people say 'I have a body' not 'I am a body'. At this level we identify with a mental construction of our psycho-physical organism and feel separate from our physical form. Thus a deeper veiling has occurred and a deeper split arises. Our ego feels separate from our body. The final phase occurs when the being identifies with only part of his Ego construct and disowns or alienates parts he is not comfortable with and categorises them as painful or undesirable.

The evolutionary movement occurs when the split or separation at each level is healed and a greater sense of unity is experienced. So the integration of the Persona, the aspects of ourselves we identify with and the Shadow, our alienated parts, leads to the experience of a healed and strengthened ego. The integration of the ego and the body will lead to the existential experience of wholeness in body and mind. The integration of the total organism with its environment will lead to the transpersonal levels of 'oneness' or 'wholeness' with all creation and a final integration will allow the creation to merge with the Creator. (See Figure 9.2.)

Another way of seeing is not so much as merging, but as a deep remembering, a casting away of our deepest veils. In Zen Buddhism they say that 'there is nothing to attain, only much to be shed'. It is a process of letting-go to our True Nature, a true voyage of universal healing. It is a peeling of the layers of the onion until the deepest truth is realised.

Returning to our discussion of thought and attitude, we can see how these can either support the process of alienation or the process of healing and integration. Unskilful or negative thinking can immerse us in the push–pull of the various polarities within us. Good–bad, pleasure–pain, hate–love, despair–joy are all poles of separation. Thoughts lock us into these counter-points until they become so entrenched that the energy behind them becomes crystallised and 'frozen'. We become so stuck in these cycles that we believe them to be our real selves. Imbalance and dis-ease are bound to result. Skilful or positive awareness can be used to investigate, to look at our lives, to change destructive ways of being into constructive ways. It can support a deeper enquiry and a deeper move-ment to wholeness and health. In a sense skilful thought and perception is a raft, until we can let go of the whole process itself and abide in what the Tibetans call 'Pure Pristine Awareness'. It is important to realise that all of these levels of dissociation are happening within us in every moment of time. Even the most subtle Primal Change from Unity into transpersonal bands is occurring moment to moment. It is a whole energetic flux occurring in the moment pulsating throughout ourselves and throughout the universe. Being a current of pulsation in the moment, its truth is also available to us in this very moment! Although, for convenience, we split the stream into phases, we *must* remember that it is a river of one truth, one energy pulsating from the source, into manifes-tation and back again. It is the Sage who fully apprehends this in the moment and re-experiences his or her deepest truth. If we remember from Chapter 1, David Bohm, a physicist, has developed a new theory of the macrocosm/microcosm relationship sometimes called the 'Holographic

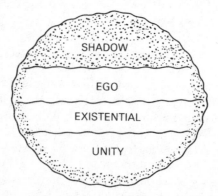

Fig. 9.2. The 'spectrum' layers: integrating the splits at each layer yields a greater and greater depth of unity

Paradigm'. In this he sees implicit laws of the universe 'enfolded' in the explicate realm of experience. Ken Wilber in *The Atman Project* uses this concept when he talks about the evolutionary and involutionary relationship:

> In order for evolution, which is the unfolding of higher structures to occur at all, those higher structures must in some sense, be present from the start: they must be enfolded as potential in the lower modes. The story of involution is simply the story of how the higher modes came to be enwrapped and enfolded in the lower states.

The important point is that the potential for both health and enlightenment is present all the time, it is already within us. In times of pain and suffering it is important to focus on this truth. Even in the depths of depression, or the pain of physical illness, the potential for health is enfolded within our very being. It is most important to realise this truth in our understanding and experience of death and dying. We view death, in our society, as something final, horrific and senseless. It is something to be talked about behind closed doors, if at all. We pretend that it always happens to someone else, but not to me, not yet anyway. We are afraid to tell others they are dying and indeed, avoid them as if it is something we can catch from them. When we meet dying people we feel uncomfortable, afraid, cut off. There is so much fear about the seeming finality of death that we shut it out and pretend it is not there. But this great fear is just an expression of our great separation. We have created this 'I' or 'me' and we are then afraid to lose it. But there is nothing to lose. We have never had 'it' to begin with and have never really lost who we really are. We have just allowed ourselves to forget.

The spiritual traditions see death as not separate from life, but as part of a grand cycle, the other side of the coin, so to speak. Death is not seen as a final ending, but as a new beginning. We see this in all traditional religions and even in traditional medical systems. Traditional medicine always had a philosophical basis to it and this always included a philosophy of the death process. Death they saw, is inexorably part of life. People must be as prepared for death as they are for dealing with their lives. In many traditions there are teachings which help a person through the death process. The familiar last rites of Christianity are a means to this end when fully understood. Eastern philosophies saw death as part of a cycle of reincarnation or rebirth. We move endlessly through many, many new lives until we are freed by a final enlightenment which is, in essence a deep remembering. Thus it was held to be important to help a person through this experience so that the next new phase or new life could have a firm and peaceful foundation to it. This preparation included death in pleasant surroundings, the presence of friends and family and the reciting or chanting of special teachings to help a person in the death experience. The best-known of these is the Tibetan Book of the Dead which takes a person through the stages of the dissolution of the elements and the entrance into a new womb. This is in marked contrast to death in the sterility of a hospital ward.

In traditional Buddhist philosophy the moment of death is considered extremely important. Since death is considered to be a portal to a new life, the quality of consciousness at death directly affects the quality of consciousness of the first moment of new life. It is also thought to affect the choice of new parents and the quality of life situation we are drawn into. Death is not thought of as something to avoid or be afraid of, but as something to *work with*. I was once studying with an elderly Buddhist monk from the forests of Burma. He was much revered in his homeland and truly emanated compassion and deep wisdom. A number of us were with him on what amounted to a five-month retreat. In the afternoons he would take a long walk in the hills and we would follow along. Although in his 86th year, he certainly out-walked us youngsters. We would then return to his room and sit in silence with him as the sun left the sky. He would very rarely speak unless someone had a question for him. One day, while we sat as darkness approached in his dimly lit room, he sat up and spoke to the person behind me. He smiled and said, 'You mustn't be afraid of dying. There is nothing to fear, you've died many times before!' the person behind me was startled and replied, 'Yes, I've been thinking of my death, dwelling on it, Venerable One. But tell me then, how should I approach this problem of Death?' The Venerable monk answered: 'There is no problem. You should approach death as you should approach life: with awareness, tranquillity and insight. If you are truly abiding in awareness and deeply realise the impermanent nature of all things while dying, then you will be born in a new life with awareness and wisdom as its foundation.'

This exchange has always stayed with me and has truly affected my relationship to death. It has, of course, also affected my relationship to life and to the healing process. One important insight for me was that life is about quality, not quantity. Life prolongation is about quantity and is tied into a consciousness locked into a time-sense. As Larry Dossey in *Space, Time and Medicine* clearly points out, the concept of a linear flowing time is a mental construct. In orthodox medicine the prolongation of life is paramount; in traditional medicine the present quality of life, including this quality of dying is paramount. As Larry Dossey points out, 'length of life is meaningless for the reason that passage of linear time does not occur in nature.' In the 'New Physics' we are seeing that events in different parts of the universe are not dependent on a concept of time for their relationship. It is the quality of the present moment which is important. In traditional Taoism, the sage does not strive after longevity (unlike popular Taoism) but follows the Way of Things or Tao in *the present moment*. Health on many levels results. This has profoundly affected my own private polarity therapy practice where I try to facilitate a better quality of life in the present and leave the question of 'time' to a higher Source.

Dr Stone stressed in all of his work that life is given to us so that we can learn. It is only through meeting the resistance of form that lessons can be learned. In *Polarity Therapy* he writes:

> . . . the learning of lessons through the play of matter is the reason for our being here, and not easy sailing in pleasures without experience and resistance. Only from resistance and the impact of energy upon matter can we learn the nature of these forces . . . Freedom of play, of choice, of action and reaction is the only way we can enjoy ourselves and learn like all children do. As long as we learn from life and forget ourselves, we are growing and living. But when the mind demands and becomes egoistic . . . when it wishes to set up its own rule and condition, then it suffers from the impact of cross currents of forces, which it opposes by its efforts and plans.

Life is a great opportunity for us to learn how we bind ourselves. How we veil ourselves. It can be a beautiful journey of letting go and following the present moment. Our freedom of action gives us the opportunity to explore our world with awareness and full consciousness. It allows us to peel off the various layers of our conditioned onion. Dr Stone further writes in his *Mystic Bible*:

> The desire which brought us down has its latent force deep within the soul, which precipitates it into involution and experience. Only by testing our desires in the energy fields of resistance of mind, emotions and matter can we be convinced mentally; and through experience, emotionally; and through suffering physically. That completes the gamut of our mental process and prowess in action and in life, as experience and proof of our own desire and folly in our cleverness.

Many ancient traditions see ego desire as the 'first cause' of our suffering. But it is only in this physical world that we can test these desires and, hopefully, see them for what they are. We tend to be controlled by our desires and urges. In life we have the opportunity to take back control, not by suppressing them, but by seeing into them and letting them go. Our energies are bound up in mental, emotional and physical processes and it is only by truly experiencing them that we can unbind them and open ourselves to health and well-being. The great struggle is to free ourselves from our inner conflicts and inner splits. Dr Stone writes in *Energy*:

> It is important to know of and understand this proceses of the involution of the soul into matter, because all the finer principles and vehicles and lines of force are still with us, buried within this form. That is the reason we have so much conflict within ourselves and are constantly searching for our lost estate, seeking our higher essences and trying to discover ourselves.
>
> The truth still lies deep within us and our outer desires and inner truths can be in constant conflict. This is a conflict of the Spirit. Do we follow the surface tension of things, the peripheral mesh of needs, desires and aversions or do we rediscover the truth at the heart of things and thereby resolve this conflict, this split?

Ken Wilber in *The Atman Project* echoes this theme,

> The soul must seek Unity through the constraints of the present stage, which is not yet Unity . . . each individual wants only Atman (i.e. Unity-ed), but wants it under conditions that prevent it . . . And that is why human desire is insatiable, why all joys yearn for infinity – all a person wants is Atman, all he finds are symbolic substitutes for it.

What we yearn for is a deeper truth, a deeper Unity, and what we get in the world are shadows of it, sex, power, fleeting joy, temporary security. But since the truth *is* inside, it *can be* available to us and the split, the conflict *can be* healed. Life is not to be feared, it is not to run away from, but is a wonderful place to learn the lessons we all so deeply need to learn. At a very basic level, we create our own world by our beliefs, judgements and conditioned ways of perceiving. We lose touch with the basic openness of things, the great open potential within us all.

Working with our energy system is a wonderful way to explore our conditioned relationships. All of creation is energy and it is our energetic blocks which entrap us in patterns of imbalance and ill health. Bringing awareness to this flow, whether through body-work, diet, exercise or counselling, starts to free our energies and increase our vitality. It gives us more room to manoeuvre in, more space to explore ourselves in.

It is important, I believe, to see ourselves in the context of the world around us. Not just as an isolated ego full of its own urges and needs, but as part of the grand interplay of energies in the universe as a whole. That is why I started the book with a chapter on the macrocosm as an expression of our own inner being. Krishnamurti used to say, 'You are the world,' and, indeed, the world is you. It is one whole movement, one whole dance. Our energies are in resonance with everything around us and we can either experience and encourage that resonance, or hide ever more deeply in our veils of conditioning. But no matter how deeply we hide, how cut off both from ourselves and others we feel, the potential for change, for health, is always within. When our minds are quiet and our hearts are open we can perceive the universal quality of love which pervades the universe and holds it together. Love, compassion and kindness are not concepts or ideals but a living experience of the oneness of all things and our essential connectedness to the deepest of all Sources.

I would like to finish here with a quote from Dr Stone. A study guide, which I hope will be helpful to those who wish to explore Dr Stone's writings, follows.

> Tuning in with the Infinite is a practical idea, if applied and understood. Man is not as helpless as he feels and thinks he is, if he could only tune in on his inner energies and deeper hidden resources of life itself.

Appendix: Study Guide to Dr Stone's Writings on Polarity Therapy

by Franklyn Sills R.P.T.
*Director of The Polarity Therapy
Education Trust (UK)*
© *Franklyn Sills*

The Polarity Therapy Educational Trust runs three-year training courses in all aspects of Polarity Therapy. For information, contact:
The Registrar, 11 The Lee, Allesley Park, Coventry CV5 9HY

The Educational Trust is a member of the British Polarity Council, an umbrella body which oversees the practice of Polarity Therapy in the United Kingdom. The Council's contact address is:
British Polarity Council, Monomark House, 27 Old Gloucester Street. London, WC1N 3XX

Preface to the study guide

Over the years, many students of Polarity Therapy have agonised over the organisation and interpretation of Dr Stone's books. In both organisation and style, many have found the books a difficult puzzle to unravel. The study guide presented here is a shorthand which will hopefully help organise one's approach to these books.

Dr Stone worked with the 'stuff' of life. He understood the underlying energies of mind and matter and their interplay in health and disease. He recognised that subtle energies manifest on many levels from the subtlest energy patterns, to the coarsened energies of the nervous system and of the musculoskeletal system. He was very practical about applying this knowledge and worked on as many of these levels as possible. The appendices have been organised to reflect these levels of approach. Dr Stone worked intimately with the Five Elements of the Ayurvedic medical system of India: Ether, Air, Fire, Water, Earth. These terms represent phases of energy which govern the various mental, emotional and physiological processes of man.

The interplay of the Five Elements is the crux of Polarity Therapy. All theory, all technique, all practical applications must relate to this understanding. The majority of categories in the appendices relate to the various levels of energy that Dr Stone worked with. The Five Elements are the subtlest level of work. These include diagnostic techniques, specific techniques for the release of blockages in the energy fields and techniques for the simulation and balancing of the energy flow relating to each element.

The nervous system is the next level of energy worked with. This is a 'step-down' energy system which brings the subtler Five Element interrelationships into physical manifestation. This work includes specific techniques for the parasympathetic, sympathetic and central nervous systems. Cranial theory and cranial-pelvic polarity work are an integral part of this work. Energy imbalances manifest in physical form as structural imbalances and Dr Stone developed a complete system of gentle structural work as a final balancing factor.

Although the best-known aspect of Polarity Therapy is therapeutic touch, equally important are the naturopathic, dietary and exercise processes that Dr Stone made an integral part of his healing system. Cleansing and health-building diets and Dr Stone's own 'Polarity Yoga' are the most important aspects of these and are covered in the appendices. Naturopathic procedures are sprinkled throughout the books and close reading is needed to glean the most from it. The use of beets as a drawing agent, colonic cleansing and therapeutic use of precious metals are just a few of the many subjects covered. The following appendices have been written in the hope that they can help both students and practitioners find a way into these wonderful volumes. They are laid out as follows:

I.   On Reading Dr Stone: a close reading of one of Dr Stone's passages.
II.   Wireless Anatomy: the basic or 'core' energy system.
III.   Energy Harmonics: the basic energy relationships and reflexes.
IV.   General Theory: a listing of page references dealing with energy theory, cosmology, naturopathic practices, diagnostic procedures and much more.
V.   Five Elements: page references of Five Element theory.
VI – X. Ether, Air, Fire, Water, Earth: separate sections organising the technique charts according to the energy patterns they relate to.
XI.   Nervous System: charts relating to the Parasympathetic and Sympathetic nervous systems.
XII.   Central Nervous System: cranial and cranial–pelvic techniques.
XIII.   Structural and Spinal Relationships: charts relating to spinal and structural balancing.
XIV.   Nutrition and Cleansing Diets: charts and pamphlets relating to diet and nutrition.
XV.   Polarity Exercise: charts and pamphlets relating to polarity exercises.

I. On Reading Dr Stone

Dr Stone's books were written in chronological order over many years and were not laid out as a step-by-step guide. To compound this problem, Dr Stone's writing style was very dense. There is an incredible amount of information, with sweeping implications, in each sentence and paragraph. If one is unfamiliar with the basic principles involved, much can be missed or misunderstood. In the following example from Book I *Energy*, we will explore some basic concepts which lay a

foundation for Polarity Therapy work and will also see the implications of just a few
of Dr Stone's sentences.

> Polarity is the law of opposites in their finer attraction from center to center.
> Unity is the merging of these currents into one Essence. Creation brings forth
> opposites by its centrifugal force, like a fountain spray of manifestation
> flowing out to the limits of the cosmos and of each pattern unit . . . Centers of
> energy are essential for creation of forms and their generation. It is essential
> that energy be concentrated and work according to definite patterns and
> designs, or exhaustion would take place.
>
> *Energy* pp. 14 and 15

Here, in a very condensed form, are the basic principles of polarity movement, of the
cyclical nature of life and, indeed, of the grand plan of the cosmos. Let's look closely
at these sentences and see their implications.

> Polarity is the law of opposites in their finer attraction from center to center.
> Unity is the merging of these currents into one essence.

Dr Stone is presenting a universal law, the Law of Polarity. The movement of
opposites is implicit in all of manifestation. To have life, to have movement,
polarities must be active. The movement of temperature, electricity, nuclear energy
are just a few manifestations of polarity relationships. At a deeper level, this law
governs the movement of subtler energies 'in their finer attraction from center to
center'. Energy must arise from a center, much as electricity must arise from a
generating plant. Energy which arises from a centre must eventually return to it.
Again, for electricity to be generated, a complete circuit must form from the
generating plant to the user, back to the plant. For this movement a polarity
relationship must be present. Thus, an electrical charge moves only when there is a
positive–negative polar relationship. There also must be a neutral field for the energy
to move through. For instance, a copper wire is a neutral field which carries the
current arising from the source. The movement of energy in all its manifested forms
has been called 'The Polarity Principle'. Simply stated it says that energy must arise
from a centre, move through a neutral field via a polarity relationship and must
eventually be drawn back to the original source.

When Dr Stone writes about the polarity movement 'from center to center', he is
talking about the grand scheme of the universe! For physical manifestation to occur,
energy must move from subtle centres to coarser ones. The more intense energy of
the subtler centres must be 'stepped down', much like the action of a transformer
which steps down the intensity of electrical energy from a higher to less intense form.
Traditional cultures have called the 'primal centre' or first cause by various names,
Tao, Godhead, Brahman, Purusha, to name but a few. From this primal centre,
various step-down phases of energy occur in which polarities are drawn 'in their finer
attraction' into less intense centres. These transform higher vibrational energies into
coarser forms. After numerous stages, energies finally 'condense' into physical form.
At each centre, when the energies are drawn together, they merge into one neutral
Essence. This unity occurs at each centre. Remembering that energies which leave a
centre must eventually return to it, we now have the possibility of merging in full
unity with the Primal Source itself. This has been the basis of many traditional
philosophies and religions, the foundation of the mystic experience, of what has been

called enlightenment. Dr Stone called this return phase of energy the evolutionary phase.

> Creation brings forth opposites by its centrifugal force, like a fountain spray of manifestation flowing out to the limits of the cosmos and of each pattern unit.

As we have seen, polarities must arise from a source. The source of energy has been seen to be the creative intelligence at the heart of existence itself. Polarity movement occurs via a positive, expansive centrifugal action which pushes the paired opposites out from the source into manifestation. This, in Eastern cultures, has been called the 'Primal Change'. The Chinese talk of yin and yang polarity relationships. The Indians talk of the three Gunas: sattvas, rajas and tamas; the neutral, positive and negative phases of polarity movement. This 'fountain spray of manifestation' flows 'out to the limits of the cosmos' through a number of step-down phases and becomes coarser at each successive phase. Finally, the energy becomes so coarse that it 'condenses' into physical form. To describe this, Dr Stone has also used the analogy of 'surface tension'. Energy moves away from the Source until the impulse that moved it reaches a 'point of exhaustion'. It can be visualised like a vast sphere expanding away from the source in all directions. At the point of exhaustion the energy flow has lost impetus, has coarsened, and a surface tension is created. It is at the periphery of the sphere, at the surface tension, that energy condenses into physical form. This occurs at the limit of the centrifugal force which originally brought forth the polarity relationship or 'pattern unit'. Each 'pattern unit' is an expression of a polarity relationship and is limited by the nature of the original impulse from the source. The nature of a polarity relationship is 'patterned' within the source and is thus called by Dr Stone a 'pattern unit'.

> Centers of energy are essential for creation of forms and their generation. It is essential that energy be concentrated and work according to define patterns and designs, or exhaustion would take place.

As we have seen, energy must arise from a centre or source. Form is nothing less than a manifestation of energy arising from the source. The ancient Chinese used to say that form is at the periphery of reality. At its heart is the Tao. Outer manifestation is but a coarse expression of this inner truth. Without a 'centre of energy' or source nothing would arise. As we have seen after energy arises from the source it is concentrated at the periphery of manifestation. At the periphery, these energies manifest according to 'definite patterns'. High and low, hot and cold, positive and negative are manifest according to these patterns which are inherent in the source itself. This concentration of energy into physical form is necessary as a crucial pivot point where the outward expansive phase of energy is concentrated and halted in preparation for the inward contractive return phase. That which has been pushed out from the source can thus be drawn back. If this concentration of energy at the periphery did not occur, then energies would soon, like ripples in a pond, expend themselves in greater and greater dissipation. Thus, physical form is at the extreme edge of the expansive or centrifugal phase of energy movement. It is at the 'surface tension' of the cosmic bubble. From here, a return to the source is now possible. As Dr Stone has said, 'the first becomes the last and the last becomes the first'. Physical form is a necessary phase of this process and is crucial as a 'springboard for all spiritual practice'.

The understanding of centres and energy flow is an important background to understanding the flow of subtle energy in the body. The energy flow in the body follows the same patterns as in the universe as a whole. We are indeed a microcosm reflecting a greater universal truth.

II. *Wireless Anatomy*

At the heart of Polarity Therapy is the subtle energy system with which it works. Dr Stone used the ancient Indian model of energy with its deep understanding of the mind–body dynamic. The Indian system is similar to other traditions around the world; the Tibetans, Chinese, Egyptians and Greeks had a similar understanding. This was an understanding which saw man not as an entity separate from the universe around him, but as an expression of the whole, a microcosm in a vast macrocosmic dance. In this way of perceiving the world, man and nature, natural cycles and God are not separate systems or realms, but are integral movements of one vast energy pattern. Not only that, but each part of the system, in a wonderful paradox, contains the whole. The whole is within the part, much like every cell of the human body contains all the information necessary to produce a complete being. Dr Stone expressed this as a universal law, 'as above, so below'.

The formation of the subtle energy system or wireless anatomy of man mirrors the movement of energy in the universe as a whole. At the heart of this is the play of consciousness or awareness that is an expression of the source itself. This play of consciousness has been called by many traditional names. It is best-known in the West as the soul, a unique expression of the whole within every living creature. The wireless anatomy of man is in turn an expression of this cosmic play. Referring to Chart 2, Book II, *Wireless Anatomy*, we see the six energy centres in their proper relationship. Dr Stone named the centres according to the quality of energy emanating from them. These terms are the traditional Five Elements of Indian medicine, Tibetan medicine and Buddhist and Greek philosophy. They are Ether, Air, Fire, Water and Earth. We will talk about these in more detail in the later appendices.

The first energy centre formed in the physical body is at the brow. This centre, formed as energy, in its travel from the primal source, has coarsened and has condensed in a new, now physical, energy centre. The Brow Centre is located between the eyes. From here, via three energy currents, a series of step-down phases occur which form five more energy centres, traditionally called chakras. The three currents which energise and link the six chakra centres are *pingala*, a positive-charged spiral current, *ida*, a negatively-charged spiral current and *sushumna*, a vertical neutral current. Pingala and ida spiral down either side of the spine and form the chakras at their cross-over points. The sushumna is a neutral current which flows in the spine and is a neutral core which links each centre. As energy spirals down from centre to centre, the quality of energy at each centre becomes less intense, coarser and less conscious. The sphere of influence of each chakra becomes coarser and more contracted with each step-down phase. The chakras below the Brow Centre are named after the Five Elements of Ayurvedic medicine. They are the Ether Centre in the throat, the Air Centre in the chest, the Fire Centre in the umbilicus, the Water Centre in the pelvis and the Earth Centre in the anal region. We can see these centres and currents represented in Chart 2, Book II, *Wireless Anatomy*. In Chart 2, Book I, *Energy*, we can see the anatomical relationships of these centres.

At each energy centre or chakra, a field of energy arises which Dr Stone called the 'oval fields'. These are seen in Chart I, Book II and Chart 6, Book III. For energy to move, there must be a field to support its movement. These pulsating oval fields provide a ground or medium which allows the movement of other energy patterns across them. Although there are six chakras (the seventh or 'crown' chakra is really not a pulsating energy centre, but is rather a centre of potential enlightenment), there are only five oval fields. This is because the last two chakras are of such a low vibration and low intensity that they can only drive one oval field between them. The ovals are named for the dominant quality of movement through them. For instance, the oval field round the fire chakra is named the earth oval due to the processing and movement of food and faeces through this area.

To complete the 'core' energy system are three currents which arise from the chakra system. These three currents mirror the three poles of polarity movement. There is a neutral 'Airy' current line, the East–West or Transverse current, seen in the Evolutionary Energy Series (25 charts), Charts 2 and 3, and negative 'Watery' currents called the Long Line currents, seen in Charts 3, 5, 6, 7, 8, Book II. The East–West current arises from the top and bottom of the neutral sushumna and transversely spirals around the body. Its function is that of intercommunication and binding. The spiral Fire current arises from the Fire Centre at the umbilicus and spirals vertically to encompasss the whole of the energy system. It provides energy for warmth, movement and distribution of internal vitality. Finally the Long Line currents emanate individually from each chakra centre. Each Long Line current is of the quality of energy most like that of its centre. Thus the current emanating from the Water chakra is called the Water current. They expand outward from each chakra and pulsate in vertical bands around the body. Their function is to regulate and monitor the physiology of the body and to relate the internal to the external through the five senses. The following charts map out the Wireless Anatomy of Man:

Book	Chart/page	Content
Bk I	Ch. 2, p. 44	Anatomical location of chakras
Bk II	Ch. 1, p. 8	Chakras and oval fields
	Ch. 2, p. 9	Chakras and central currents
	Ch. 3, p. 10	Composite chart
	Chs. 5, 6, 7, 8, pp. 12–15	Long Line currents
	Ch. 7, p. 14	East–West currents
Bk III	Ch. 6, p. 50	Oval field relationships
Bk V	Ch. 3, p. 32	Long Line currents
Bk V	Ch. 8, p. 51	Oval field relationships
EES	Ch. 1	Long Line currents
(25 charts)		
	Ch. 2, 3	Fire currents

Charts dealing with specific energy patterns for the Five Elements are listed below with each special element.

III. Energy Harmonics and Reflexes

As we have seen, we live in an ordered universe. Energy flows in ordered phases and patterns. The patterns of energy in the universe are determined by the energy centre from which they flow. These patterns are orderly and are mutually interdependent.

The subtle energies of the body are no exception to this rule. Due to the ordered sweep of energy from the Brow Centre down and to the movement of the various energy patterns from each chakra centre, a complex interweaving of energies is produced. This network of interpenetrating energies forms an 'interference pattern' which underpins physical form. This can be likened to a hologram whose existence is based on the interference pattern created by the criss-crossing of its related energy fields. It is the balanced and open flow of the related patterns which maintains the integrity of the hologram. Likewise, it is the open and balanced flow of the various energy patterns of the body which maintains the integrity and health of the individual.

As these energy patterns criss-cross and interpenetrate, complex harmonics and reflexes are set up. A harmonic is a relationship where the qualities of energy will resonate with each other. If you strike middle 'C' on a piano all other 'C's will also vibrate. Thus, in an energy field, like qualities of energy will harmonically 'resonate' with each other. This interweaving of energies sets up a series of reflexes in the body which are in harmonic resonance with each other. Dr Stone continually talks of the triad and triune relationships of an energy pattern. Energy flows in its positive, neutral and negative pole relationships. This flow sets up positive, neutral and negative pole body relationships. In situations of energy blockage and imbalance, all three aspects of the energy relationships must be taken into account. They are the 'harmonics' of that particular energy flow. An imbalance in one 'pole' of a relationship will have repercussions throughout all of its harmonic relationships. Chart 4, Book II shows these as general polarity zone harmonics. This becomes more complex when the therapist starts to deal with the harmonics of the five elements and of their interrelationships. General charts of energy harmonics and reflexes are as follows:

Charts in Appendix II above give 'core energy' patterns

Book	Chart/page	Content
Bk II	Ch. 4, p. 11	Polarity zone harmonics
	Ch. 17, p. 24	Thumb-web and ankle reflexes
	Ch. 33, p. 40	Ankle and joint reflexes
	pp. 62–71	General theory, including types of touch
Bk III	Ch. 3, pp. 37–44	Diagnostic reflex areas
	Chs. 4, 5, pp. 45–49	Lateral reflexes
Bk V	Chs. 4, 5, pp. 35–42	Foot and hand reflexes
	Ch. 7, pp. 48–50	Face diagnosis
	Ch. 8, pp. 51–55	Diagnostic oval field relationships
EES	Chs. 5, 6	Horizontal reflex areas
EES	Ch. 21	Tongue diagnosis

IV. General Theory

Dr Stone's books deserve and need close reading. A principle in one paragraph may be clarified and made practical in another seemingly unrelated section. A paragraph in one book may be further expanded in another. Listed in the following page references are a mixture of general theory, cosmology, naturopathic practices, diagnostic procedures and much more. It is up to the inquisitive student to carefully read and cross-reference these passages. They are listed here as a guide for this purpose.

Book	Chart/page	Content Summary
Bk I	pp. 2–43	Energy theory; energy in health and disease; Five Element theory; introduction to nutrition; naturopathic practices; mind–body interrelationship; caduceus; theory of conception.
Bk I	Ch. 3, pp. 46–47	Polarity Triad theory
	pp. 54–75	Mind-matter relationship, function of mind, prana, hypnosis, pain, psychology, centrifugal-centripetal relationships, acute versus chronic conditions, naturopathic practices
	pp. 90–93	Soul progress, conditioning
Appendix Bk I	pp. 1–8	Energy currents, Five Elements
	pp. 17–28	Use of gold and silver, body relationships, use of proportion in polarity therapy, fever, response in treatment, cycle of nutrition
Bk II	pp. 1–4	General principles, summary of principles
Bk II	Ch. 12, p. 19	Tree of life
	Chs. 14–16, pp. 21–23	Muscle relationships and reflexes
Bk III	pp. 1–26	Polarity principle, limitations in matter, triune polarity patterns, three bodies of man, polarity body relationships, mind and matter, involutionary–evolutionary energy cycles, mental blueprints and the energy field, five-element theory, structural balance, brachial plexus, health and disease, summary of principles
	Ch. 1, pp. 26–30	The caduceus, energy theory, polarity principle
	Ch. 2, pp. 31–36	Life Force patterns, life circuit of the heart, pulse reading, the body as end product of imbalance, health and disease principles
	Ch. 3, pp. 37–44	Diagnostic areas, polarity relationships, diagnostic procedures, treatment in acute or in chronic conditions, polarity principles
Bk V	Ch. 1, pp. 1–14	Vitality and energy, the 'Vital Flame', involution-evolution, vital balance for health, conception and birth, bodily systems and the elements, Soul and Mind, the unconscious and psychiatry, hypnosis, faith

	p. 79	Client responses
	pp. 96–97	Fever
	pp. 98–105	Use of precious metals in healing
EES	Ch. 10	Chakras
	Ch. 11	Spiritual regions
	Ch. 16	Primal energy patterns

Booklets	Content/summary
'A Brief Explanation of the Emerald Tablet of Hermes'	Explanation of an alchemical formula
'Polarity Therapy Principles and Practice'	General principles, principles of treatment, hypotension vs hypertension
'Energy Tracing Notes'	General theory

V. The Five Elements

Polarity Therapy, as practised by Dr Stone, is based on a deep theoretical and practical understanding of the Five Elements. Dr Stone used the Ayurvedic system of elements as his model. He found within it a clear knowledge of both the psychological and physical ramifications of imbalanced energy and a clear presentation of the underlying energies involved. The Five Elements are names given to the qualities of energy which arise from the different chakra centres. These energies are also manifestations of qualities of consciousness and thus have vast implications in the understanding of health and disease. One's quality of consciousness and one's patterns of behaviour are at the root of these processes.

The general movement of energy in both man and the cosmos is governed by the three Gunas. They are much like the Chinese concept of Yin and Yang. The Gunas are principles of energy movement through its poles: sattvas, the neutral phase; Rajas, the positive phase and Tamas, the negative phase. As we have seen, all energy must move through these phases. The Gunas, as principles of energy movement, outline its flow. The Five Elements, as expressions of the quality of this movement, define its progression.

The Five Elements delineate the quality, the energy patterns and the sphere of influence of each chakra centre. Each element represents a phase of both energy and consciousness. They define an 'orb' of energy patterns and functions which arise from each chakra. At each step-down phase there are corresponding differences in the quality and intensity of each energy orb. The first centre, the Ether Centre, is the subtlest; the last centre, the Earth Centre, is the coarsest. All five qualities of energy are found everywhere in the body, but each is in predominance in its own sphere of psychological and physiological activity. The lower the chakra centre, the more restricted the quality of consciousness and the coarser the quality of energy vibration. The Brow Centre is most expansive and has the potential for an all-encompassing perception of the universe. The Earth Centre is least conscious, most contracted and deals with a limited realm of expression.

The progression of the Elements can be viewed as a cycle where an outward, motor centrifugal phase flows from Ether to Earth and an inward, sensory centripetal phase flow from Earth back to Ether. Energy blockage can occur anywhere in this cyclical movement. This can be viewed in very practical terms. If we take the building of a house, we have the Ether phase of a 'field of need' for the new house, the Air phase of thinking and planning, the Fire phase of putting energy into its creation, the Water phase of grounding the ideas in the nuts and bolts of building and the Earth phase of completion. We then cycle back to Ether when we take possession of the new house and have a new 'field' for family life. We can get stuck in any of these phases and the cycle will never reach completion. It is the same in the body. Through processes of thought and emotion we can become blocked and imbalanced in any phase of energy and any quality of consciousness. This blocking will prevent a completed circuit or cycle of energy to occur and imbalance and disease processes will ensue. Health is the unblocking of these energy relationships and this process is the foundation of Polarity Therapy. The following is a list of specific page references which deal with Five Element theory. It must be stressed, however, that aspects of this theory run like an unbroken thread through all of Dr Stone's writings, and references to it are found throughout the books.

Book	Chart/page
Bk I	Chs. 4, 5, pp. 48–53, 64–5
Bk I	Ch. 6, pp. 76–7
Appendix Bk I	pp. 9–11
Bk III	pp. 32–3
Bk III	Ch. 6, pp. 50–3

Private Notes for Students of Polarity Therapy Conventions (Pentamirus Relationships).

VI–X. Five Element Appendices

The following is a listing of the basic charts which deal with the practical application of technique in relationship to the Five Elements. Each element has various energy patterns and energy harmonics which arise from the chakra centres. These patterns of energy form relationships in the body which can be used therapeutically. At the time of conception, energy patterns arise which set up polarity relationships for each element. These relationships were called 'Triads' by Dr Stone as they relate each element to its positive, neutral and negative poles in the body. The techniques are intended to open, stimulate and balance the qualities of energy moving through each triad. It is a complex intermeshing of elemental energies and the polarity therapist must know the various energy patterns of each element to be truly effective (See Book I, Energy, Charts 4 and 5).

VI. Ether

The Ether element is the ground or field from which the other elements arise. Dr Stone called it the 'one river from which the other four rivers arise'. Ether is a ground element, a unified field which creates subtle space for the movement of the other elements. Its basic quality is stillness, harmony and balance. It is the closest element in quality to the neutral centre of the Source and is the neutral ground for the manifestation of the mind–body complex. It has no triad relationship in the body as it is the neutral field from which the other active elements arise. The triads are relationships of energy movement. Ether is the quality of stillness at the heart of this movement. Its chakra centre is located at the throat and the neuter field of the neck is a manifestation of it.

The Ether centre in the neck is a place of interconnection and communication. It is an area which relates to all other elements and is commonly congested and blocked. There are various techniques geared to unblock this area and to relate it to the other elements. There are diaphragm and scapula reflexes in the neck which relate to Air; digestive reflexes which relate to Fire; pelvis and perineal reflexes which relate to Water and colon reflexes which relate to Earth. Blockages in the neck can further relate to structural imbalance in the pelvis and spine and these too must be dealt with in the course of treatment.

The Ether element governs the emotions in general and combines with the other elements to create various qualities of emotion. It governs the specific emotion of grief. Those who have truly grieved know that the neck and throat must be open for grief to flow freely. The attribute of movement which it governs is a combined Ether–Air relationship called 'lengthening'. Ether allows the expansion of other qualities of energy through its space, Air governs the general quality of this movement. Ether governs the sense of hearing, the subtlest of the senses. In combination with Fire, Ether governs sleep; with Water it manifests as saliva, and with Earth its expression is seen in the hairs of the body.

Ether treatments are geared to allow the patient to contact their neutral core and to generally create stillness and balance. Gentle, sattvic treatments can be extremely powerful as a sattvic touch will resonate with all neutral centres. The following are basic charts which deal with practical applications of Ether techniques.

Book	Chart/page	Content
Appendix Bk I	p. 15	Neck release
Bk II	Chs. 39–42, pp. 46–9	Neck release
Bk II	Ch. 33, p. 46	Neutral joint relationships
Bk II	Ch. 41, p. 48	Fig. 1, Neck release
Appendix Bk II	Ch. 59	Neutral joint relationships

See also Appendix on Cranial Therapy

VII. Air

The Air element is the first step-down from Ether. It is the first quality of energy which manifests from the neutral etheric field. The Air element is focused in the heart centre and governs qualities of conscious desire. The positive potential of this quality of energy is in desire for liberation and a return to the source. Its expression in the world is seen in true compassion, an all-encompassing love that is not tied to ego need and which truly understands the roots of suffering. The Air element also governs mental activity and thought. A person stuck in thought, who does not bring their ideas and plans to fruition, is stuck in the Airy realm. The person may appear dreamy or may be anxious, scattered and indecisive. The emotional quality governed by Air can be blocked by a physical closing of the heart area seen through a chronically contracted diaphragm, tense shoulders and a congested rib-cage.

The Air element governs movement in general and combines with the other elements to create various qualities of movement. The expression of Air in the world is that of speed and motion. It is the congested flow of this quality of energy which precedes rigidity in both mental and physical processes. A rigid person may not be able to flow with new ideas or approaches. Likewise, an imbalance in the Air element may underlie rigid, congested joints. The Air element governs the lungs, respiration, kidneys, adrenals, ductless glands, the nervous system and, in conjunction with Earth, the colon. In combination with Fire, it governs thirst, with Water it manifests as sweat and with Earth its expression is seen in the skin. Dry skin conditions, excessive sweating and excessive thirst may indicate an Air imbalance.

The Triad relationship for the Air element relates the chest and shoulder area to the kidney, colon, thighs and ankles. Two triad relationships result. One relates to the back of the body and one to the front.

⊕	φ	ϴ
shoulders	kidneys adrenals	ankles

⊕	φ	ϴ
chest/lungs	colon	calves

There are many techniques which act to balance these energy relationships and reflexes, and the basic charts are outlined below.

Book	Chart/page	Content
General balance		
Bk I	Chs. 6, 7, pp. 76–80	General release and balance Air–Water relationships
Bk II	Chs. 28, 29, pp. 35, 36	Balance Air–Water relationships, diaphragm relationships
Bk IV	pp. 30–44	Heart sequence, general series for balancing energies of the heart
Bk IV	Ch. 13, pp. 49–52	Fig. 2, Air–Water balance and respiratory release
Positive Pole		
Bk II	Ch. 36, p. 43	Scapula lift
Bk II	Ch. 41, p. 48	Thoracic release
Bk II	Ch. 45, p. 54	Shoulder and thoracic release
Bk II	Ch. 46, p. 55	Scapula release
Bk II	Ch. 49, p. 58	Neck/occiput release (gaseous release)
Appendix Bk II	Ch. 57, p. 78	Shoulder/chest release (also relates to digestive reflexes)
Bk IV	Ch. 7, p. 35	Scapula and neck release
Bk IV	Ch. 13, pp. 49–52	Fig. 1, Respiratory release through cerebro-spinal fluid
Neutral and Negative Poles		
Bk IV	Ch. 8, pp. 37–8	Neutral diaphragm to positive shoulders
Bk III	pp. 90–102	Gaseous Release Sequence, neutral colon to positive pole reflexes

Appendix Bk II	Chs. 60, 61, pp. 81–2	Neutral colon to negative pole calves
Bk V	Ch. 13, pp. 80–1	Vital colon balance, neck (positive), colon (neutral), calves (negative)
Bk V	Ch. 11, pp. 71–2	Vital kidney Balance, shoulders (positive), kidneys (neutral), ankles (negative)

VIII. Fire

The Fire element is the second step-down from Ether. It is the rajasic, impulsive phase of energy which is the driving force behind bodily functions. Air governs movement, Fire governs the direction of that movement. It is the driving vital force of the body's energy system. It provides the warmth of healing and its umbilical centre is the reservoir of vital energy reserves.

The Fire element governs the intellect. Colloquial expressions such as 'a fiery intellect', or 'quickness of mind' express this quality of the Fire element. Fire also governs the emotional qualities of anger and resentment. It can be constructively channelled into assertiveness, intellectual clarity and forgiveness. A person who holds back their fire in the world may have trouble getting their needs met and may channel their fire into seething resentment or may disconnect from the Fiery feelings completely and internalise them as insecurity, self-denigration, depression and powerlessness. A person who uses their Fire in an imbalanced way may be power-orientated, manipulative and emotionally or physically violent. A person with strong and balanced Fire would have good vital energy reserves, clarity of mind and purpose and an insightful intellect capable of cutting through confusion and turmoil.

Fire governs the sense of sight and the quality of insight. In combination with Air it produces shaking, with Water it manifests as urine and with Earth its expression is seen as blood vessels. It governs hunger and digestion and its balance is necessary for internal temperature control, a balanced metabolism and, in conjunction with Water, a strong self-healing ability. Fire governs the digestive system and its organs and provides both the subtle and coarse centres for the production and dissemination of warmth and vital energy.

A person with an imbalance in Fire may have digestive problems and poor circulation. He may have periods of the day when he is overcome by sluggishness, tired eyes and low energy.

The triad relationship for the Fire element relates the eyes and head generally to the solar plexus and thighs.

$$\oplus \qquad \phi \qquad \Theta$$

eyes   solar plexus   thighs
Fire oval field   umbilical area
of head

The following charts outline basic techniques that work with each pole and which also stimulate balance and disperse Fire through its various patterns.

Book	Chart/page	Content
Positive Pole		
Appendix Bk II	Ch. 58, p. 79	Simulation of Fire through ear reflexes (other positive pole techniques using occipital and eyebrow reflexes are also used)
Neutral Pole		
Bk II	Ch. 20, p. 27	Release of abdominal area
Bk III	Ch. 9, Fig. 3, p. 60	Umbilicus to inner thigh release
Bk V	p. 82	Polarising across fire centre
Negative Pole		
Bk II	Ch. 32, p. 39	Thigh and reflex releases
Bk III	Ch. 9, Fig. 1, p. 60	Inner thigh release
Bk III	Ch. 19, p. 85	Thigh and umbilicus releases
Sequences		
Bk III	Chs. 7, 8, pp. 54–9	Stimulation and balance of Fire elements through the Fire Principle Current
Bk IV	pp. 30–41	Heart energy sequence balancing energy patterns of heart; Fire and Air releases
EES	Ch. 4	Fire dispersal techniques
EES	Ch. 18	Fire dispersal patterns

IX. Water

The Water element is the next step down from Fire. In this sphere of energy, the movement from the source has coarsened and the quality of its expression has become less conscious. Thus, the Water realm of energy is one of unconscious emotions and attachments. It is felt as deep feelings and gut responses. The Water Centre is focused in the pelvic area and governs these deep feelings which can manifest on one hand as emotional attachment and on the other as an ability to let go and flow. An imbalance may express itself as over-sensitivity. Unconscious patterns may become overwhelming and reactions may seem irrational. Watery holding may relate to sexual issues as the Water element governs procreation and sexual urge. Imbalance may be physically seen as pelvic tension, excess flesh in the pelvic area and a general tendency for water retention in its triad areas. The Water element is the phase of energy which seeks the lowest level and grounds our energies to earth.

A blockage in this grounding flow, generally in the pelvic area, may result in an apparent airy quality of spaciness or scatteredness. The real key may be unconscious emotional holdings in the Water element sphere and the subsequent lack of grounding.

The Water element is the energy of procreation, renewal and healing. Intuitive, creative urges can stem from here. It governs the generative system, the lymphatic system and secretory glands. It governs the sexual fluids and the sperm and ovum. The solids in the body which fall under its sphere of influence are fats and flesh. The Water element also governs the function of binding and cohesion in the body, and it is, in that sense, the element which maintains the integrity of physical form. Its triad relationships relate to the chest and breasts, the pelvis and generative organs and the feet.

⊕	φ	θ
1. breasts (chest)	generative organs (pelvis)	feet
2. neck	diaphragm	perineal floor
3. shoulders	buttocks	achilles tendon area

As the Water element governs the movement of energy to earth, it is logical that it also governs the feet. The feet connect us to earth and our relationship to this grounding can be seen in them. The feet are the last body part in which energy is expressed in its outward, centrifugal phase. There energy tends to become 'earthed' and sluggish and the feet are an expression of this crystallised phase. The history of the whole body becomes crystallised in the feet and this makes them an important diagnostic tool. The following charts work with the Water element relationships in the body. They cover basic triad work, perineal work, Five-Pointed Star work and many other relationships. An important Water energy relationship covered is that of the perineum (floor of the pelvis) to its various reflex relationships.

Book	Chart/page	Content
Positive to Neutral Pole		
Bk I	Chs. 6, 7, pp. 76–80	'Balancing by Contour', pelvis to positive pole relationships above
Appendix Bk I	p. 15	North pole stretches to open positive pole of neck (the neck is the positive pole of the perineum)
Bk II	Ch. 19, p. 26	Pelvis release with stretch at positive pole of neck.
Bk II	Ch. 27, p. 34	Pelvic relationships to neutral pole of diaphragm and positive pole of jaw.
Bk II	Ch. 28, p. 35	Pelvic relationship to positive pole above.
Bk II	Ch. 29, p. 36	Subtle balance of Water and Air elements through the poles of the diaphragm.
Neutral Pole		
Bk II	Ch. 25, p. 32	Pelvic and inguinal ligament release
Bk II	Ch. 26, p. 33	Pelvic releases
Bk II	Ch. 34, p. 41	Pelvic and hip releases
Bk II	Ch. 35, p. 42	Pelvic release
Bk III	Ch. 20, p. 87	Pelvic release
Neutral to Negative Pole		
Bk V	Ch. 14, pp. 83–7	Pelvic balancing (see also foot reflexes in Appendix III).
Perineal Work – Positive-Neutral-Negative Poles		
Bk I	Ch. 8, pp. 81–9	Perineal releases
Appendix Bk I	pp. 12–14	Perineal releases
Bk II	Chs. 30, 31, pp. 37–8	Perineal reflexes
EES	Ch. 8	Perineal to spine releases (see also Appendix on the nervous system).

Book	Chart/page	Content
General Work		
Appendix to Bk II	Ch. 62, p. 83	Posterior motor Water element reflexes
EES	Ch. 7	Prostate drain and reflex
EES	Ch 9	Lymphatic drain

X. *Earth*

The Earth element is the final step-down of subtle energy from Ether. Its chakra centre is the last of the five centres which govern physical form. It is located in the anal region and its spinal focus is at the junction of the sacrum and coccyx. The Earth element represents the coarsest quality of manifestation of the core energy system. As Earth represents the coarsest and least conscious phase of energy, inertia and resistance reach their peak in its sphere. Laziness and loss of awareness can result if one is caught up in its sphere. Fear can arise if one is attached to its manifestation as physical form.

Earth governs the crystallisation of energy into form and creates support and foundation in the world. It represents the conclusion of a process or cycle and defines the limits of physical manifestation. As it is the final stage of the 'involutionary' process of energy moving from the source into form, it is a crucial pivot point for a return flow of energy back to the source in an 'evolutionary' phase. 'That which is last becomes first' is an ancient saying which expresses this potential return phase. In creating support and groundedness in the world, it provides the basis for courage and a springboard for letting go of attachment and ego need. A person with a balanced and open quality of energy governed by the Earth element would be seen to be 'grounded' and stable in physical form. If its flow is blocked and its patterns in contraction and attachment to physical form is strong, fear and instability can result. This may manifest as an undue fear about the body's well-being and an inability to be grounded in the practical things of the world.

The Earth element governs the form and condition of the colon and rectum and, with the Air element, the elimination of the body's solid waste products. An imbalance may disrupt the eliminative function and become manifest as a 'holding on' as in constipation, or as an inability to 'earth' the digestive process as in diarrhoea. Chronic constipation may be due to fearfully holding on to physical and emotional needs while chronic diarrhoea may be due to an anxious and fearful inability to be grouned in the things of the world. An 'earthed' body type may be excessively padded, muscular, block-like in form, thick-necked and may have a 'dense' overall look.

The Earth triad relationships are the neck at the positive pole, the colon at the neutral pole and the knees at the negative pole. Thus, a fear response, which is governed by the Earth element, may result in a tightened and painful neck, diarrhoea and a loss of grounding seen by shaky and weak knees.

$$\oplus \qquad \phi \qquad \theta$$

neck   colon   knees

The Earth element technique is covered by the following charts. Earth also governs the structural work which is detailed in a following appendix.

Book	Chart/page	Content
Neutral and Negative Poles		
Appendix Bk II	Chs. 60, 61, pp. 81, 82	Colon to negative calve reflexes
Positive, Neutral, Negative Poles		
Book V	Ch. 13, pp. 81–2	Balancing via all three poles of the Earth triad.

XI. Nervous System

The nervous system is a sphere of energy which directly enlivens and controls physical form. It is a final step-down of subtle energy into the mind/body complex. Its physical manifestation is a stepped down harmonic of the subtle energies of the chakra system. Thus, the various nerve plexuses are controlled by chakra centres of similar, but subtler, energies. Chart 17 in the Evolutionary Energy Series of 25 charts gives vital background information for nervous system technique. The fiery, rajasic principle has its harmonic in the sympathetic nervous system. It is the system which prepares and stimulates the body for action. The Airy, sattvic principle has its harmonic in the parasympathetic system. It is the system which calms and creates relaxation in the body. It stimulates digestion as this function must be carried out in a state of calm. The water tamasic principle has its harmonic in the central or cerebro-spinal nervous system. It is the system which brings thought into a final conscious manifestation as action or speech. The following charts relate to techniques for the sympathetic and parasympathetic nervous system. Technique for the central nervous system is covered in the next appendix under 'cranial and cranial-pelvic therapy'. Generally speaking, Parasympathetic Techniques fall under 'perineal techniques' and Sympathetic Techniques fall under 'coccygeal techniques'. The perineum is a negative pole of the parasympathetic system and the coccyx, via the sacral/coccygeal ganglion, is a negative pole of the sympathetic system.

Parasympathetic and Sympathetic

Book	Chart/page	Content
Bk I	Ch. 8, pp. 81, 89	Perineal treatment
App. Bk I	pp. 10, 12–14	Perineal information
Book II	Chs. 30, 31, pp. 37, 38	Perineal contact points
Book IV	pp. 14, 16	General energy relationships, positive to negative poles of the nervous system.
Bk V	p. 73	Perineal and spinal release
EES	Ch. 8	Perineal and spinal contacts parasympathetic and sympathetic contacts
EES	Ch. 17	Theory on the nervous system
EES	Ch. 19	Sympathetic contact areas
EES	Ch. 20	Sympathetic and parasympathetic contact areas

XII. *Central Nervous System: Cranial and Cranial-Pelvic Technique*

The central nervous system can be best influenced by working with its main fluid, the cerebrospinal fluid. This fluid is a shock-absorbent and acts as a storage field and conveyor for subtler etheric energies. There is evidence that it actually flows along nerve fibres as they leave the spinal column and thus conveys these subtle energies throughout the body. Its movement creates a subtle, but extremely important rhythmic flow called variously the cranial rhythmic impulse, the cranial-sacral impulse and the cranial respiratory impulse. I prefer the term 'cranio rhythmic impulse' as it best captures the quality of its movement. The impulse is most easily felt in the cranium, spine and pelvis, but can be palpated anywhere in the body. A healthy central nervous system is reflected by its open and balanced movement. There are many forms of cranial holds and techniques used in Polarity Therapy which are unfortunately not illustrated in the books. Holds which work with the positive pole, the cranium and the negative pole, the pelvis, are referred to in the charts, and some are illustrated.

Cranial and cranial-pelvic therapy is a powerful sattvic balancer. Proper understanding and application of its technique can profoundly affect all aspects of the nervous system and thus, all aspects of the mind/body complex. Its sattvic techniques also resonate with all other sattvic qualities of energy and thus influence core energy in its subtlest form. A listing of cranial–pelvic body relationships is given, followed by appropriate chart references. The Polarity Therapist works on the subtle flow of cerebrospinal fluid and on the energies which underlie that flow.

Cranial-Pelvic Relationships

⊕ Pole	⊖ Pole
Occiput	Sacrum
Sphenoid	Coccyx
Parietals	Innominates, iliac crest
Temporals	Ischium, acetabulum (hip socket)
Mandible	Pubic symphysis
Frontals	Pelvic basin under lower abdomen
Maxilla	Inguinal ligament

Book	Chart/page	Content
Bk II	Ch. 13, p. 20	Geometric relationships
Bk III	Ch. 43, pp. 50, 51	Cranial moulding
Bk II	Ch. 44, pp. 52, 53	Special sense locations
Bk III	Ch. 12, pp. 67, 68	Sphenoid–coccygeal relationships
Bk III	Ch. 13, pp. 69–73	Cranial–pelvic relationships
Bk III	Chs. 15, 16, pp. 76–9	Cranial–pelvic relationships
Bk IV	pp. 11–13	Cranial–pelvic relationships
Bk IV	pp. 49–52	Cerebrospinal fluid pump – can be applied all the way down spine to sacrum
Bk V	Ch. 8, pp. 51, 55	Cranial–pelvic bony correspondences
Bk V	Chs. 16, 17, 18, pp. 90–2	Cranial–pelvic relationships

XIII. *Structural and Spinal Relationships*

Dr Stone worked with three phases of imbalance in the body. The structural level is the final phase of blockage and distortion in this triune pattern. The first or sattvic phase is the subtlest. It is of the chakras and the Five Elements. This steps down to the nervous system (which has its own triune relationship of the Parasympathetic, Sympathetic and Central Nervous Systems). The nervous system in turn transfers these energy imbalances to the physical body and this is seen as structural imbalance. Dr Stone talks about this in Book I, *Energy*, p. 75: 'Energy impulses are from above downward. Structural reflexes are from below upward. Sympathetic and Parasympathetic nerve reflexes also respond from below upward. All sensory impulses are from without inward.'

Subtle energy impulses from the Brow Centre downwards and from the core outwards. The nervous system and the structural system are governed by these subtler impulses and become imbalanced relative to them via a reflex action from below upward. The sensory or incoming phase of subtle energy returns from the periphery inwards and feeds back information to the core.

Dr Stone was both an osteopath and chiropractor. He was able to relate the subtler imbalances to the grosser physical imbalances and developed a structural system based on these interrelationships. He used a Gravity Test Board (Plumb Line Board) for diagnostic purposes and integrated the structural work with work on the subtle energies and the nervous system. The structural work was practised 'from the bottom up' and was based on the fact that structure above is dependent on the foundation and balance of the structure below. The focus of the balancing work is the innominate (hip) bones and the sacrum. The sacrum is a wedge-shaped, upside-down pyramid which rests on the innominate bones. It was called 'the mysterious sacrum' by Dr Stone due to the complex energy patterns and the structural variations found within it. Sacrum means 'sacred bone'. It relates energetically to the two lowest chakras and it is the negative pole of the nervous system and spine. It is an area of energy crystallisation. Energies become sluggish and crystallised there and these blockages can be a focus for many physical imbalances. Dr Stone developed techniques which open and balance both its energy and its structural relationships. Once the pelvis is balanced, the structure above (the lumbar, thoracic and cervical areas of the spine) can be more easily worked on and a longer-lasting balance can result. The following charts are listed as body area technique in a general order from the bottom to the top of the body.

Book	Chart/page	Content
Theory and Diagnosis		
Bk II	Ch. 13, p. 20	Geometric relationships; lines of force and energy currents
Bk II	Ch. 18, p. 25	Measuring for short leg
Bk III	Chs. 10, 11 pp. 62–6	Gravity Test Board and structural theory
Book IV	pp. 7–9	Gravity test-board procedure
Bk IV	Ch. 2, pp. 10–13	Polarity structural relationships
Bk IV	pp. 26–9	Short leg theory
Bk V	Ch. 2, pp. 15–31	Specific and general theory
Bk V	Ch. 10, pp. 58–9	Gravity Test Board

Book	Chart/page	Content
Pelvic Reflexes		
(see also parasympathetic and sympathetic nervous system reflexes)		
Appendix Bk II	Chs. 54, 55, 56 pp. 75–7	Reflex releases (ankle-hip-sacroiliac and occiput reflexes)
Bk I	Ch. 6, p. 76	Anterior and posterior gravity lines for
	Ch. 7, pp. 78–80	diagnosis and correction of structural distortions
Hip and Sacral Balance		
Bk II	Ch. 34, p. 41	The innominate release and balance
Bk III	Ch. 20, pp. 87–9 pp. 24, 25	Pelvic and hip release
Appendix Bk II	Ch. 53, p. 74	Thigh and pelvic muscle release
(note: nervous system and pelvic reflexes above combine with these techniques)		
Bk IV	pp. 3, 4 Ch. 1, pp. 5, 6	Sacral theory
Bk IV	Chs. 2, 3, pp. 10–19	General theory and structural imbalance in relationship to the sacrum
Bk II	Ch. 19, Fig. 2, p. 26	Correction for anterior sacral base
Bk II	Ch. 21, p. 28	Sacral release by pressure
Appendix Bk II	p. 16	Sacral and hip pressure adjustment
Bk III	Ch. 14, pp. 74–5	
Bk IV	pp. 22–3	Sacral balancing techniques
Bk IV	Ch. 15, Fig. 1	
Bk IV	Ch. 4, pp. 20–1	Sacral balancing techniques (contd)
EES	Ch. 22	
Bk V	pp. 69–70	Sacro-iliac balance
General Spinal Techniques		
Bk II	Ch. 22, p. 29	General spinal muscle release
Bk II	Chs. 23, 24, pp. 30, 31	Muscle relaxation via energy current stimulation or inhibition; 'S' release along vertebrae
Bk III	Ch. 18, pp. 83–4	Spinal polarisation
Bk IV	pp. 24–5	
Appendix Bk I	p. 16	Pressure adjustment for posterior
Bk V	p. 73	vertebrae and spinal curves, spinal muscle relaxation
Lumbar Techniques		
Bk II	Ch. 34, p. 41	Rotational stretch through lumbars
EES	Ch. 23	Lumbar release and curve adjustment
Thoracic Technique		
Bk II	Ch. 41, p. 48	Upper thoracic release and balance
Bk II	Chs. 47, 48, pp. 56–7	High shoulder/thoracic curve release
Bk III	Ch. 50, p. 59	Upper thoracic release
Cervical Technique		
Bk II	Chs. 39, 40, 42 pp. 46, 47, 49	Cervical releases
Bk V	pp. 69–70	North pole stretch

Spinal Harmonics and Specific Releases

Bk V	Ch. 2, pp. 15–31	Spinal harmonics and local vertebral
Appendix Bk I	p. 10	correction
Bk V	Ch. 15, pp. 88, 89	Spinal harmonic balance in sitting position
Bk V	Ch. 19, pp. 93–5	Foot reflexes to spinal vertebrae (used in conjunction with spinal harmonics)

Note: Spinal harmonics also relate to general nervous system balance and the sympathetic nervous system.

XIV. *Nutrition and Cleansing Diets*

Dr Stone used naturopathic dietary principles and procedures for internal cleansing and health building. Due to imbalances in body function, to poor diet and to pollutants, detoxification and eliminative organs become overloaded and toxic wastes accumulate in body tissues. Dr Stone developed a cleansing diet which consists of a morning 'liver flush' to help in detoxification and of vegetables and fruit in mostly raw form to aid the eliminative process. A cleansing tea is also taken throughout the day. After a period on the cleansing diet, other foods are gradually added in to see their individual effects and a health-building diet is developed.

Dr Stone also understood food in relationship to its energy content. Food types were categorised according to the Five Elements (actually the four active elements of Air, Fire, Water and Earth) and were prescribed to the patient according to their energy imbalances and needs. The following booklets and page references contain much information about internal cleansing, nutrition and naturopathic principles.

Book	Chart/page	Content
Bk I	pp. 4, 11	Energy relationships
Appendix Bk I	pp. 26–8	Nutritional information
Book III	pp. 105–12	Energy relationships and the Polarity Diet
EES	Chs. 24, 25	Energy relationships
Health Building		Much information about diet and naturopathic principles
A purifying diet		The purifying diet (now included in 'Health Building')

XV. *Polarity Exercises*

Dr Stone emphasised self-help procedures. He wanted patients to start taking responsibility for their own health. He developed specific exercises which help to maintain an open and balanced flow of vital energy. These exercises can be given as a general series or as a specific set in relationship to the patient's specific imbalances. The different exercises also relate to the Five Elements and each exercise stimulates different qualities of energy. They can thus be given in specific sequences to work with either Air, Fire, Water or Earth imbalances and also generally to bring the system to an Ether balance. The following chart lists page references for these exercises.

Summary chart: food relationships*

	AIR	FIRE	WATER	EARTH
Nutritional relationship	Stimulates, oxidation, nourishes, oxidising element in blood stream and nervous system, cleansing foods aid in flushing system out, as air stimulates movement, is necessary in right amount to help augment fire.	High in protein simulates appetite and digestive function, increase circulation and all motor actions, impulse behind cleansing activities. Increases vital energy; tonifies liver, gall bladder, duodenum.	Eliminators, purgatives, high in minerals, builds new tissues, controls secretions of mucous membranes and skin, flushes kidneys, water in the general matrix which holds body structures together.	High mineral content, earth foods easily assimilated but slowly eliminated. Satisfies hunger, draws out toxins when applied externally. 'Grounding' energetically.
Taste (stimulates that element)	Sour	Bitter	Salty	Sweet
Grows	High above the ground, in trees.	Waist to chest high.	Above ground, on or near it.	Underground and some nearest to surface on ground.
Food types	Fruits, nuts, acid foods, fermented foods	Cereals, grains, legumes, pulses, (beans, lentils), seeds.	Leafy greens, squash, melons, milk, dairy	Roots, tubers, herb roots, edible bulbs, honey, hard cheeses.
Specific foods	*All fruit and nuts* *Acids:* pineapple citrus tomatoes rhubarb strawberries *Fermented:* cultured dairy products yeasts	*All cereals, grains, pulses, seeds.* *Bitters:* endive escarole dandelion watercress *High in protein:* All beans, pulses, peas, lentils, oats corn, wheat, rice, millet. *Stimulants:* ginger, garlic, onions, leeks.	*All leafy greens, squash, melons* *Mucus formers:* milk and milk products. High sodium (salt) celery, cucumber	*All roots, tubers* *Sweets:* sugar, honey, etc. *Starches:* potatoes, root vegetables. *Mucus formers:* cheese products.
Temperament	Highly nervous, highly sensitive, 'electric' type person.	Vital, active, person, much mental and physical drive.	Persons of highly emotional (Watery) nature, easily moved to tears, sadness.	Rugged constitution, hard physical labour leads simple life.

Source note* Much of the information here was compiled by Dr James Said DC.

Book	Chart/page	Content
Bk II	Ch. 52, p. 61	General water stimulation, 'energy pump', clears head congestion at its negative pole
Appendix Bk II	Chs. 63, 64, pp. 84	Squatting techniques
Bk IV	pp. 45–6, 47–8	Diaphragm release, brachial plexus and neck release
Bk V	Ch. 9, pp. 56–7	Vital posture balance, etheric balance
EES	Chs. 13, 14, 15	Ha! Breath exercises
Easy Stretching Postures (booklet)		Squatting variations, general theory
Energy Tracing	pp. 10–14	Pyramid squats, cliffhanger exercise, general theory

Liverflush and Purifying Diet

Liverflush Tea

(This is made first, so it will be ready for drinking immediately following the Liver Flush below.)

1 tsp liquorice root, 1 tsp aniseed, 1 tsp peppermint leaves, 1 tsp fenugreek seeds, 1 tsp fennel seeds, 4 slices of ginger root cut 1/8" thick. 1 tsp flax seed (or linseed).

Boil the ginger root 3 minutes in 1½ pints of water. Then pour this over the other ingredients and let simmer, covered, 10–15 minutes while you prepare the Liver Flush.

The Liverflush

Mix together in a blender if you have one:

The juice of one grapefruit or several oranges
4–6 tbsp fresh lemon or lime juice (double the amount of olive oil)
1–3 tbsp pure, cold-pressed olive oil
1–3 crushed cloves of garlic
optional: grated ginger and dash of cayenne papper.

Drink this. Then drink a glassful of Liverflush tea, without honey, while it is hot. During the day, drink as many cups of the tea as possible, with honey if desired.

An hour or two later, have some fresh citrus juice or other fresh fruit juice (apples, pears, apricots, grapes, etc.) or some fresh vegetable juice (mixture of carrot, cabbage, celery, beet, etc.).

From lunchtime on, eat plentifully of leafy green and other vegetables, such as lettuce, carrots, turnips, squash, spinach, onion, leeks, celery, cabbage, broccoli, cauliflower, string beans, radishes, cucumbers, beets and their tops, and also sprouts (alfalfa, fenugreek, mung bean, soy bean, lentil). One may also eat fruits such as apples, pears, grapes, peaches, prunes, figs, raisins, fresh berries.

One should eat all of these in raw form as much as possible, but they may also be steamed, baked or made into soups, *but do not fry*. A moderate amount of raw nuts, preferably almonds, may be eaten.

DO NOT EAT meat, fish, chicken, eggs, starches (potato, rice, bread, cereal), sugar (honey or maple syrup are permissible), milk or milk products, coffee, regular tea, alcohol, drugs – not even aspirin. Do not use aluminium cookware.

Recommended readings on diet by Dr Randolf Stone: *A Purifying Diet; Health Building* (particularly pp. 23–42 and 53–75), and 'Summary, supplement to *Health Building*.

Basic Health-Building Diet

Morning

First thing: A modified liver flush made up of 1–3 tablespoons cold-pressed oil (olive or almond oil) blended with three times the amount of fresh lemon juice. Then drink two cups of hot water with the juice of one half to one lime or lemon per cup.

At least one hour later: if a more substantial breakfast is needed: soak raisins, dates or figs overnight. Add to a porridge made of three-fourths millet and one-fourth fenugreek seed. Add, if desired, 1–2 dozen peeled almonds.

Beverages

During the morning and the rest of the day take hot water with lime or lemon and honey in it. A simple cleansing tea made from ginger root, fenugreek seed and peppermint flavoured with lemon and sweetened with honey may be taken. The regular cleansing tea (see purifying diet) may also be used. Fresh fruit or vegetable juices may be drunk. Eliminate alcohol, coffee and black tea.

Noon meal

Sprouted legumes (pulses) with steamed, boiled or baked vegetables or a large mixed raw salad with sprouts. Fruit salads may also be used as the main course on their own. Do not fry any foods.

Evening meal

Fresh fruits and warm milk may be taken or a more substantial porridge of wheat, oats, corn or millet may be made and fresh sweet fruit (not citrus) or dried fruit may be added. A porridge may also be made as a non-sweet savoury dish with herbs and mild spices.

Index

acupuncture 46
Ahamkara 8, 9
Air (as element) 56, 57, 59–64, 173–5
Air Centre (or Heart Centre),
   and Air element 60, 61, 95, 105, 108
   blockage in 140
   and emotional shock 41
   and fields of elixir 47
   location 28, 30, 167
   and love 61, 105
   and triads 58
Air Element relationships 105–9
Air foods 56, 59, 147
Air Oval Field,
   diagram of 30, 38
   and Earth oval 40
   effects of 64, 105
   and energy type 39
   named after 29
Air Triad 58, 60, 61, 63, 106, 107, 108
Air type (constitutional) 96, 98
Airy current see East-West current
Allan 94, 95, 98, 99, 100
animals 143–4
armouring 149
Astral Realm 24
Ayurvedic Tradition 8–10, 25, 46, 167,
   171

Bell, John 15
Bioenergetics 84, 149
blockages, energy 49, 80–3, 89, 93–4,
   136, 162, 164
body–mind separation 156–7
body reading 94–9
body structure 136–41
body-work 87–8, 100

Bohm, David 15, 16, 19, 20, 158
Brahman 8–9
Breaths, Life 124–8
Brow Centre,
   and fields of elixir 47
   location in body 28, 30, 167
   location of physical manifestation of
      energy 26–7, 34, 47, 51, 171
   qualities 47, 51, 171
   Third Eye 26
   in Tibetan tradition 53
Buddhism 81–2, 83, 147, 148, 149,
   157–8, 160

cardiac rhythm 124–5
Causal Realm 24, 127
centres,
   definition 29
   derivation from Ayurvedic tradition
      xii, 167
   diagram of 28, 30
   and Five Elements 47–9, 57, 58, 171
   and Oval Fields 38–9
   types 28, 51–5
see also Air, Brow, Crown, Earth, Ether,
   Fire, Water
cerebrospinal fluid (CSF) 126, 127, 132,
   134, 180
chakras see centres
Chart, Foetal 50
chi 10, 46, 47, 149
Chi Kung 47, 149
connective tissue see fascia
constitutional types 96–7, 98
contact areas 132–3
Core Energy system 30
cranial holds 134, 136, 180

cranial osteopathy 127, 132–4
cranial rhythm 124–6, 127, 134, 180
'Crown' centre or chakra 29, 168
crystallisation 86, 119, 149
currents 31–3, 35, 130–1, 168
    see also East–West, Long Line, Spiral

death 159–60
Descartes, Réné 2, 15
diets 89, 142–8, 183, 185–6
Dossey, Larry 160

Earth (as element) 56, 57, 75–8, 178–9
Earth Centre,
    location 28, 30, 167
    qualities 44, 49, 171
    realm of action 75
Earth Element relationships 120–3
Earth foods 56, 59, 147
Earth Oval Field 30, 38, 39, 40
Earth Triad 75, 76, 77, 121, 122
Earth type (constitutional) 97, 99
East–West Current 31, 33, 168
ectomorph 96, 98
Einstein, Albert 2
elements see Five Elements, Air, Earth,
    Ether, Fire, Water
elixir, fields of 47
encysting 83, 84
endomorph 97, 98
Energetic Fields & Transitions 38–44
energy,
    and Air 60
    in Ayurvedic tradition xii, 9–10, 25
    blockages 49, 80–3, 89, 93–4, 136,
        162, 164
    and Brow Centre 26–7, 34, 47, 51, 136
    and centres see Centres
    and cerebrospinal fluid 126, 127, 134,
        180
    and chakras see Centres
    completion 81
    concept of 1, 3–4
    and Earth 75
    and Ether 51
    evolution & involution 10, 20–5, 81,
        91, 145, 159
    and exercise 148
    fields & transitions 38–44
    and fire 64, 67, 68

    and Five Element patterns 87, 100–1,
        144
    and food 144–5
    and form 124–41
    in Gunas 8, 9, 25–6, 28, 47, 104, 166,
        171
    harmonics 168–9
    and health 79–80, 88–90
    in Hologrammatic model 13–14
    and illness 85
    and individual responsibility 88–90,
        153
    kundalini 138
    and laziness 148
    mind 127
    and nervous system 128–9
    and Oval Fields see Oval Fields
    phases of 46, 49
    physical manifestation of 26–8, 34,
        47, 51, 136, 166
    in Polarity Principle 10–12, 165
    Primary 47, 48
    and pulsation 10, 11, 34–6, 46–7
    in Tao 5–8, 19
    and triads 55, 58, 60
    and water 69, 72
entropy 148
Ether (as element) 51–5, 56, 57, 172–3
Ether Centre,
    location 28, 30
    named after 29
    qualities 47, 51–5, 167
Ether Element relationships 102–4
Ether Oval Field 29, 30, 38, 39, 40
evolution 10, 20–5, 81, 91, 145, 159
exercise xii, 148–55, 183–5
Eye Centre see Brow Centre

fascia 39–40, 41
fear 88, 121, 123, 145, 159
fields see Energetic, Oval, motor
fields of elixir 47
fiery current see Spiral Current
Fire (as element) 56, 57, 64–9, 175–6
Fire Centre,
    location 28, 30, 66, 167
    qualities 64, 67
Fire current see Spiral Current
Fire Element relationships 109–13
Fire foods 56, 59, 147

Fire Oval Field 30, 38, 39, 40
Fire Principle Current 109, 111
Fire Triad 64, 65, 66, 67, 109, 110, 113
Fire type 96, 98
Five Elements,
  and chakras 29
  definition xii, 7, 163
  and food 56, 59, 144–5
  and health 92–123
  and illness 90–1
  origin 9
  patterns 47, 87, 100–1, 144
  and polarity therapy 93–102
  relationships 10, 45–7
  types 47–78, 167, 171–9
  see also Air, Earth, Ether, Fire, Water
Five-Pointed Star Pattern 117, 118, 119,
  120
flus 127
Foetal Chart 50
Foetal Triads 49–50
foods 56, 59, 68–9, 89, 142–8, 183
Freud, Sigmund 84

Generative Centre see Water Centre
George 119, 120
Gregory 149–50, 152
grief 53, 152
Gunas 8, 9, 25–6, 28, 47, 104, 166, 171

Ha! Breath Exercises 152, 153, 154
Harry 82–3
health building 86–7, 89, 90
  and diet 145, 148, 186
  and exercise 153
hearing 53, 55
Heart Centre see Air Centre
Heisenberg 15
heteronomy 15, 16, 17
holds, cranial 134, 136
Hologrammatic Model 13–14, 15, 18
Holographic Paradigm 158
holonomy 15, 17

ida 27, 47, 167
illness, path to 85
individual's responsibility 88–90, 142,
  153
interlaced triangles 130
inverted triangles 129

involution 10, 20–5, 81, 91, 145, 159
iridology 66

Jenny 85–6

Krishnamurti 162
Kum Nye 149
Kun Zhi 24
kundalini energy 138

Lao Tzu 75
Lappé, Frances Moore 143
laws of heteronomy 15, 16
laws of holonomy 15
Life Breaths 124–8
liver 147
liverflush 147, 185
Long Life Currents 31, 33, 129, 130, 168
Lower, Alexander 84

Mahat 8, 9
mesomorph 96, 98
mind energy 127
motor fields 41, 43–4

Naval Centre see Fire Centre
Needleman, Jacob 83, 84
nervous system 128–36, 135, 136, 179–
  80
Newton, Isaac 2

Oval Fields 29–32, 38–40, 41–4, 127,
  130, 168
ovum 49, 50

Paranudi-Swami 67
parasympathetic contact areas 132
pelvic centres see Earth Centre, Water
  Centre
phases 35, 49
physical body structures 136–41
Pierrakos, John 84
pingala 27, 47, 167
Plank 2
polarity,
  definition of 3–4, 20, 165
  general, in body 36
Polarity Exercises xiii, 149–55, 183–5
Polarity Principle 4, 10–12, 15, 17–18,
  20–1, 37, 165

Polarity Purifying Diet 147, 185–6
Polarity therapy,
　appeal of xiii
　beginnings xi
　and bioenergetics 84
　and body-work 87–8
　and diet 144
　guide to Dr Stone on 163–86
　intention/object of 79, 80
　methods of 92–102
　and sacrum 137
　types of touch in 104–5
Polarity Yoga 149–55, 183–5
Polarity Zone Chart 35, 37, 101
Prakhita 8, 9
prana 10, 34, 45, 80, 124
Primal Source 19, 26, 51
Primary Energy 47, 48
protein production 143
pulsations 10, 11, 34–7, 46–7, 81, 124
purusha 8, 9
pyramid postures 149, 150, 151

Rajas 8, 9, 25, 26, 64, 104, 166, 171
Reich, Wilhelm 84, 149
respiratory rhythm 124–5
rhythms 124–6, 134

sacrum 43–4, 134, 135, 137, 138, 140,
　181
Satchakranirupana 67
sattvas 8, 9, 25, 26, 104, 166, 171
sleep 55
smell 100
sound 149, 152
spectrum of consciousness 156–7, 158
sperm 49, 50
spinal harmonics 138, 139, 181
Spiral Current 31, 33, 112, 130, 168
Star Pattern, Five-Pointed 117, 118,
　119, 120
Step-Down process 22, 23, 24, 46, 164
Still, Andrew Taylor 127
Stone, Randolph,
　and Air 105
　and body structure 136, 137, 138
　and clients 92–3
　and connective tissue 41
　and cranial rhythm 126, 134
　and crystallisations 119, 149
　and CSF 126–7, 134

　and currents 31, 89
　defined polarity 20–1
　and diet 147, 148
　and Earth 76, 98
　and energy 3–4, 21, 22, 34, 79, 80, 81,
　　83, 89, 93, 124, 126–7, 131
　and Ether Centre 51
　and exercises 148, 149, 152
　and fire 109
　and first & last 49, 76
　and Five Elements 46, 49
　and Foetal Chart 50
　guide to writings 163–86
　and health 79, 87, 91, 92
　and life 161–2
　and motor fields 44
　and nervous system 123, 128, 129, 131
　osteopath xi, 78, 123
　and oval fields 29, 30–1, 38
　and Polarity Principle 10, 15, 20
　and Polarity Zone Chart 35
　and Primal Source 19
　and pulsation 10, 30–1
　and thoughts/attitudes 86–7, 91,
　　161–2
　and triads 55
　and water 13
　and Wireless Anatomy xii, 22, 46
sushumna 28, 47, 126, 129, 138, 167
Sutherland, William 126, 127
sympathetic contact areas 133

Tai Chi 5, 6
Tai Chi T'u 5, 6
Tamas 8, 9, 25, 26, 104, 166, 171
Tan T'iens 47
Taoism 5–8, 18–19, 51, 52–3, 76, 82,
　108, 160
taste 55, 56
tea 147–8, 185
therapist-client relationship 92–3
therapeutic touch xii, 104–5
Third Eye 26
thought, crystallisation of, into physical
　form 83–6
Three Life Breaths 124–8
Throats Centre see Ether Centre
Tibetan Book of the Dead 159
tissue, connective see fascia
touch,
　therapeutic xii

types of 104–5
transitions 40, 41, 42
Transverse Current 31, 33, 168
Triads,
    Air 58, 60, 61, 63, 106, 107, 108
    in body reading 94, 98, 99
    and centres 58
    definition 55
    Earth 75, 76, 77, 121, 122
    Fire 64, 65, 66, 67, 109, 110, 113
    Foetal 49–50
    and spinal harmonics 138, 139
    Water 70, 72, 73, 114, 115
triangles,
    interlaced 130
    inverted 129
    in motor fields 43–4

Upledger, John 126

vegetarianism 143–4

Water (as element) 56, 57, 69–75, 113,
    176–8
Water Centre 28, 30, 47, 69, 167
Water Element relationships 113–20
Water foods 56, 59, 147
Water Oval Field 30, 38, 39
Water Triad 70, 72, 73, 114, 115
Water type (constitutional) 97, 98–9
watery current see Long Line Current
Wilber, Ken 156, 159, 162
Wireless Anatomy xii, 46, 167–8
Woodroffe, John 67
worldview of East 2–3
worldview of West 1–2
Wu Chi 5, 6

Yin & Yang 5, 12, 19, 70, 129, 131–2,
    166, 171
Young, Arthur 18